# Negotiation Alchemy

# Negotiation Alchemy:
## Global Skills Inspiring and Transforming Diverging Worlds

Nancy Erbe

Berkeley Public Policy Press
Institute of Governmental Studies
University of California, Berkeley
2011

Printed in the United States.

**Library of Congress Cataloging-in-Publication Data**

Negotiation alchemy : global skills that inspire and transform diverging worlds / Nancy Erbe, editor.
p. cm.
Includes bibliographical references and index.
ISBN 978-0-87772-438-4
1. Mediation. 2. Conflict management—Case studies. 3. Dispute resolution (Law)—Social aspects. I. Erbe, Nancy.
HM1126.N44 2011
303.6'9—dc23

2011023960

## Dedication

This book is lovingly dedicated to my mother Diane, a professional teacher who danced with me and encouraged joy in exploration, learning and creative expression every day, my gifted inspirational engineer father Richard who nurtured me since birth and helped me prove that girls could excel in math and physics too, my soul partner Suraji who passionately cares for all people fighting for their rights, my grandfather Henry who enjoyed life while standing for workers' right to decency, my grandmothers Lisette and Nanna and aunts who modeled strong empowered women, my great aunt Lynn who also served in World War II and actively encouraged my peace work, and all the immigrants, nationalities and languages in my family who taught me to persist in the face of odds and relish this life and world. Thank God they and others still believe that true democracy is worth the struggle.

## Acknowledgment of Permissions and Copyrights

An earlier version of Section III appears in Al-Hakim & Jin (2010). *Innovation In Business and Enterprise.* Hershey, PA: Business Science Reference, 209-223.

An earlier version of Section IV is published as Nancy Erbe, *The Global Popularity and Promise of Facilitative ADR,* 18 TEMP. INT'L & COMP. L.J. 343 (2004).

An earlier version of Section V is published as Nancy Erbe, *Negotiating and Mediating Peace in Africa,* 9 PEPPERDINE DISP. RES. L.J. 457 (2003).

Section VI is reproduced with permission of Harvard Law School from the earlier publication Nancy Erbe, *Appreciating Mediation's Global Role in Promoting Good Governance,* 11 HARVARD NEGOT. L. REV. 355 (2006); permission conveyed through Copyright Clearance, Inc.

# Contents

# Acknowledgements

This reader was researched and written with a collective who I respect and appreciate very much. Their names and work are identified throughout the book. I would also like to acknowledge and thank the book's reviewers. Colonel Swaranjit Singh know the costs and challenges of war, terrorism, violence and peacebuilding intimately. Professor Ahmet Sozen has worked for peace his entire professional and academic career. Professor Augustine ("Gus") Martin is an appreciated colleague and the author of Sage's leading best seller on terrorism. Former student Mandala Pham brought her rich multicultural experience and her passion for negotiation, conflict resolution and peacebuilding. I am also grateful to my former editors who diligently helped me polish this work at the journals and books that previously published: *Harvard Negotiation Law Journal, Pepperdine Journal of Dispute Resolution, Temple Journal of Comparative and International Law, the 4R Journal of the Education Section, Association for Conflict Resolution*, the Sage *Encyclopedia of Governance, Business Research Yearbook, Innovation in Business and Enterprise, Journal of the International Ombudsman*, and *Seeds Bearing Fruit Pan African Peace Action for the Twenty-First Century*. The important final editing was done by Maria Wolf for publication by the Institute of Governmental Studies at the University of California, Berkeley, under its Director Ethan Rarick and with the encouragement and support of Professor Chris Ansell. Thank you. This reader was piloted in my Key Issues in Peacebuilding class at California State University Dominguez Hills. I wish to extend a special appreciation to my students who took the time to give me valued feedback: Lisa La, Anthony Leavell, Ongele Harris, Richard Quiloan, Adrianna Gehr, Jeremy Napial, Courtney Hudson, Heather Saint, John Lira and Raven Harris. I appreciate all of my students; how they continually stimulate and encourage me with their interest in and passion for peace. Last, but not least, thanks to the many “unsung heroes” around the globe who moment by moment, day by day, chose to do the right thing, care about another and otherwise build the peace present today. Without you and your efforts, our societies and quality of life would dramatically deteriorate. Suffering would increase. I salute all of you.

# Introduction and Rationale

Welcome to *Negotiation Alchemy: Global Skills Inspiring and Transforming Diverging Worlds.* The author has been invited to assist, coach, and facilitate the cross ethnic process described throughout this reader for over two decades. While her efforts began in the multicultural communities of the United States, her clients and students to-date come from over 70 different countries.

Like many professors of negotiation and dispute resolution in the United States, the author's career began as a trial lawyer and lawyer-mediator facilitating early settlement of a wide range of lawsuits, from business to divorce. After she was approached several times to assist with cross-cultural conflict and particularly after she was asked to do so outside the States, she began to research how conflicts were being handled in other countries. As a result, unlike most scholars of negotiation and dispute resolution, the author's scholarship focuses on conflict process outside the States as well as within, particularly the best of multicultural process present today.

Peace studies and international relations are just beginning to include participatory conflict process in their literature. The largest comparable body of literature is found in intercultural communication and negotiation. Since this literature is often comparative—comparing the styles of two cultures (e.g., Chinese and American), the reader will find that this collection of articles is new in exploring the ways mediated, or assisted, conflict process can bring several cultural approaches together to design a multicultural process that facilitates relationship building, understanding, negotiation of differences, creative problem solving and otherwise creates lasting goodwill.

*Negotiation Alchemy: Global Skills Inspiring and Transforming Diverging Worlds* is not a traditional textbook or traditional reader. Like a reader, it brings together and presents several articles and chapters published before—in *Harvard Negotiation Law Journal* and other publications concerned with dispute resolution, international law, business innovation and African peacebuilding. Unlike most readers that collect and introduce several short articles, this reader presents a few short introductory pieces and then focuses on four chapter and multichapter length articles. To help the reader, these articles have been divided into shorter sections, with explanations and skill building activities. Language has also been edited to be as plain and simple as possible while still maintaining the original meaning. (Since the concepts and processes will be new to many readers, they are advised to keep a dictionary close by while they are reading and regularly reference it, along with the book's glossary).

*Negotiation Alchemy: Global Skills Inspiring and Transforming Diverging Worlds* will introduce the emerging potential and promise of skillfully facilitated conflict process to professionals and students who wish to make an important difference with cross-cultural dialogue, resource disputes, and other critical challenges, local and global. Readers who fully engage themselves in beginning to understand the new processes introduced here and exploring their own awareness and skills with the activities at the end of each section will be equipped to begin offering their strengths and proposing new promising alternatives to address their most important concerns and causes. Readers will discover that while these processes are new, they already have several skills and attitudes to contribute to these processes. They will also learn exactly which skills and attitudes they must develop and improve to become the charismatic and trusted leader of such process.

It is important to understand that the study and practice of facilitated, or assisted, multicultural conflict process and negotiation is inherently creative and dynamic. There can never be a set formula for crafting such complex shifting practice. Arguably, its practitioners are artists skillfully co-designing a particular process with all those concerned.

Courses teaching the fundamental skills must engage students in role-play practice, applied analysis, and reflection that includes constant observation of self and others, and evaluation of effectiveness through gathering honest, diverse feedback. It is the author's belief and experience, though, that students are best served and equipped by beginning this process with an inventory of personal strengths and natural talents. Perhaps like other artists, the sensitive nature required for insightful and empathetic mediation can be easily discouraged by harsh insensitive criticism or its own perfectionist self-critic. The field of peacebuilding cannot afford to lose the gifts and contributions of the sensitive students and professionals it most needs to move forward.

The study of negotiation, conflict resolution, and peacebuilding (NCRP) is also highly interdisciplinary and thus sometimes challenging to those who have only studied one discipline. NCRP must draw upon the disciplines of anthropology, communications, labor studies, law, peace studies, political science, psychology, and sociology—to name a few of its primary contributors. This reader is designed to be a rich resource for university students and professionals who are interested in learning how popular conflict skills can be used to effectively reduce violence and bullying, create the best of multicultural dialogue, collaboration and community, build peace in the midst of violent conflict, and advance democracy in several different practical ways. The content is directed to academics and professional courses of instruction whose subject areas include conflict resolution, environmental and urban planning, peace and development studies, international relations, international social work, intercultural communication, innovation, community development, and related subjects. It can be incorporated into many different classes and seminars, especially if used as supplementary literature introducing new and promising global and multicultural processes. The intended level of instruction is undergraduate and master's level university students as well as many professionals challenged by conflict: doctors without borders, engineers, planners, human resource directors, law enforcement officers, nurses, ombuds, public managers, social workers, and teachers—to name some of the most common students of these processes. Prerequisites recommended are courses that introduce the core processes of interest based negotiation and facilitated or skilled mediation (to be contrasted with the common alternative where a respected authority, elder or expert directs the parties to conflict).

## Course Overview and Pedagogy

*Negotiation Alchemy* introduces the reader to the role skilled mediation can play in reducing violence, building multicultural relationships and inclusive, participatory democracy. It reviews several real world case studies showing the details of effective process explored and elaborated from different perspectives in this collection of articles.

The pedagogical approach of *Negotiation Alchemy: Global Skills Inspiring and Transforming Diverging Worlds* reflects the approach commonly used in teaching negotiation, mediation, and other conflict resolution skills. In line with adult learning principles and practices, it is applied, interactive, and reflective. Students "learn by doing," evaluating what they have done and creating as well as implementing plans for improvement. They do this individually and through group work—the latter is particularly popular. (Note: Several excellent resources already exist for group activities. Readers may appreciate the author's interactive case study curriculum *Holding These Truths: Empowerment and Recognition in Action* available through the same publisher as this book). Here such activities follow each section. Since much new information is presented, instructors may wish to incorporate more traditional ways of assessing information comprehension in addition to the exercises provided at the end of each section.

## Chapter Guide

This volume is organized into six thematic sections, each consisting of two to three parts. Appendices guiding the interested reader in learning more about the conflicts in the Balkans, Cameroon, Nepal, and Ukraine, and a glossary index are included at the end of the text. The first section introduces citizen's diplomacy with a short introduction to nonviolent resistance as well as new uses of conflict resolution. The most popular processes appear to be interest-based negotiation and facilitated mediation—at least for cross ethnic process. These processes are also introduced. The introduction for mediation includes links with democracy building.

The second section reviews the essential role of nonviolent resistance with peacebuilding (along with government use of force) but also introduces the necessity of creating peace in addition to resisting injustice. Two articles are shared that describe specific conflict tools and skills that the author has found promising with containing and preventing violent conflict with youthful offenders and bullies.

Violence is often what readers will envision as conflict resolution's most important challenge with cross-ethnic conflict. The emerging global reality though is that cross-ethnic interaction is more often nonviolent and holds increasing promise for stimulating creative innovation. Thus, the third section reviews the specific conflict resolution techniques that the author's multicultural and minority classrooms have found optimal. The focus is innovation through building cross-cultural relationships and collaboration. This section also more thoroughly introduces the steps and skills of facilitated mediation. Thus the reader is better prepared for understanding the processes and case studies described in subsequent sections.

Cross-ethnic violence does describe one of the most gruesome and challenging realities facing many countries today. The fourth section describes how participants in cross-cultural dialogue evaluate optimal multicultural leadership and process. This dialogue occurred in the Balkans during its war and Cameroon post-violent conflict; through court mandated mediation in Nepal, and cross ethnic community mediation in Ukraine. Somehow skilled mediators found ways to facilitate cross-ethnic dialogue in the face of fierce minority prejudice and violent conflict. It is interesting to note that two of these parts of the world have experienced dramatic societal transformation since the time of the cross-ethnic processes described. The Balkans found their way out of tragic war. Nepal ousted its monarchy. One wonders if the community empowerment described in this section contributed to such important change.

The fifth section goes further and deeper in exploring the detailed process that has proven successful in Cameroon. It also shares the thoughts of four African authors who are educated in the skills and processes described in this book. Each is from a different African nation and profession. As a lawyer-ombuds, theologian-pastor, historian-activist, and journalist-filmmaker, they share their hopes and visions for addressing some of the toughest conflict and challenge facing their country and continent. They share their experience and recommendations about how these tools are helping and could further help their communities.

The sixth section explores the question that naturally flows from reading the previous case studies regarding mediation's success and potential with cross-ethnic conflict: can such mediation also help in building and advancing democracy within the United States and around the world? This section not only presents facilitative mediation's many parallels with democratization within nation-states but also its potential with building necessary global governance to decide critical issues that concern all like sustainable development, through guiding genuinely inclusive and effective participatory process and fair viable community partnerships. It is divided into several parts so that readers can digest and discuss each one separately.

Section I

# "Ordinary" People Are Building Peace with Conflict Tools

> Peace culture is a culture that promotes peaceable diversity. . . . *The ceaseless culture creating activity that characterizes the social body involves interaction at every level, from the intrapersonal . . . to the interpersonal in household, neighborhood, and community, on through successive levels of civic organization from city to the United Nations.* . . . Because there is a constant interpenetration of levels, the societal capacity for aggression or peacebuilding, depends on patterns developed in every domain, from the individual and the interpersonal to the national, and interenvironmental (emphasis added) UNESCO.

Traditionally when peace is mentioned, most think of what scholars refer to as negative peace or the absence of war. In recent years, the scholarly definition of peace has expanded to include positive peace—a much more complex and dynamic concept involving second track, or citizen, as well as traditional peacebuilding. While sudden attack can shatter innocent lives unexpectedly, peace rarely surprises. Instead, it must be a purposeful choice that is built and carried on over time.

This section introduces informal citizen, or second track diplomacy, with a brief introduction to nonviolent resistance along with their most popular conflict resolution processes: negotiation and mediation. In its introduction of mediation, it will also begin introducing the connections between facilitated, or skillful, mediation and democracy building as described by good governance scholars.

# Part 1: Introducing Second Track Diplomacy

Second track or people diplomacy encompasses all informal efforts at peacebuilding to prevent war or restore society after war, through the development of culture and institutions that sustain peace. "Track two" peacebuilding stands in contrast to first track, or traditional and formal international diplomacy, where officially designated representatives, such as heads of state and ambassadors, come together for political reasons. High profile nongovernmental organizations and citizen activists are often publicized with unofficial diplomacy. A wide range of less visible stakeholders, however, can be quite influential in nonrepresentative activities and forums. In many conflicts, the stakeholders are not publicized. Those interested in studying multitrack diplomacy must ask: who is acting to prevent conflict? Is anyone effectively mediating difference?

Even our Nobel Prize inspirations like Dr. Martin Luther King Jr. and Archbishop Desmond Tutu of South Africa, however, give us only an introduction to one of the essential citizen processes present in the modern picture of peace. Their skillful and strategic use of nonviolent resistance, or noncooperation with media exposure of injustice, exercised with strong local and global support, is worthy of study and understanding by all working for global awareness and justice. It begins to introduce how an ordinary person can join, or even create and lead, causes that make key differences.

The power of nonviolent resistance can be practiced at a micro conflict process level as well as the community and political level. Parties to conflict can consistently refuse to cooperate with any behavior or attitude they oppose and instead, like Gandhi or Dr. King, emulate higher ground again and again. Parties to conflict can go even further and build strategic alliances to support and publicize the best of such nonviolent strategy. The time is ripe to see a movement insisting on higher moral ground with global conflict resolution. If every person would discipline themselves to only cooperate with that (acts, relationships, employers, decisions) that reflect their values, principles, and ideals, one can imagine how incredibly transformative such non-cooperation would be—for the individual, their groups, and society as a whole.

Yet even Gandhi, arguably the world's greatest inspiration, strategist, and teacher of nonviolent resistance, would likely agree that India's liberation from oppression was only the first step forward and sadly, actually increased violence between warring Hindus and Muslims. Building peace requires more than independence—no matter how important liberation may be. The continuing violence in liberated Iraq after years of costly warfare brings this painful and troubling reality close to all Americans.

An honest witness to history is forced to admit this sobering truth—that no matter the size or force of the army and the level of weapons built, brute military force alone, or the threat of that force, has not built peace that lasts or spreads throughout all of any society's communities—poor as well as rich. Government force, whether military or law enforcement, and citizen resistance, or force, through nonviolence—both can only play limited roles in building peace.

This book will not attempt to study governments' current or best role in building peace. Many books of political science address this debate. Instead, this book attempts to introduce a much less studied effort with building peace. The growing role of the average person or professional concerned with violent conflict, cross racial and ethnic fighting, and a range of injustices is shared. These actors are discovering that while injustice, oppression, and bullying can and must be resisted, peace must be created and co-created. While peace work used to be seen, at least within the Western world, as primarily protesting war in some other country, contemporary peacebuilding recognizes that domestic efforts are as important as garnering outside support. Anyone who has experienced domestic or community violence appreciates the challenge intimately. In the best of societies, law enforcement and rule of law can provide some help and hopefully protection, but those at risk must be prepared to take the lead, strategize, rally resources, and build whatever is needed for safety and well-being.

The growing emergence of grassroots peacebuilding reflects contemporary concerns. In some parts of the world, for example, security, in its traditional military sense, has not been a concern for years. Instead, challenges that require regional and local cooperation, like resource disputes, are a priority. Actors concerned with environmental and other complex global tension, like ethnic conflict, are pioneering a multistakeholder process that includes many of the actors listed below.

Second track diplomacy mirrors and parallels the widespread transfer of powers, rights and functions to organizations within civil society. Our most powerful international actors are no longer necessarily the heads of state but include transnational corporations, churches, and nongovernmental organizations like Amnesty International and Web-based campaigns like Avaaz.org and Human Rights Watch. General Electric, in one instance, is credited with promoting peaceful conflict resolution between India and Pakistan. Philanthropy, finance institutions, professional and labor groups, academia, and media also play roles as opinion leaders and evaluative researchers demonstrating worth of investment and thus persuading funders to continue support.

Naturally, involvement of these stakeholders alone does not guarantee diplomacy. Transnational corporations and churches have been instrumental to violent and corrupt dynamics, including notorious war crimes. In such circumstances, developing civic society strong enough to weaken, or at least check and publicize, authoritarian abuse of power reflects track two diplomacy. Strong citizens are less likely to be manipulated by governments leading genocide, for example. Empowering communities in the face of self-interested political leadership is man's best; perhaps only, option for building peace. Seeking and protecting political leadership whose interest is embedded in their community's welfare is one of many critical challenges.

Private stakeholders, like those named above, are often best situated to respond to particular needs. They may have practical insight and information not readily available to government. Civil society is most often acknowledged for closeness to people. Furthermore, civil society groups are often more flexible than government bureaucracies, allowing them to act swiftly and more creatively to newly arising issues and concerns.

Visionary initiative can create unexpected opportunities. Those who can operate flexibly, with access to people and networks that can be mobilized quickly, can take this lead. The Oslo Accords, as one instance, were preceded by months of informal communication preparing the ground for formal negotiation through building relationships and identifying common ground.

Increasingly, formal and informal diplomacy merge. The negotiation of South Africa's transitional constitution brought official and track two diplomacy together. It opened meetings to the public through a media campaign, made materials accessible with the Internet, and widely circulated a draft constitution for review, comment, and objection. Government and business need independent watchdogs to oversee and stimulate their best. Nongovernmental organizations often serve as these watchdogs.

At its best, informal community diplomacy fills critical gaps in international capacity. Intranational and cross-ethnic disputes often fall outside international authority. Without track two alternatives, minority ethnic groups may see their only option as violent effort for independence. With track two diplomacy, those involved have opportunities to gain understanding, transform costly destructive attitudes, build bridges and balance between rights and responsibilities, and create lasting resolution. Concrete ways for citizens to develop democratic capacities are common.

Likewise, emerging international law and mechanisms explain growth in unofficial diplomacy. Traditionally, international was literally interpreted as between two nation-states. Now, however, citizens are free to bring grievances, such as human rights violations, outside their state of citizenship. Business can craft arbitration of disputes and avoid national forums. The international community and its organizations can call and create truth and reconciliation and other forums to investigate the blame of a nation's citizens and leaders. Restorative justice's role in emerging international systems is a strong example of second track diplomacy. Truth and reconciliation commissions engage interested community, including victims of crime and nongovernmental organizations, in negotiating repair of harm with offenders admitting responsibility.

Track two diplomacy raises questions about the impact of independent uncoordinated efforts—potentially problematic if at odds with formal government efforts. Yet given the seemingly impossible challenges traditional diplomacy faces, imagined in an ideal world is that unofficial diplomacy supports formal diplomacy. Perhaps it can even create the conditions necessary for official efforts to succeed. If second track diplomacy can relieve some of the formal pressure and fix a few failings and limits, institutional systems are freed to strengthen capacity and realize ideals. Some government agents are recognizing this potential and initiating multitrack partnering. The multistakeholder process involving Europe's Convention on Access to Information, Public Participation in Decision-making and Justice in Environmental Matter, as one instance, is heralded as a model for multilateral policymaking, emulating democratization of global institutions.

Which professions are most motivated to make the commitment to track two diplomacy and play this essential leadership role? Unfortunately, many nongovernmental organizations appear more renowned for their competition over funding than their proactive community partnering and effective peacebuilding. (Fortunately there are others like the International Red Cross with strong reputations and roles.) History shows that despite religion's role with fueling war, prejudice, and hatred, religious leaders of many different faiths represent a likely profession to organize against the worst of exploitation and oppression. Occasionally, labor leaders join them in exercising the moral courage and influence needed to advance their communities' most important needs. Once in a while a grieving parent, like the mothers who started Mothers Against Drunk Driving or those who have lost children and loved ones to war, e.g., Women Waging Peace Network, emerge from their sorrow to lead movements, speak truth to power, and otherwise help change the conditions of their tragedy.

One would imagine more social workers, politicians, and law enforcement officers being moved to serve their communities, and perhaps they do—in daily unrecognized service. In some war-torn societies, doctors and nurses are the surprising trusted impartial mediators—but too often unequipped and untrained to effectively respond to conflict or lead community change.

While the public enjoys creating and honoring heroes, unlike medicine or literature, leaders in peacebuilding and conflict resolution never act alone. They must build critical alliances and rally collective support like Desmond Tutu did during South Africa's apartheid. Ordinary human behavior, in contrast, is too often bullying or manipulating family and other group members into conformity and submission. It takes extraordinary sensitivity and skill "to walk the middle" without being labeled as and suspected to be a traitor. Our greatest inspirations must live exceptional rather than ordinary lives. Having suffered horrifying tragedy, they nevertheless declare "I have no enemy," stay open to hearing and deeply understanding all embroiled in conflict, seek and discover common ground, and co-create optimal response for all concerned. The most effective inspire others to do the same.

All living inspirations, past and present, demonstrate effective use of conflict resolution skills and tools. Gandhi, as his story is told, was first an unsuccessful Oxford educated lawyer who failed to establish a practice in India. He nevertheless was well prepared for clever rebuttals when later interrogated in British courts, but more importantly, became a smart strategist who aligned with Western media and persuaded the Indian masses. Barack Obama, community organizer and lawyer, evoked such memories as he traveled the States during his campaign. He added a modern strategy. Like former candidate Howard Dean, he knew how to persuade and organize the youngest voters electronically as well as through traditional media. Contemporary use of conflict resolution skills and tools for building peace does the same.

It is likely that there are many unsung heroes of social justice and peace-building that most will never know. Federal district court judge Thelton Henderson is one noteworthy example of the tough impartiality described throughout this book. As a judge rather than a mediator, he has shown consistent assertion of the moral boundaries embedded in the United States Constitution—in the face of great political opposition. His judicial oversight against cruel and unusual punishment in California prisons brings to mind the judicial oversight that was required to begin ending segregation in United States public schools and the ombuds oversight of international agencies described later in this book.

## Part 2: Introducing Skillful Negotiation

Negotiation embraces many strategies and tactics exercised to influence agreement in efforts to create value, solve problems, and resolve disputes. Bargaining encompasses a broad array of simple two-party to complex multiparty encounters, domestic and international.

### Optimally Distributive and Integrative

When the average person envisions negotiation, they often see what is referred to in negotiation literature as the distributive dance. This is a simple linear model, with what is termed a "fixed pie," or limited resources to be divided, such as water. Negotiating the price of a home or car further shows the simplistic and straightforward distributive dynamics. The buyer or seller begins with an opening offer, demand, or position. The other party responds with a counter offer or demand. Through a series of moves and countermoves, the parties proceed to "split the difference"—the distance between the two offers, with a predictable dance of proportional and responsive concessions until they reach agreement through compromise.

Most negotiations, however, do not merely involve a "fixed pie" to be divided. They encompass complex layers of interests and needs to be explored, identified and satisfied, rather than split. Integrative in contrast to distributive bargaining assumes interdependence. It is designed to handle complexity. It expects that different stakeholders will define desired outcomes in their own subjective ways. It does not equate such difference in perspectives with distributive positioning. Instead, diverse perspectives are studied and reframed in search for options maximizing satisfaction, without requiring change in mandate.

Roger Fisher, founder of the Harvard Negotiation Project, introduced and popularized interest analysis as an alternative to positional, or power-based, bargaining. Rather than expecting political leaders to abandon their postures, they are analyzed. Then the principals' underlying interests are used to stimulate creative problem-solving.

In contrast, framing a complex conflict with linear logic as a simple "either/or" win-lose paradigm can polarize. Overly confident distributive moves risk escalating hostility, eroding trust, and otherwise inciting unproductive moves, particularly with conflict involving groups. A study of United States lawyers described the least effective with words like arrogant, stubborn, unethical, and egotistic. A study of multicultural leadership of conflict process in four parts of the world likewise described the least effective as closed minded, judgmental, insensitive, negative, and indifferent. Even if a party succeeds in forcing its desire, the agreement is unlikely to last. The risk of public scrutiny and negative publicity is high.

Distributive bargaining in the international arena makes most sense with truly "fixed pies." Even then, it must be exercised with skill and strategy to avoid incurring the costs described above.

United Nations and other international case study evaluating negotiation indicate that integrative approaches as a whole generally result in superior outcomes. Simple logic advocates that agreements reached by consensus are more sustainable and easier to implement than those imposed. Mediators, or facilitators of negotiation, are increasingly recognized as contributing necessary sophistication when parties lack knowledge and experience with integrative bargaining. In the global study of multicultural leadership mentioned above, careful listening alone can lead to progress, particularly with cross-ethnic negotiation.

A student of conflict resolution, whose family immigrated to the United States from Afghanistan shortly after his birth, credits the coming together of ethnic factions in Afghanistan to integrative bargaining. His intriguing perspective asserts that after a long history of distributive failures, resolution was only possible after finally attempting interest- based negotiation for the first time.

## Proven Research and Theories

Most negotiation research and resultant theories are criticized for not translating into pragmatic usefulness. Short-term laboratory studies fail to simulate complex conflict. Howard Raiffa, renown games theorist, in working as an international administrator had an opportunity to test his paradigms' practicality and found that negotiators often fail to act in rational, coherent ways.

A few studies, however, are noteworthy exceptions. They demonstrate that while many rational models and theories are not capable of predicting diverse cultural as well as irrational behavior, they can provide insight capable of making critical difference.

Robert Axelrod provides one important example. He did extensive mathematical research attempting to identify optimal strategy for transforming aggressive tactics to collaborative bargaining. The results indicated the following. Beginning negotiation cooperatively and giving generously builds goodwill. Otherwise a defensive, hostile climate is created. Transforming broken trust is harder than beginning in ways that earn and build trust. The other's goodwill, however, cannot be assumed. Negotiators must be vigilant—alert and prepared to respond strategically to each countermove, move by move, like a game of chess. If an opponent responds aggressively, it is recommended to respond in kind to the degree necessary to inform one's opponent that the proponent is not vulnerable to attack. At that point, generously offering an olive branch, or opportunity to continue working together, gives the opponent an opportunity to collaborate once again. If the invitation is accepted, hostility has been successfully transformed to cooperation, at least for that moment. If an opponent stubbornly persists in aggression, however, the negotiator must resist.

Neil Rackham's research is another example. Scrutinizing labor-management negotiations, Rackham found that the most effective, judged so by all parties and demonstrated through durable agreement, involved these behaviors. The best were excellent gatherers of information, asking many more questions than less effective negotiators. They listened actively. They zealously sought common ground and creative options that benefited all. In contrast, the less effective frequently demonstrated unstrategic attack and wasted much energy rehearsing arguments in their minds. Thus, they failed to observe and hear what could have helped them.

## Part 3: Introducing Mediation and Its Relationship to Building Democracy

Simply defined, any force outside of a conflict mediates when it assists with that conflict's management, negotiation, resolution or transformation—even the strengthening of relationships—without the use of force. If all parties to a conflict agree, a third-party individual, state, group, or organization not involved in the conflict and often described as impartial, can intervene.

Conflict mediation is growing dramatically, threefold or more, as state power declines. New regional, international, and civil society conflict mechanisms reframe global shifts. The focus is shifting from sovereigns to international community. Confrontation is not the only option with the emergence of negotiated collaboration. As a result, control is giving way to shared capacities. Present definitions of good governance stress civil society rather than government. They deconstruct political will into articulation of interests, exercise of rights, and mediation of differences. Conflict mediation can be and is equated with governance. Likewise, democratic governance is advocated as effective conflict mediation. Informal conflict mediation can satisfy many needs and challenges outside the purview of formal governance, at all levels of society. For example, the majority of significant global conflict is intrastate and ethnic—beyond international law's mandate. In response, more and more new programs are training activists and other members of civil society, along with international diplomats and lawyers, in the skills and attitudes of facilitative conflict mediation. Good governance, for the purposes of this book, will be defined as the optimal exertion of societal influence, or effective democratic culture. The emerging role of mediation with building democratic capacity will be elaborated in great detail in the last section of this book.

## Contemporary Conflict Mediation Bridges Traditional Distinctions between Roles and Responsibilities of States and Citizens

Multilevel analysis is necessary to understand evolving conflict mediation. Traditionally, heads of state and state representatives mediate international conflict through exercising their power of authority, and promising resources or other support. Distributive bargaining, or negotiating division, has predominated. State-compelled mediation is still prevalent, particularly with high profile crisis, but increasingly complemented with more collaborative mediation initiated by civil society and international organizations like the United Nations. As described earlier, integrative bargaining aims to avoid division through constructing innovative, collective possibilities. Conflict is framed as partnering to search for options that consider all interests—how might we respect sovereignty and ethnic self-determination, for example. Collaborative mediation aspires to increase sustainable (durable) resolution through building civil society cooperation rather than dependence on state oversight.

States and international organizations are attempting to respond to the changing global order by institutionalizing mediation. Transnational corporations are following this lead. As a result, conflict mediation is both centralized in government programs, domestic and international, and institutionalized within transnational corporations. At the same time, though, mediation is also decentralized. Any member of civil society is free to start informal, and sometimes formal, mediation. Thus, conflict mediation is institutionalized yet simultaneously acts as a means for institutional reform, providing an alternative to untrustworthy, nonresponsive, and partial systems.

Some contend that civil society's roles with contemporary governance are providing broad, inclusive public participation and overseeing accountability. Business' responsibility is to promote efficient effectiveness. Government facilitates rule of law, with transparency. These lines, however, are increasingly blurred. Civil society, for example, can participate in negotiated rule-making and thus create rule of law.

## Linkages between Conflict Mediation and Governance

Many linkages, explicit and implicit, exist between conflict mediation and the changing nature of governance. Consequently, conflict mediation has potential to build or erode governance. At its best, democratic mediation, in contrast to state-compelled solutions, bridges legal systems, crosses cultures, promises transparency, and builds relationships rather than destroys them.

Citizen participation in conflict mediation is increasingly personal as well as representative. Multistakeholder process, like the negotiation of South Africa's Peace Accords, includes more of those affected by decisions, interested parties like nongovernmental organizations, and state representatives. The United Nations Economic Commission for Europe's Convention on Access to Information, Public Participation in Decisionmaking and Access to Justice in Environmental Matter also included nongovernmental organizations in the design of its negotiation process and negotiation. It is lauded as a model for multilateral policymaking, or democratization of international institutions.

The office of ombuds is yet another form of conflict mediation and governance growing in popularity. The office created by the International Finance Corporation and Multilateral Investment Guarantee Agency is one well-studied example. The ethical principles and independent oversight of the ombuds office prioritize civil society's interests in transparency, responsiveness, and robust accountability through a designated independent third party.

The model offered by international commercial arbitration is spreading as a preferred ombuds-like governance structure. Parties to conflict select three member panels—one chosen by each party or approved by all. A nongovernmental representative with an established reputation for impartiality, like the International Red Cross, may be one of the trusted panelists. Panels mediate conflict and provide oversight to ensure good faith.

Interesting challenges and questions arise with changing governance and conflict mediation. What space do states and international organizations have for negotiating with civil society within their mandates? Will increasing accountability with human rights quiet demands for ethnic self-determination? As civil society initiates more and more sustained and collaborative conflict mediation to advance democracy, how will such effort interface or impact state territorial integrity?

## Conclusion

Surprisingly, these conflict resolution skills and processes have received relatively little attention with peacebuilding despite the promise they are showing with cross ethnic conflict and their remarkable parallels to democratic governance. Scholars and professionals seem primarily focused on traditional diplomacy, realist politics, and the role of international institutions and rule of law, or authoritarian processes. While these remain critical areas of concern, they have yet to show that they have capacity to effectively address the globe's most troubling violence and insurgency—at least by themselves and without doing something new. Due to their limits and failures, during the last several years individuals and groups have been forced to seek and create their own options for protection and empowerment such as immigration to nations with trustworthy rule of law and safe havens, and reliance on international human rights.

If power politics, or the eternal war to dominate for short-term gain and loss continues, with widespread tolerance for ruthless brutality, manipulation, and wealth for a privileged few, how can citizens committed to democracy ensure growth in the fair rule of law and shared prosperity as well as security? It is particularly essential that those from the most powerful nations do whatever they can to ensure that the power of their nations is not abused. Otherwise, democracy's credibility will continue to be discredited as self-interested hypocrisy. The ironic tension present today cannot be denied. The democratic nations must remain the most powerful to counter and contain widespread and ruthless disregard for life. At the same time, they must find a way to promote, nurture, and emulate true democracy where all concerned participate equally and are treated equally, at least in regards to fundamental human rights.

Promoting conflict resolution tools and processes as pragmatic steps to democracy building may seem like a utopian dream. The fact remains that the majority of armed conflicts end through negotiation. Citizens around the world continue to organize and influence history. Science and technology have received steady interest and investment since ancient times in countries like Egypt, Greece, India, and China. In comparison, peace and conflict studies are relatively young, with research for only about the last 50 years. Thus, any solid conclusions about peace and conflict resolution's potential deserve more time. Conflict resolution as an academic discipline is even younger—emerging as a more common program in just the last 30 years. Combining conflict resolution skill education with peace studies did not occur until recent years.

Why has mediation and other conflict process and skill not received the serious scholarly consideration its potential appears to warrant? In the United States, the court system, particularly that overwhelmed with small claims, quickly embraced mediation, giving it the stigma of a process worth trying when not much is at stake. Corporations, government agencies, and other powerful organizations praised such informal process as a means to minimize conflict's costs. Unfortunately, commercial interest often influenced a highly partisan rather than impartial process. Thousands hoping to earn extra income as mediators enrolled in 40-hour training courses and advertised their newly discovered and quickly developed skill as mediation. Given the relative infancy of mediation's professional use, the skills and knowledge offered were too often elementary rather than masterful.

Fortunately, as will be described throughout this book, visionary practitioners concerned with their communities' futures have simultaneously been experimenting with mediation and related skills. Some of the obstacles that they face in their attempts to fulfill these processes' global promise include the following: (1) widespread passivity in waiting for a "friendly enemy" before engaging rather than exercising necessary leadership, (2) general ignorance about the conflict resolution and peacebuilding options and alternatives presented in this book, (3) common knowledge of conflict resolution language masking lack of necessary skill and advanced competence, and (4) at least within the United States, predictable avoidance of personal encounter with the most emotional and contentious—tough—conflict, even within the conflict resolution practitioner community. This may reflect the earlier described commercial profitmaking focus with its attendant cost analysis.

This book aspires to begin equipping those interested in effectively meeting these challenges. It introduces several negotiation and mediation skills and processes showing promise with bridging ethnic divides—even violent. After an introduction explaining how the following practices also have relevance at the global, or macro, level of peacebuilding, the next section presents two articles. They describe how the mediation practices of negotiating ground rules, suspending judgment, careful listening, and compassionate mentoring are showing promise with reducing the violent behavior of youth offenders. The following section describes in detail how these same and other mediation tools can be used to build cross-ethnic community and structure rich creative problemsolving. That section is followed by two sharing case study examples and success stories applying these mediation steps and skills in the midst of cross-ethnic violence in the Balkans and Cameroon, as well as for minority empowerment and inclusion in the face of prejudice and oppression in Nepal and Ukraine.

## Comments and Questions

1. Identify one or more of your concerns related to peacebuilding. In response to this/these concern(s), write one or more goals that you would like to achieve in addressing your concern at each of these levels of peacebuilding: personal, community, national, and international. Share and discuss through an interactive social networking site.

2. Observe yourself cooperating and not cooperating as you experience an ordinary day. Do you only cooperate with that which reflects your personal values or do you allow others to dictate your actions? Do you ever find yourself betraying your values? How might you not cooperate with what you find to be unjust?

3. Do you see yourself as involved with track two diplomacy or people's peacebuilding, whether in your local community or with a global cause? If so, include a description and evaluation of your involvement and experience in your introduction from activity 1. This evaluation can be quite simple, stating your perception of what was most helpful, what was not, and what you would do differently in the future.

   If your answer is no, can you imagine yourself involved with peacebuilding? Describe your ideal image. You are also welcome and encouraged to include this in the goals you created from doing activity 1 above.

4. What is your experience with and knowledge of negotiation? Include a description with your introduction. You are welcome to include the study and use of negotiation in one or more of your goals.

5. What is your experience with and knowledge of mediation? Include a description with your introduction. You are welcome to include the study and use of mediation in one or more of your goals.

## Bibliography and Recommended Reading

Dukes, F. 1996. *Resolving Public Conflict: Transforming Community and Governance*. Manchester, United Kingdom: Manchester University.

Erbe, N. 2006. "Appreciating Alternative Dispute Resolution's Global Role with Good Governance." 11 *Harv. Negot. L. R.* 355–419.

———. 2005a. "Communications Theory and Restorative Justice: Approaches to Proactive Conflict Resolution." XII *Business Research Yearbook*, 696–700.

———. 2005b. "Optimal Strategy with Global Disputes: Blending the Best of Distributive and Integrative Bargaining." XII *Business Research Yearbook*, 748–52.

———. 2004. The Global Popularity and Promise of Facilitative ADR. 18 *Temple Int'l. & Comp. L. J.* 343–89.

———. 2004. "Appreciating Alternative Dispute Resolution's Global Role with Good Governance." Paper presented at the biennial conference for graduate students studying conflict, Boston, Mass., October.

———. 2003. *Holding These Truths: Empowerment and Recognition in Action* (an interactive case study curriculum for multicultural conflict resolution). Berkeley: Public Policy Press.

Hemmati, M. 2002. *Multi-Stakeholder Processes for Governance.* London; Sterling, Va.: Earthscan Publications.

Raiffa, H., J. Richardson, and D. Metcalfe, D. 2003. *Negotiation Analysis: The Science and Art of Decision Making*. Cambridge: Harvard University Press.

Schneider, A. 2002". Shattering Negotiation Myths: Empirical Evidence on the Effectiveness of Negotiation Styles." 7 *Harv. Negot. L. Rev.* 143–243.

Section II

# Conflict Resolution Can Decrease Violence and Bullying

> Peacemaking is marked by experimentation. There is no right way to go about creating peaceful communities and a peaceful world. Working for peace will differ according to context (Herr and Herr 1998).

It is a common cliché for American yoga enthusiasts and others new to meditation to say that a person must first have peace within to begin building peace outside. Perhaps this is a glib and indirect excuse for not taking the time to seriously consider what is needed to advance the most troubling of conditions around us. Admittedly, with peace studies and conflict resolution as relatively new fields of practice and academic study, few have received much guidance and information about what is needed.

Unfortunately, even social scientists differ in their assessments of best practices for reducing youth and gang violence. Communities like Los Angeles have been fiercely critiqued for their failure to evaluate the effectiveness of projects funded to address youth and gang violence. Literally millions of dollars have been invested in purported intervention without any requirement that those receiving funds test and prove their practices. In fact, in the mid-nineties, the state of California closed its Office of Criminal Justice Planning rather than respond to criticism that taxpayer money was being sent into a costly dark hole with no accountability. While this section cannot begin to replace this lack, it will attempt to raise awareness and concern about this gap. It will do so through sharing some of the ways that conflict resolution tools and skills are showing promise in reducing violent interpersonal conflict with high risk young people. Law enforcement has done this with detailed study of effective hostage negotiation. Hopefully, this section will stimulate and encourage others to also study effective conflict resolution with violent conflict.

As introduced in Section I, while scholars may limit "negative peace" to the absence of war, most scholars of peace also study and describe what they call "positive peace," or the many conditions and institutions that play a role in containing and challenging destructive human behavior. From this perspective, peace is built in degrees. When a person takes the time to seriously reflect on the nature of peace, they realize that peace is not a static destination but inherently involves complex layers of everchanging dynamics. Prominent peace scholar Elise Boulding defined peace culture as the ceaseless culture creating activity that characterizes the social body and involves interaction at every level, from the intrapersonal . . . to the interpersonal—in household, neighborhood, and community, on through successive levels of civic organization from city to the United Nations. . . . Because there is a constant interpenetration of levels, the societal capacity for aggression or peacebuilding depends on patterns developed in every domain, from the individual and the interpersonal to the national, and interenvironmental.

From this complex perspective, peacebuilding has parallels to other seemingly ordinary yet critically important life tasks, like day-to-day parenting to informed and active participation in preserving democracies that maintain moral boundaries for equally protecting all citizens, particularly those most vulnerable, like children.

Recently George Mubanga, a journalist from Zambia who helped lay the foundation for South Africa's Truth and Reconciliation process, expressed the belief that without authoritarian control, or dominance, societal structures will eventually crumble and fall—a challenging perspective for an academic community intent on teaching mastery of power balancing and other key conflict resolution skills facilitating democratic collaboration. As mentioned earlier, this book will not attempt to resolve any debate regarding the appropriate balance between state power (including law enforcement—presumably noncorrupt and truly just) and people power in democratically negotiating peace and justice. The author teaches negotiation, conflict resolution, and peacebuilding to students from around the world including those from war- and violence-torn societies like Lebanon and Nigeria and those working with gang and other violence within the United States. She sees dramatic contrast between students' strong enthusiasm for conflict resolution tools and the relative lack of skilled practice in the world today.

Is the enthusiasm of students representing over 70 countries misplaced? They include successful professionals and intellectuals: lawyers, engineers, and medical students. Some have multiple graduate degrees. They are joined by peace scholars who assert that emerging democratic practice reduces societal violence.

The articles included in this section are intended to stimulate thought and discussion about the ways effective conflict resolution skills can reduce and contain violent conflict and bullying. They stress the importance of negotiating boundaries with all concerned. Consistent respect for these good faith rules of engagement protects good will from being exploited and abused. It simultaneously ensures the power balancing, or equal treatment and democratic participation described throughout this book, and is absolutely necessary for process credibility and legitimacy.

While domestic scholars and practitioners often frame impartiality as an ethical principle, the global case studies and evaluative research described throughout this book reveal that impartiality might be the most important criteria for evaluating the skill of those mediating cross cultural conflict. This impartiality in action is far from neutral. Instead, it is described as encompassing intrapersonal states of consciousness as well as interpersonal choices: (1) a consistent commitment to suspend judgment regarding all concerned and offer an open mind that is free from bias and prejudice towards the party(ies) in conflict—evidenced in the mediator actions as all are encouraged and treated in equivalent ways and perceive their participation as equal and fair, (2) sincere interest in hearing and deeply understanding those in conflict, and (3) the ability to listen carefully and accurately.

Of course, it is likely that the majority of practicing mediators see themselves as impartial even in cases where observers have documented that the mediator is allowing only men to speak while the women present listen and the outcomes for parties of minority social standing are less than those for parties of greater standing. Research of self serving bias shows that most Americans studied view themselves through a flattering light, minimizing, rationalizing, excusing, and even denying their weaknesses and faults. Unless the average American mediator commits to rigorous self scrutiny through somehow finding a way to receive honest feedback from those who do not belong to that mediator's in-group of loyal supporters, they may never find a way to bridge cultural difference and build deep trust.

On a larger macro peacebuilding level, these intragroup and intergroup communication challenges matter as well. While ethnic conflict is inevitably layered and complex, with political as well as personal motivations, and dependent on power dynamics, a quick look at several contemporary tragedies reveals much popular, or intragroup and intrapersonal, support for political polarization and use of violence.

During the author's stay in Cyprus as a Fulbright Senior Specialist in Peace Studies and Conflict Resolution, she met more than one Greek Cypriot with painful regrets that they had not spoken up and done more to act against their community's ostracizing of Turkish Cypriots. Teaching conflict resolution to Israelis and Palestinians in Norway during the late 1990s, Israelis said that their parents did and could not know of their communication and contact with Palestinians. They were fearful of parental condemnation.

On the other hand, facilitating cross-ethnic dialogue with the Nansen Network during the Balkans war and watching the subsequent nonviolent overthrow of Milosevic was to intimately know the power of people when organized and committed to change through nonviolent resistance. When in Cyprus, more than one Greek Cypriot informed the author that they would not "waste her time" introducing her to intolerant members of their community. Yet, at the same time, they acknowledged the critical importance of eradicating inflammatory and destructive prejudice at its roots through education. Courageously, a team of Turkish and Greek Cypriot teachers determined to write a shared history for their schools—one that educates children about their full island rather than allowing self serving bias and antagonism to fuel and justify propaganda that vilifies and blames "the other" and omits, excuses, rationalizes, and even denies, personal role and responsibility.

Another research-based option in the face of bullying and other less than constructive behavior is called "generous tit for tat," or forgiveness math. It was introduced earlier but deserves to be described again. When practiced skillfully, it can have remarkable impact. Generous tit for tat describes an optimal formula for negotiating long-term gain. In simple terms, it involves, like nonviolent resistance, a commitment to not react or reciprocate to nasty tactics with the same, but, instead, to disarm nastiness by not giving it any of what is normally expected. Instead, the nonreactor surprises the bully and then attempts to influence the other to maximize their own interest through mutual and creative cooperation.

Of course, the challenge and risk with this clever and rarely understood formula is that the other side, particularly hardened bullies, may nevertheless persist in attempting to exploit and abuse generosity for short-term domination and gain. The most aggressive and violent of opposition may not be intelligent or aware enough to recognize the opportunity extended. They may have such a habit and history of violence that they cannot readily or easily manage themselves or even see their most important interests.

The conflict resolution tools introduced in the articles presented at the end of this section offer vital "next steps" that are proving themselves in practice. If a bully is not capable of acting in their own interests, they need to be offered strong guidance in doing so. A masterful negotiator or mediator has several ways to diffuse and manage the above situation: (1) negotiating no violence boundaries that actively engage and commit all parties in terms they understand and can realistically honor, (2) helping all parties save face through suspending all personal judgment and offering sincere validation and interest, (3) careful and accurate listening for important insight, and (4) guiding negotiation with the best of creative problem solving (to be explained in the next section).

Skilled professional law enforcement officers are deeply aware of the power of these tools as they describe the best of what occurs during hostage and other crisis negotiations. No society has yet to demonstrate their full potential as tools for proactive prevention and containment of violence. Norway, however, as one example, has shown remarkable results with its schoolwide antibullying program, stressing consistent assertion of no violence parameters.

It is important to note that these skills are not presented as a magic panacea guaranteed to end all violence. Their success depends entirely on the skill and consciousness (awareness-sensitivity) of the negotiator and the wisdom, intelligence, and responsiveness of the others involved. The most arrogant and disturbed of bullies may refuse to negotiate, get a sick thrill out of violence, or demand ego domination. At the international level, those with the most power are likely to continue to be tempted to exploit and abuse their power for short-term gain. Anthropologists of war have studied and documented repeated political manipulation of masses for private gain.

At these times of micro and macro impasse, parties must be prepared to protect themselves from abuse—just like wives must empower themselves enough to leave violent husbands/fathers and somehow find safe hidden shelter and parents in gang-infested communities and schools must commit to protecting their children—sometimes leaving their neighborhoods entirely. Likewise, citizens must become political and act to protect their interests and limit political damage. As Gandhi and Dr. King exemplified with their nonviolent resistance, peacebuilders must constantly strategize ways of not cooperating with oppressors and publicizing brutal ways to those willing to support just resolution.

Contrary to popular contemporary approach with violent and threatening opponents, what is being recommended here is a graceful yet strong and firm diplomatic disengagement ("exit") *after* attempting negotiation, seeking information and insight, and building relationship and influence. In negotiation, information truly is power. Most of the world is unskilled in negotiation and conflict resolution. Waiting for another's lead will more often than not be futile. Cutting off any opportunity to learn more about or influence a challenging party may be quite foolhardy.

The following articles present two real world success stories with dramatically reducing the violent behavior of youth criminals—one in a treatment facility for repeat offenders, and the other in a Los Angeles high school. Two authors share their conflict resolution experience and insight after using the conflict tools introduced above with gang affiliated youth.

## Part 1: The Power of Negotiated "Ground Rules" When Negotiated with Violent Youth and Monitored by Observant Concerned Adults Who Listen, Validate and Problem-Solve

Fifteen years ago the author was asked to design an intervention program for juvenile offenders, 10 to 18 years old, with long-term histories of violent and defiant behavior. She had taught in and out of school community education, to students, ages six to 15, from a poor community facing many problems, most commonly, absent and addicted parents, but had otherwise primarily used an evaluative and authoritative approach to violence and other disciplinary problems in public schools. With an evaluative approach to conflict and negotiation, those involved have "asked the evaluator . . . to decide the issue or resolve the conflict" (Erbe 2004). (As an attorney-mediator, the author served as counsel for public schools in the late 1980s.) Here, though, as a facilitative mediator of two years, she responded to her directive with enthusiasm for exploring such mediation's potential. "The facilitator's main task is to help the group increase effectiveness by improving its process" (Erbe 2004). The results astounded all concerned. Violent and defiant behavior decreased by more than 50 percent in less than six months.

The author's current classrooms are much different, teaching conflict resolution in graduate and undergraduate programs for peacebuilding. Students, however, attempt the same process, using facilitative mediation as a model for creating and committing to cultures of peace.

They start with negotiating detailed ground rules. With the special education students described earlier, a day-long planning retreat invited all stakeholders, including counselors, students, and teachers, to thoroughly brainstorm problem behaviors and otherwise use the mediation process to negotiate and reach consensus regarding what should happen in response to each problem. The result was a group agreement that scrupulously spelled out the community's "ground rules" and enforcement process. Likewise, students of peacebuilding may be asked to identify all behaviors that they see as problematic or contrary to a culture of peace. They then negotiate and agree to responsive class guidelines.

As in the best of facilitative mediation, all concerns and interests are valid. All present are encouraged to speak. The majority cannot overrule the minority. Students, for example, cannot gang up against their teacher and agree to talk during class. On the other hand, power balancing occurs. All must be satisfied with their agreement.

New mediators, like new teachers, may assume a more evaluative or directive approach to ground rules, introducing and trying to enforce their own expectations or demands. When parties agree to and choose an evaluative style, no problems arise.

Seasoned practitioners, however, both mediators and teachers, have likely faced the party, student, or parent who questions and challenges their authority. In such moments, persistence with imposing one's "way" can be a recipe for disaster—inciting an escalating and even entrenched power struggle. In contrast, facilitative mediation as a model for classroom management is effective because teachers, like mediators, are skilled in careful listening, facilitate inclusive discussion towards problem solving (active learning), and otherwise model the best of mediator skills.

Negotiating ground rules by consensus is only the first step. In the author's experience, the most effective teachers and mediators also do the following. They quickly, gently but firmly, and, most important, respectfully, name the breach of the agreed rule. They do not erode their credibility and strength as leaders, perhaps in an attempt to garner popularity, through ignoring, tolerating, minimizing, or laughing off disrespect for group boundaries. Instead, they consciously "separate the people from the problem" by asserting the relevant rule without shaming, attacking, or attempting to control and punish the perceived offender. They initially appeal to the power of group consensus. If thorough, the class has already decided what the teacher will do in the face of repeated defiance or disrespect.

Special education students may also require frequent private mini-mediations. While additional problem-solving sessions are labor intensive, such proactive "parenting" can reap invaluable information, insight, and rapport to strengthen long-term classroom management. Teachers do not need to be the mediators in these special sessions. In the special education case beginning this section, staff, with high school diplomas and less, proved gifted listeners, mentors, and mediators once they received necessary training.

Researcher Rackham, in studying labor-management negotiations, discovered that the best of negotiators: (1) gather quality information through skillful questioning and active listening, (2) zealously search for common ground, and (3) strongly commit to creating mutually satisfactory and beneficial solutions. Based on classroom and special education success, the author encourages teachers and others working with challenging conflict to prioritize mastery of these skills. They form the heart of facilitative mediation and can dramatically enhance classroom management and effectiveness, when exercised skillfully, with strength.

## Part 2: The Power of Appreciative Mentoring

> Attention now seems to be focused on our children. . . . It seems we are saying they are to blame. . . . Our children are not the problem. The violent behavior of a small percentage not only ignores . . . the immense goodness of the majority but scapegoats them for a situation generations of adults have perpetuated (Horn 1993).

Upon opening in 2006, Santee High School (Los Angeles) experienced a two-day violent eruption, resulting in 34 arrests. Principal Carbino took immediate, comprehensive, and sustained action, interviewing his community (gang members, business owners, and families), negotiating a school safe zone, and taking several other actions detailed below. The results were stunning. Violence became near nonexistent.

The authors of this section, Nancy Erbe and her former student Aneisa Bolton, share many years working directly with youth and schools—as an attorney representing a school district with its disciplinary and special education concerns, trainer coaching teachers across the nation in conflict resolution curriculum, the head of a treatment program for repeat violent offenders, ages 10 to 17, and the mentor to high risk youth and felons. One of the authors grew up in Long Beach, California, and was a teen during the eruption in youth/gang violence publicized by the popular movie Freedom Writers. In this section they would like to speak to concerned educators and community. They aspire to share their most important insight for preventing and intervening with youth violence and gang involvement that is validated by Santee High and other real world case study success.

## Gang members and violent youth are as unique and distinct from each other as any other young person and likely require individualized response.

Principal Carbino believes that the most important action he took in extinguishing school violence was securing funding for a large team of counselors who identified student mental health needs and responded appropriately to the 10 percent of his students identified as responsible for violent behavior and in need of treatment. In conversations, the authors see local community, even highly educated ones, regularly equate drug addiction and color with gang status. They also lump children with adult offenders, and otherwise create vague, confusing and erroneous overgeneralizations. Even as late as 2005 the California Youth Authority did the same. Only when confronted by a lawsuit did it finally start to distinguish between youth and their specific needs. Educators and all concerned with young people must do the same. It is particularly important that we distinguish between youth on gangs' periphery and hard core criminals. The 14-year-old sucking her thumb in the privacy of her social worker's office while she describes her rape on the streets is worlds apart from 35- to 60-year-old criminals coldly calculating drug business strategy. Unless concerned communities accurately separate them, in perception and response, authorities say we risk increasing both general delinquency and gang involvement.

## Children without protection will seek protection and sometimes unknowingly endanger themselves more.

Young people are victimized many times more than they victimize. In Long Beach, for example, where in 2006 the police department reported 55 gangs responsible for 177 shootings, only four youth, ages 10-17, were arrested for homicide. In contrast, over a thousand youth were victims of violent crimes in 2004. The violent children the authors have known best have not been protected by parents or anyone else. They have been violently victimized—repeatedly, more often than not by their parents. One was nearly smothered at birth by her mother. Two gang-affiliated children the authors knew reported joining gangs innocently, without awareness of the risks and pressure involved, and intentionally, to receive protection from other gangs on the street. Fortunately, communities like Long Beach are catching on and creating alternative safe havens, shelters just like have been created for victims of domestic abuse.

**All youth need at least one concerned wise mentor who partners in daily troubleshooting and validates and encourages nonviolent behavior. This mentor does not need to be an educator or adult . Research, however, shows that a positive adult in a child's life improves the child's resiliency in the face of risk.**

Principal Carbino of Santee High prioritized regular conversations with all his parents. He also sent his ninth graders to intensive conflict resolution and leadership training at the authors' university, California State Dominguez Hills. Natural student leaders were identified to form governing peace councils, responsible for overseeing and coaching school peacebuilding and violence prevention. In the authors' experience, all similar successes emphasize such mentoring.

One of the authors observed the success of her mentoring in several environments where she taught at-risk youth. Here she will describe her approach at an alternative high school program in San Pedro California for youth that were not allowed into traditional high schools because of criminal records, truancy and other disciplinary problems. She focused on making meaningful connections with her students by first gaining understanding of their interests, talents, and gifts. She would then look for ways to connect their interests and strengths with ideas for their future. For example, if she discovered that a student was an artist, she would see if he or she was interested in enrolling in a graphic arts program. Thus interests became selling points for staying in school and encouraging students to make better decisions when they were away from campus, exemplifying the type of seemingly simple mentoring that can make dramatic difference with young people who lack such guidance and concern for their futures.

Not that this mentoring is necessarily easy. Youth that have experienced trauma are extremely intuitive. Authentic and sincere communication with them is imperative. Their survival sometimes depends on "intuitively reading" people and environments correctly. They will likely know if someone is not sincere in their communication.

Some students have been so traumatized that it takes months for them to trust a new adult and open up to that adult. One particular student that comes to mind would barely speak and was very unresponsive to attempts to connect with her. A concerned adult did not push her but tried to remain consistent in showing concern while respecting the student's need for her boundaries. That same adult noticed that this student loved to read "romance" novels. She used this love of reading as a mechanism to encourage her to continue education beyond the alternative high school program. The student is now in college and is a teacher's assistant for a local adult school in South Central Los Angeles.

In facilitating teacher trainings in many schools across the country, it is surprising to see how many educators are afraid of their students. One technique that one of the authors regularly taught educators to help them build rapport with their students was consciously giving students a warm welcome by saying hello and shaking their hand at the beginning of the school day and even going a little further by saying I am glad you are here today. Some of the educator responses were quite shocking ranging from "I don't have time to greet my students" to "Is the school going to give me hand sanitizer?" Of course this is not reflective of all teachers, but there were enough of these types of responses to cause great concern about teachers' attitude toward students.

The authors have found, hopefully along with most of the readers, that the small things adults do on a daily basis can make an enormous difference in the life of youth while also creating a positive learning environment: treating all young people with respect and dignity, looking for talents and gifts within each student, and most importantly, consistently expressing a sincere desire to have a positive impact in their lives. Resilience research concurs, over and over again, identifying the presence of a supportive and caring adult in the lives of children and youth who succeed despite adversity (Masten and Garmezy 1985).

Before presenting the articles demonstrating how the conflict tools introduced in this section work with communities facing and engaging in cross-ethnic violence, the next section will describe the same tools in greater detail as well as present additional mediation steps and skills that the author's classrooms are using to effectively build cross-cultural conversation, relationships, and collaboration for creative problem-solving. The author's classrooms include former gang members, students who have tragically lost family to gang violence, and students from several countries, including some that are war torn and conflict infested. Their experience has relevance to other cross-ethnic conflict and violence. More importantly, this section introduces the reader to many of the facilitative mediation stages and skills that will be reviewed in later sections. As readers will eventually appreciate, a highly skilled and aware mediator who facilitates party self determination equally, or impartially, rather than telling them what to do, is key to the success stories shared throughout this book.

## Notes and Questions

1. Some Questions for Reflective Practice

   Consider a group from class or outside of class while asking the following questions:

Do all of my group members (parties to conflict, etc.) participate?

Equally? If not, what might encourage more inclusive participation?

Do my group members perceive me as:

Treating them equally?

(Note: This does not refer to academic performance but, instead, the unconditional regard that humanist psychologist Carl Rogers promoted as facilitating personal growth. Do all students feel accepted, esteemed and encouraged independently of academic and social performance?)

Suspending judgment?

Welcoming and encouraging all points of view?

Encouraging active participation, serious discussion and honest disclosure of their most important concerns, such as harassment, bullying and discrimination?

Carefully listening to gain deep understanding?

2. If you were to propose "ground rules" for the above group to build a culture of peace, what would you include?

3. What are your ideas for reducing youth violence and gang affiliation in the schools and communities you know?

## Bibliography and Recommended Reading

The Advancement Project. 2007. Citywide Gang Activity Reduction Strategy: Phase III Report.

Erbe, N. 2004. "The Global Popularity and Promise of Facilitative ADR." *Temple Intl. & Comp. L. J.* 18 (2): 346, 353.

———. 2003. *Holding These Truths: Empowerment and Recognition In Action* (an interactive case study curriculum for multicultural dispute resolution). Berkeley, Calif.: Berkeley Public Policy Press.

Herr, Judy Zimmern, and Robert Herr. 1998. *Transforming Violence: Linking Local and Global Peacebuilding.* Scottdale, Pa.: Herald Press.

Horn, Reverend Gilbert J. 1993. Colorado Council of Churches.

Long Beach Commission on Youth and Children. 2006. Annual Report.

Masten, A., and N. Garmezy. 1985. "Risk, Vulnerability, and Protective Factors in Developmental Psychopathology." In *Advances in Clinical Child Psychology*, vol. 8, ed. B. Lahey and A. Kazdin. New York: Plenum Press, 1-52.

Section III

# Facilitative Mediation Sparks Innovation through Skill

> "(O)ne encourages the other to communicate. One allows free expression, seeks understanding and avoids value judgments that stifle. One shows desire and capacity to listen without anticipating, interfering . . . warping meanings into preconceived interpretations. Assumptions and prejudgments are minimized" (Johannesen 1996).

> "A party gives recognition . . . when: He realizes that he feels secure enough to stop thinking exclusively about his own situation and to focus to some degree on . . . the other. . . . He consciously lets go of his own viewpoint and tries to see things through the other's perspective" (Bush and Folger 1994).

> "The word *question* is derived from the Latin *quaerere* (to seek), which is the same root as the word for *quest*. A creative life is a continued quest, and good questions are useful guides. We have found that the most useful questions are open ended: they allow a fresh, unanticipated answer to emerge" (Goleman 1995).

The previous section and this one represent two ends of a peacebuilding continuum. At one end is containment and reduction of violence. At the other is the best of innovation. In the middle is difference: ethnic, religious and all other fueling conflict. To effectively navigate this continuum several skills are required—at the level of mastery.

The last section introduced how some conflict resolution skills are demonstrating promise in reducing violent behavior and alliances. Before presenting real world case studies of how these and other conflict skills are also proving popular and promising in violent cross-ethnic conflicts around the world, this section will more thoroughly introduce the conflict skills used in a masterful process. The next section will directly compare and contrast facilitative and evaluative mediation and assert that facilitative, or highly skilled, mediation is what is advocated for cross-cultural process in these global case studies.

This section introduces the connections between facilitated negotiation, or mediation, and optimal multicultural relationships. Ironically, and wonderfully, the same skills that effectively contain and bridge difference in the face of violent conflict can also facilitate the brilliant innovation that emerges when difference is welcomed and embraced.

While this section, with its focus on creative innovation, may at first glance seem worlds away from violent conflict, it is actually a critical and necessary part of peacebuilding. Without creative and open minds, the ideas needed to build peace will never surface.

It begins with scholarly links between cultural diversity and ingenuity. It shows how skilled negotiation and mediation can create and sustain the cooperative conditions promoted by scholars for nurturing innovation. Research evaluating ideal multicultural process will be shared. The author hopes that understanding these specifics will encourage many to adopt excellent practices in their pursuit of innovation. Daniel Goleman describes this as schooling in emotional intelligence (Goleman 1995). He believes that competitive advantage requires cooperative training in the social skills described here. Exemplary collaboration is necessary to fully leverage global strengths and opportunities.

For readers unfamiliar with contemporary scholarship, this chapter exemplifies the growing academic use of qualitative research for in-depth exploration of the real world complexities and nuances faced today. One popular example of qualitative methods is the case study. Laurence Lynn of the University of Chicago is one of many respected proponents acknowledging that, in the face of complex problems, like the relationship between diversity and innovation, there is no one right or best answer (Lynn 1999). In response, case analysis must necessarily draw upon the entire body of behavioral and social science and make use of it in myriad ways. "The reasoning process is more experiential and associative, involving pattern recognition and intuition, than it is logical . . . or scientific reasoning (Lynn 1999)." This does not mean that traditional quantitative statistical analysis is not also valued as demonstrated by this book's reference to varied studies. In fact, ideally the qualitative research introduced in this section will be used to inform and shape rich longitudinal studies designed to identify the variables that can be repeated to produce optimal innovation. Without preliminary qualitative exploration, like that presented in this chapter, however, research risks being overly simplistic (Lewicki, Barry, and Saunders 2007). "Several important qualitative . . . activities inform most, if not all, quantitative projects (Druckman 2005)."

Yet even if the qualitative data presented here is used to create more informed behavioral categories for future research, today's stakeholders cannot rely on traditional research alone. Because of the complex and dynamic problems global actors constantly face, unfortunately more often than not without the benefit of relevant research, they must somehow learn to conduct their own applied research on an on-going basis (Bordens and Abbott 1999). For example, in the field of negotiation, much research has studied Japanese and American behavior, leaving the rest of world cultures a negotiation mystery (Lewicki, Barry, and Saunders 2007). Applied research, aiming to investigate real-world problems as they arise, must attempt to fill this gap as much as possible. Thus this section also intends to guide applied research and shape actual success through providing negotiation and mediation structures that have effectively created cross-cultural communication and stimulated innovation.

The author's work mirrors the shifting realities of contemporary global community. More and more workers are being asked to work as part of cross functional teams that include various cultures. Their ability to effectively cooperate with each other in performing tasks is key to success. Here experience and insight, along with research-based knowledge, is offered so that global actors can act proactively rather than reactively. The proactive path maximizes the potential of diverse teams while avoiding the enormous costs of destructive conflict and loss from failure. Practices are shared for structuring groups in ways that effectively stimulate the synergy of difference: the exact structure that the majority of the author's clients and students from around the world embrace with great enthusiasm. They generate creative passion and avoid the many pitfalls that often arise.

## Part 1: Diversity Fuels Innovation

Diversity is often linked to heightened creativity whether finding new answers to questions, developing new perspectives, or solving problems with fresh solutions (Fink 2003). One expert, who has studied companies effectively fostering innovation, states that "innovation communities recognize that diversity is important for growth and development" (Dundon 2002. Other experts go so far as saying that "diversity fuels innovation" (Skarzynski and Gibson 2008). Still others assert that the greater an organization's diversity, the better its chance for launching innovation (Snyder and Duarte, 2008). At the very least, enough diverse ideas must be available to combine them into novel and varied patterns.

### Diversity's Potential for Innovation

Broadly defined, the diversity promoted as enhancing creativity includes not only ethnic and gender difference but also expertise, life experience, perspective, and function. In the contemporary workplace, more and more employees are what Peter Drucker calls knowledge workers, like computer programmers, who must work as part of cross-functional teams. While multicultural diversity will be stressed here, all difference, whether in style, background, profession, philosophy, or ability, has potential to spark innovation. History abounds with examples of creative partnerships and teams where disparate members complement and stimulate each other.

The reasons for this resonance between variety and creativity will be elaborated throughout this section. To begin, diversity's potential for conflict, ironically, when facilitated skillfully, creates the conditions linked with innovation. By its very nature, difference creates the disequilibrium and new questions that many believe must be present to spark innovation: "original thinking . . . (or) something never created before" (Tubbs 1995). Conflict can also create motivation. It is possible that a group facing escalating tensions and struggling with difference will be fueled to greater heights of innovation in its attempts to move forward. In light of what scholars have learned about the creative process, it is likely in fact that the best of innovators and innovation will emerge from struggling with frustration and discomfort (Deutsch 1973). Brilliant "aha" insight is reported after periods of concentrated effort focused on more familiar territory followed by apparent impasse resulting in shifting perspective.

## Challenges Inherent in Diverse Communities and Creative Problem Solving

So why is the world not seeing more innovation as a natural result of its growing multicultural communities? Instead, "creative thinking and reasoning, while vitally important to effective groups and teams, is hard to find in the real world" (Johnson and Johnson 2000). More visible is the innovation of Japanese companies, who at the management level can be about as homogeneous as can be imagined. Yet, taking the auto industry as one prominent example, Japanese managers have been remarkably successful in launching popularly received innovation. In contrast, a creative endeavor like the recent election of Barack Obama in the United States, where people from a wide range of life experiences; economic and ethnic groups aligned to create an event and movement truly new—one that had never occurred before, is remarkably difficult to find. The reason is likely the need, rarely met, for skillful collaboration effectively embracing the conflict and challenge predictably arising in the face of difference (Triandis 2003). Research indicates that cross-cultural negotiations generally yield poorer outcomes than negotiations within one's own cultural group or between similar cultures (Lewicki, Barry, and Saunders 2007).

To bring something new into existence, explore new opportunities, and change, those concerned must be sufficiently motivated (Deutsch 1973). Different perspectives, or ways of viewing a problem or situation, are automatically present with diverse cultures. Conflict itself can generate needed motivation. As will be elaborated later in this book, however, ethnic difference alone has been found to dramatically threaten core identity. This may sound overly dramatic until one considers the following explanation. "Identity [is] defined as an abiding sense of selfhood that is the core of what makes life predictable to an individual. . . . To have no ability to anticipate events is essentially to experience terror. . . . Events which threaten to invalidate the core sense of identity will elicit defensive responses aimed at avoiding psychic and/or physical annihilation" (Erbe 2003).

So, at the very least, those threatened by ethnic difference may show defensive response. They attempt to "defend" their identity and create a sense of security by mentally minimizing and otherwise distorting the very difference that is needed to create innovation. Or they may project and anticipate rejection and threat where they do not exist.

The theories of coordinated management of meaning and confrontation episodes in particular describe how difference can easily lead to destructive rather than creative understanding. Coordinated management of meaning focuses on the rules and expectations that individuals bring to any communication. It explains how when individuals share understandings and expectations they are likely to interpret cues of communication in similar ways. When they come from cultures with different communication norms and practices, however, they risk violating each other's expectations, offending, and otherwise (often unknowingly) inciting conflict.

The day-to-day routine of the contemporary workplace provides numerous examples of how difference alone easily leads to misunderstanding. Many employees understand little, if anything, of cultures, functions, and perspectives other than their own. They can easily construe innocent difference as intentionally disrespectful and even hostile. Seemingly simple communication practices like interruption, timing, eye contact, and tone can start long-standing conflict with costly consequence. Even in the author's conflict resolution classrooms, it is challenging for students to understand, for example, that interruption and direct eye contact communicate passion and genuine interest to some. Others feel deep offense and irritation. They perceive disrespect even when respect is intended. Working with engineers at one of the United States' most successful global technical corporations, the author encountered much suspicion, frustration, and impatience when attempting to explain that a group of Japanese managers needed time to confer with each other. The Japanese tradition of consensus building had nothing to do with American engineers. Yet these engineers felt disrespected. On the other hand, many cultures around the world feel disrespected when American employees insist on business, or task focus, first and foremost. Such Americans are seen as insensitive to business relationships.

## Intentional Perspective Taking Facilitates Innovative Process

Research of closed minded individuals demonstrates that they are more likely to act with the defensive responses described above, frequently rejecting information that is potentially threatening to their perspective. Such rigidity counters the flexibility needed for creativity. At the very least, information gathering suffers. At its worst, destructive conflict is incited. Furthermore, participants will not likely be aware that they are limiting themselves to a narrow perspective and blocking construction of complex ideas. To most observers, they will simply appear to be disagreeing with each other, showing yielding, dominating and compromising—"splitting the difference or meeting each other half way."

Researchers examining creativity promote the opposite—that different perspectives and information are actively sought. Multicultural teams tasked with innovation must somehow respond to difference with openness and curiosity rather than closed defensiveness. They must initiate the practice that William Gordon termed compressed conflict—to force themselves to perceive an object or concept from two or more frames of reference; in short, perspective-taking. This is similar to a creative negotiation process. Researcher Rackham found that the best negotiators listened actively to ensure understanding, while the less effective were more likely to argue. Those intent on innovation must be encouraged to engage in dialogue and even controversy with each other regarding their ideas, opinions, assumptions, experience, and perspective.

Some experts say that creativity requires conflict (Deutsch and Coleman 2000). To create top quality innovation, those involved must not only be open and curious about new ideas but actively work to maximize diverse possibilities and sustain vigorous critique of those options—not to destroy or discard, but to further create.

Somehow innovators must find ways to avoid or effectively address the hesitation, judgment, and doubt that often arise when truly fresh ideas emerge. Otherwise, innovative efforts will be inhibited and possibly defeated. In response to these challenges, this section advocates schooling in the best of collaboration. In the author's experience, skilled collaboration is proving itself as an effective facilitator of innovation with multicultural teams. Perspective taking is just one example of its helpful approach and tools. While collaboration does not ensure innovation, team members trained to skillfully negotiate and mediate are better equipped to avoid defensive and destructive reactions. At the very least, they will share a commitment to active exploration rather than mere judgment and reaction. Bringing diverse people together to work on a common goal can start to break down deeply held stereotypes and other negative reaction. Varied research projects, including Prisoner's Dilemma, mixed motive and "generous tit for tat" mathematical research, demonstrate that maximizing gains to self interest occurs with strategic cooperation (Bevir 2007). In other words, even if team members do not create stunning innovation, their enhanced collaborative abilities will likely benefit the bottom line through enhanced and even custom designed responsiveness to long-term priorities.

The author would like to share an observation from her experience guiding diverse multicultural teams. It is possible that her students, who chose to study negotiation and mediation, and her clients, who hire an external consultant, demonstrate, through these choices, a capacity to embrace complexity, unpredictability, and ambiguity. Occasionally, though, the author has worked with individuals who appear to lack such ability. These individuals are threatened by open dialogue and difference. They often seek one "right" answer rather than creative construction of multiple models and possibilities.

Global stakeholders may need to begin their innovation process by doing some type of psychological assessment. This would help determine if participants are capable of embracing complexity and uncertainty; most importantly, of taking the risk and initiative of imagining what has not existed before. Those who are smug or simply satisfied with the status quo, who are generally passive, perhaps lacking in confidence and waiting for someone else's lead, or who generally focus on conforming and pleasing, will not be well suited to innovation. Some level of confidence, tolerance for ambiguity and frustration, and dissatisfaction with, or at least the ability to question, the status quo is required.

During Barack Obama's election, scientists studying the neurobiology of politics at the University of California, Los Angeles and New York University reported that liberals tolerate ambiguity and conflict better than conservatives because of how their brains work. Conservatives tend to block what they perceive to be "distracting" information. Frank Sulloway, a researcher at the University of California Berkeley's Institute of Personality and Social Research, says that based on the results of this study, he believes liberals should be expected to more readily accept new ideas (Gellene 2008).

The following subsection will introduce right and left brain research and discuss how both are necessary for the highest quality innovation. Not all people are suited for both. It may be that a global group decides to ask its more open minded free thinkers to create ideas and its more conservative and judgmental thinkers to critique ideas.

## Innovation's Requisite and Disparate Functions

Readers are likely familiar with what is called the "left" or rational brain and the "right" or intuitive brain. The first describes logical analysis, either/or thinking with one right answer requiring evidence and comparison against standards of performance, like what is found in science and law. The second is less systematic. It may involve flashes of unexplained insight, emotional reactions, subjective use of imagination, and artistic expression—all that business case studies attempt to stimulate as they are necessary for innovation. The best of innovation, however, must also be scrutinized by the left brain at some point.

The collaborative negotiation attitudes and skills promoted throughout this entire section require both the left and right brains and guide their use. First, participants are led in creating a safe and supportive environment encouraging and validating the right brain's subjective unique expression without judgment or critique. In-depth understanding is the goal. The step-by-step process then asks for many alternatives before engaging the left brain in its rigorous evaluation.

In looking at diversity's relationship with innovation, a natural and fascinating question is whether different professional functions and cultures exhibit different strengths in relationship to the right and left brains. Years ago, for example, the Massachusetts Institute of Technology compared Indian and American mathematicians and found that the Indian professionals often solved mathematical equations quickly in a flash of apparent intuition and use of the right brain. Americans, in contrast, were more likely to solve the same problems step by step through the application of equations. Does this mean that certain cultures are more left brained and others right brained? It appears that professional functions express a dominant preference and skill. Engineers are predictably logical and pragmatic while designers more nonverbally oriented with graphic descriptions. What matters most here is the appreciation that difference enhances creative process and is more likely to lead to true innovation.

## Part 2: Skill Mastery Is Non-negotiable

As mentioned earlier, facilitated mediation provides the skill needed to help those involved embrace difference and create innovation. As elaborated in several sections, this particular type of mediation is a popular process with unique capacity to bridge difference. It guides creative problem-solving's step-by-step process and intimately addresses the common obstacles to innovation encountered by diverse teams and organizations.

### Safety, Understanding, and Acceptance Are Likely Precursors to the Emergence of Untested Ideas

It is inherently contradictory to pressure employees into independent thinking as part of conforming to company culture. Any organization or community aspiring to nourish innovation must find a way to effectively embrace this dilemma. Scholar Goleman has found that businesses nurturing the best of innovation hire and sustain employee self initiative. The rewards can be rich. As mentioned earlier with track two diplomacy, visionary initiative regularly creates unexpected opportunities. Leaders who can operate flexibly, with access to people and networks that can be mobilized quickly, mirror the behavior of proven star employees.

In interviewing experts around the world, the author quickly learned that prohibitive difference goes far beyond the vast ethnic differences involved with global relationships. Some of the greatest challenges global practitioners face include finding ways to effectively transcend professional and functional differences such as conflicting philosophies and goals. To begin, many, if not most, professional employees are not schooled in the assumptions and approaches of collaboration. Instead, they come to a collective process prepared to promote their function's perspective rather than listen to the others present. One of the global experts interviewed by this chapter's author, for example, mentioned that scientists and engineers too often see their mandate and achievement as exclusive rather than shared and collective (Erbe 2006). They are prepared to compete rather than cooperate—at least when asked to work with nonengineers and scientists. Scholar Naomi Roht-Arriza describes a similar dilemma. She sees difference in professional vocabulary, biases, mandates, and goals as inhibiting development projects worldwide (Roht-Arriza 2004). At their worst, perspectives are myopic and approaches rigid—destined to incite conflict, defensive reaction and distance rather than build productive relations.

Fortunately, as will be stressed again and again, facilitated negotiation, or mediation, has inherent capacity to bridge difference, without asking any of the players to change their approach or thinking. It creatively builds through using the very difference that would otherwise block innovation. It begins to do this by asking all participants to start their creative process focusing on the perspective taking mentioned earlier, or getting to know and understand all present. Perspective taking describes the popular "walking in another's shoes," or attempting to see through another's eyes and experience. In the global evaluation that will be shared later, such perspective taking was one of the most lauded cross-cultural practices, particularly in Cameroon and throughout the Balkans. Many students of negotiation and mediation, as well as participants, see facilitative mediation as naturally promoting cultural understanding through emphasis on storytelling. Hearing others humanizes them. In the process elaborated here, participants normally report increased appreciation for each other and growth in positive climate.

Participants are further coached in consciously suspending judgment and thus avoiding reactive blocks. In studying groups, scholar Gibb found defensive communication and climate in response to criticism, judgment, other evaluation, and even "cold silence" and nonresponse. Not surprisingly, he concluded that such groups wasted more time with ego protecting discussions and accomplished less than more supportive groups. A conscious commitment to suspending judgment must be the first step to creating a climate where innovation can flourish.

In the author's advanced classes, suspending judgment has been the most popular choice when naming helpful behaviors (Erbe 2003). It has been three times more popular than any other. Likewise, in the evaluative survey of multicultural group process that the author conducted in the Balkans, Cameroon, Nepal, and Ukraine, positive climate was listed as the second most important requirement for an effective experience (Erbe 2004). Respect was the most popular way of describing this positive commitment. Other words used included support, serious interest and concentration, concern, trust, a cooperative attitude, empathy, humane, and "good spirit." Psychologist Carl Rogers used the term unconditional regard. After a lifetime of research, he named unconditional regard as instrumental to growth. When suspension of judgment is consistently offered, group members feel free to test out ideas without fear of stigma. Conversely, the worst members of cross cultural process are seen as lacking deep understanding (Erbe 2004). They are criticized for failing to suspend judgment and otherwise demonstrating insensitivity to others.

The most innovative, productive, and successful employees appear to be found within organizations consistently giving them strong regard. Harvard political scientist Putnam has developed the concept of social capital to describe the difference observed between effective and ineffective governance (Reuben 2005). Strong social capital describes public trust of institutions, resulting connection, cooperation (reciprocity), and civic virtue or generous giving. In contrast, less effective governance correlates with distrust, unhealthy competition, and alienation.

Researchers of organizational behavior have carried this study of social capital into the workplace. Their research documents the value of management behavior like responsiveness, or listening to and implementing employee ideas, investment in priority common interests, and investment in the employee interests that matter most to them. Other studies show that institutions can retain employees through listening to and implementing employee ideas as well as investing in their interests. Such a contemporary workplace is described as a collaborative partnering between employees and employers. Both are stakeholders "sharing strengths for mutual gain" as long as their individual interests are served. Loyalty and job security become irrelevant if counter to self-interest. As a result, employers are more attuned to employee's authentic needs.

Only a minimal or surface level of social capital can be mandated in the workplace. Civic virtues like respect and cooperation must be inspired and nurtured rather than forced (Cohen 2001). Even if organizational policy commands polite behavior, such policy would be difficult to enforce. Assuming organizational stakeholders are successfully intimidated, the resultant social capital will likely fall far short of that encouraged by reciprocal respect. Thus, as with legal influence, organizational influence is at its best when it mediates rather than dictates social capital. Just as children at a certain age respond more to their peers than the authority of parents, the more an organization can encourage its members to create a culture of responsiveness the better.

One way that an organization can begin building its social capital in order to attract and retain stellar innovators is to create an ombuds office responsible for responding to employee concerns. The very best ombuds have a reputation for compassion and support—exactly what is needed to create the environment promoted here. The term "Organizational Ombudsman" was first used by Mary Rowe of the Massachusetts Institute of Technology in the mid-1980s. Rowe defined the term as: "a confidential and informal information resource, communications channel, complaint-handler and dispute resolver, and a person who helps an organization work for change" (Rowe 1995). In recent years, international agencies, transnational corporations, and universities are the main places where organizational ombuds can be found (Erbe and Sebok 2008). In a recent survey, organizational ombuds indicated that their second most popular role was training employees in the collaborative skills described throughout this section and book.

Until a business or community creates strong social capital, however, they must somehow create environments where employees and members feel safe and secure in expressing themselves freely. One scholar describes this state as relaxed but alert. Achieving this ease can be particularly challenging in times of economic insecurity and frequent employment turnover. Compounding these natural stresses, in a survey of organizational ombuds last year, their greatest reported challenge was confronting historically abusive working environments—the sad but true opposite of the social capital described above.

A small step towards creating the safety needed for innovation to flourish is to give teams the authority to create their own process parameters. The purpose is ensuring that all participants feel comfortable and respected with open expression of ideas and opinions. Team members may decide, for example, to agree to anonymity—that creative ideas will not be linked with team member names until management has demonstrated unequivocal buy-in. Such ground rules, or negotiated understandings, can respect and include all personal and cultural norms equally. Thus they create a solid multicultural foundation that helps everyone feel comfortable.

Students' second recommendation for building multicultural rapport is to show a true desire to understand culture in its depth along with encouragement to share uniqueness. One of their comments follows. "If something confuses you, there is nothing wrong with asking! . . . You might not understand most things that are done in a certain culture but the other person will appreciate [your willingness] to try to understand. All it takes is a little bit of enthusiasm. Being enthusiastic about the differences and the wonder of another's culture is a wonderful thing. The feelings will be reciprocated." Suspension of judgment was promoted earlier for encouraging group members to speak freely and thus allow innovation to emerge. It also plays a vital role in guiding the open mindedness necessary to fully understand another's perspective. (Related recommendations include giving sufficient time and patience to speakers whose first language is not English. Also advised is noticing nonverbal feedback regarding group members' discomfort and responding to ensure comfort).

Related to open mindedness are the flexibility and willingness to change one's perspective with new information. Research shows that the opposite, or misunderstanding, results from closed minds filled with prejudice, judgment and preconceived assumptions (Erbe 2004). All cognitive bias precludes actual experience with and an opportunity to get to know another. By choosing to defend what is familiar rather than focusing on learning what is new, less true information is received.

Of course, if open minded and flexible perspective taking of differences was easy it would occur more readily. The author would like to share some of her practices for building a positive climate where group members feel comfortable and safe with beginning to explore their difference. Surprising but true, in the face of tension, members of multicultural groups appreciate and request an easy going spirit including fun, play and humor. If group members can find a way to enjoy each other while exploring difference, this spirit will likely further enhance creativity and innovation. Some call play the midwife of creativity. It encourages imagination, hopefully reduces inhibitions and other mental constraints, and at the very least, assists innovators in relaxing with each other.

The author provides multicultural groups with a few structured activities to begin creating a friendly, fun and low risk environment. In one, over one hundred statements describe various cultural approaches to communication and decision making. Group members are asked to pick or create a few statements describing their own approaches, as well as a few statements that describe the opposite of their style. Participants then mingle, introduce their cultural preferences and attempt to rid themselves of all statements that do not describe their approach. The point of this game is to become acquainted with differences in a fun spirited activity and start to identify commonalities within the group. Group members usually build light-hearted rapport with each other and discover that difference can be quite stimulating. Once surviving open acknowledgment and articulation of difference, confidence and comfort grow. Participants normally start to see the intriguing and creative potential found within difference. If nothing else, by spending time together with elucidation of difference, the resultant knowledge benefits later creative exploration.

In another popular exercise, participants are encouraged to use visual, descriptive, poetic, and even musical metaphor to introduce themselves and their cultural perspective. This activity actively embraces the creative expression and exploration found with innovation. If participants limit themselves to rational analysis and thought alone, they will often simply revisit what has already been discovered rather than ask and see something rare and unique. Fortunately, "(p)eople are story-making creatures who long used symbols and images to convey meaning and identity" (LeBaron and Welch 2005).

## Optimal Multicultural Process Is Inclusive with Equal Participation Built on Common Ground

Once group members begin to know each other through low risk activities like those described above, they often recognize similarities, or common ground, as well as difference. These commonalities offer a resilient platform for multicultural process since they are pre-existing and will endure beyond the group process (Lowy and Littlejohn 2006). Researcher Rackham, mentioned earlier, found that the best of negotiators zealously search for common ground. It is even more important that multicultural innovators be guided and encouraged to continually recognize and explicitly express what they share and how they resonate with others as preparation for effectively handling difference. Hearing their commonality validated over and over again inspires confidence in the group. Publicly recognizing common ground can also shift the group members' perceptual frame of reference from separate individuals to a collective unity.

One of the author's students specifically found that her group's task performance was enhanced by first taking the time to discover common connection (Erbe and Smith 2008). She found that relationship building and mutual support must begin before facing collective challenge. Once group members effectively built alliance so that they trusted each other to some degree, she saw less defensiveness and improved communication and understanding. Group members were able to openly share complaints and critique with each other. In her words, everyone seemed to contribute ideas and accept critiques without ego.

This inclusive democratic approach to process strongly promotes creativity. No one is asked to conform to another's norm or change their uniqueness in any way. No opinion is discounted or ignored. Instead, difference is already seen, from the very beginning of working together, as richly enhancing the group experience.

Researchers Sternberg and Williams found that the most effective corporate groups emulate this democratic process. Innate intelligence and talent do not matter as much as equal participation of team members—that no one dominates and no one refuses to participate. Sternberg and Williams' findings match the author's global evaluation of multicultural groups. Respondents described the best cross-cultural experience as including all voices and encouraging active and serious participation. If a business has the organizational ombuds office introduced earlier, it might consider asking the ombuds to facilitate an impartial process that balances power and participation so that all levels of employees feel safe and encouraged. Some ombuds describe this as multipartiality: commitment to the best interests of all.

An alternative meeting forum available when higher and lower status employees are asked to be part of an innovation team and lower status employees do not feel safe is anonymous discussion on the computer. Research has found that computers create a democratic environment where all feel comfortable with participation and open expression. The downside of this approach, though, is that participants report less satisfaction with its impersonal approach.

## Skilled Listening "Mines for Gold"

Once an innovation team feels safe with each other and its dynamics mirror those described above, the discovery process can begin. The cross cultural model promoted here organizes a structured step-by-step process, with many tools, beginning with careful listening, or what one scholar calls the deep capacity to understand unarticulated needs (Skarzynski and Gibson 2008). Active listening is taught at levels, including the deeper level of meaning. Interest analysis, which at its best discerns unarticulated needs, became quite popular in the negotiation world when Roger Fisher and William Ury of the Harvard Negotiation Project promoted interest-based bargaining (Fisher and Ury 1991). In-depth identification of the interests and needs underlying a particular problem, challenge, conflict or decision is promoted as the basis for stimulating generation of creative ideas.

Related to interest identification is another skill emphasized by creativity and innovation scholars: validation, or the ability to leverage assets—process, business, community, . . . appreciate individual contributions, and celebrate successes (Kennedy and Barker 2008). Assets include all strengths, talents, and interests present in any given situation (Barge 2001). Careful listening alone can provide the most potent of validation. "Gratitude at being heard transcends all cultures. . . . This recognition leads to empowerment" (author's student).

In accord with principles of behavioral reinforcement, students of integrative and facilitated mediation are taught to consciously stress the positive meaning and need underlying any message no matter how destructive or inappropriate it may initially sound. Through reframing "toxic" language, they mine for implicit veins of gold and bring them forward, while leaving disrespectful and hostile material behind. They also learn the power of not reacting to perceived criticism and misunderstanding.

In talking to students, the author has found that the practice of frequent and conscious validation of all group members, through reframing and other communication skills, is fundamental to their feeling of safety and trust with each other (Erbe and Smith 2008). In contrast, the normal human being studied in the United States often emphasizes his or her point of view while minimizing or ignoring others' contributions. Such ethnocentrism deadens both multicultural rapport and innovative risk-taking.

To prevent impasse, students of cooperative group work are also taught concrete ways to express themselves assertively rather than aggressively. As one example, they learn to use "I statements" rather than "you statements." By taking responsibility for their own opinions and ideas, they are less likely to be heard as criticizing or attacking another group member.

Another skill involved with careful listening and linked with creativity and innovation is the ability to pose a good, challenging, astute, and insightful question. In Rackham's research, the most skillful negotiators asked two to three times more questions than the less successful. Students of conflict process are taught to frame collaborative questions to stimulate as many creative ideas as possible. They do this through explicitly incorporating the articulated and unarticulated interests they have identified in a particular context. For example, if the group is attempting to generate creative ideas for making General Motors' cars more environmentally friendly and popular with a new generation of customers, they would frame this sentence as an open-ended question, asking how can General Motors make its cars more environmentally compatible and popular with its youngest consumers?

Creativity researcher Gruber posits that "having a novel point of view is the main thing." The skilled perspective taking introduced earlier, when paired with stellar listening that combines active paraphrasing, validation, reframing, and excellent questioning, fully allows and encourages novel points of view. All involved with a particular project generously attend to deeply understanding, recognizing, and encouraging each and every point of view. Collaborative process expects that diverse stakeholders will define what is desired in highly subjective ways. Diverse novel perspectives are consciously mined and reframed in search of creative ideas.

## Skilled Teams Are the Proven Innovation Leaders

After custom framing of collaborative questions, multicultural negotiators and team members then use common brainstorming and visioning processes to create actual ideas. Once again, it is critically important that they suspend judgment and proceed with open minds. They must delay critique of ideas until several are created. The author of brainstorming, Osborn, proposed these guidelines: (1) suspend judgment, (2) the more unique the idea, the better, (3) go for quantity and speed (to circumvent judgment), (4) have fun, and (5) build off of each other's ideas. His emphasis on quantity is validated by Rackham's research, which found that the best negotiators consider at least twice as many ideas as lesser negotiators. Once again, the right questions can stimulate brainstorming, asking how about . . . ? what if . . . ? has anyone considered . . . ? and has anyone heard what they did . . . ? Some practical recommendations for creating ideas include, once again, noting and building from areas of commonality, starting "easy," and validating the ideas given.

Creativity researcher Gruber further stresses the importance of creative imagination in discovering and constructing alternatives. This is where all struggles inherent in cooperative group work can bear fruit. Research shows that teams generate more alternatives than individual innovators, demonstrating the power of collective imagination.

Contextual safety is still important. Alternatives that pose minimal threat are the most likely to go forward. The advent of computer-assisted groups is particularly interesting when studying the generation of alternatives, especially unique ideas. Studies have found that the anonymity provided in computer-facilitated group discussions can increase the number and uniqueness of ideas. Despite the lack of anonymity and resultant risk, however, team participants still report higher satisfaction in face-to-face meetings. Apparently, team members' social needs are more important to them than promised safety. Yet, since generation of innovative ideas may occur more often with anonymous computer-mediated discussion, a combination of face-to-face and computer discussions might prove best.

At the very least, innovation through diversity insists on generation and evaluation of multiple alternatives, countering the human tendency to quickly accept the first plausible alternative available—even when relatively unsatisfactory. Likewise, to a certain degree, structured cooperative process asks for the in-depth prolonged engagement linked with the most creative and highest quality innovations.

At some point in a creative process, innovators must be "forced" to synthesize their ideas, or somehow integrate divergent pieces and perspectives into a holistic progression. The facilitated collaboration described here does this, insisting that participants do their utmost to reach agreement after rigorous evaluation of their ideas. Once again, teams trained in the skills introduced in this section show enhanced ability to do such evaluation and agreement, as they are more open to each other's ideas and suggestions and thus profit from the differences present in their groups. Being able to embrace group members' scrutiny deepens analysis.

## Conclusion

When negotiators are masters of the skills introduced here or are coached by a master facilitative mediator, the creative process is enriched. This is particularly so with multicultural teams. More ideas result. Additional resources are present and offered. Social support encourages creative synergy that maximizes use of the talents and skills present. To arrive at this optimal place, however, many skills are required, including communication, perspective taking, validation, and trust building. Even more important, control of egocentrism is required. Somehow open-mindedness and curiosity must be created and nurtured.

In working with colleagues, students, and clients from about 70 different countries over the last decade and several organizations and communities in crisis, the author is struck by the disconnect and distance between rhetoric and realities. Scholars urge negotiators and teams to find the new question while diverse workforces keep many new questions to themselves. The newness being sought is often already present. The global community is rich in the variables needed for innovation. Are most of us, in truth, actually afraid to let the fresh idea emerge?

As the author's students and clients risk intimacy, they quickly feel enthusiasm and intrigue. They face their fear and become authentically curious about learning more. Difference is often not difficult when approached with an open mind. When commonalities resonate and differences are validated, all feel welcome, accepted, and valued. Such relationship building lays the foundation for more candid dialogue and critique. Collaborative negotiation and mediation provide structure and skills that sustain engagement enough to mine the riches of the global world.

Those who have studied creativity and innovation find that some level of optimism is needed. Without the confidence that humans can face uncertainty and frustration, innovation is unlikely to happen. Disagreement, misunderstanding, and even impasse will result instead.

Professional group facilitators are hired to observe team dynamics and make suggestions to improve process. Negotiation and other innovation teams, however, can be trained to observe and evaluate themselves. This is called reflective practice, developing the habit of self and other observation (witnessing), evaluating the impact and success of various behaviors, and attempting ongoing improvement (Oetzel and Ting-Toomey 2006). In effect, team members are asked to persist in continually innovating their own process, striving for the best possible relationships and results.

The organizational ombuds introduced earlier are optimally experts in generating alternatives and facilitating others' exploration of alternatives. The most effective ombuds are experts in all the skills described in this section. They can serve as resourceful models and teachers for all. Their most important skills include reframing and persuading others to understand each other's perspective in ways that strengthen rather than jeopardize relationships. Some ombuds report uncanny intuitive radar that accurately senses the unspoken. At its best, this can ignite critical innovative insight.

Those that commit to mastery of these skills can look forward to becoming bold pioneers. They may even become known for having the capacity to dare what others cannot. These skills, while foundational for encouraging innovation, are also the best of conflict resolution and prepare all to harness their strengths proactively in ways that will only enhance reputation and competitive edge.

## Notes and Questions

1. Several foundational skills are introduced in this chapter. They are listed in no particular order below. Rank the following negotiation and mediation skills, with #1 identifying your strongest skills and so forth.

   ___ Explore differences with an open mind
   ___ Examine threatening information, ideas and opinions for insight and benefit
   ___ Actively seek difference
   ___ Listen carefully with paraphrasing to ensure accurate understanding
   ___ Sustain vigorous critique of ideas to create improvement
   ___ Suspend judgment
   ___ Avoid and hold back defensive reaction, including criticism
   ___ Embrace, even enjoy, ambiguity, uncertainty and complexity, e.g., several rather than one answer
   ___ Take calculated risks
   ___ Initiate proactive response

___ Imagine new possibilities
___ Generate several options or alternatives
___ Trust own intuition
___ Think independently
___ Envision futures
___ Understand others' perspectives
___ Encourage others' communication
___ Create positive, comfortable, and low-risk climate
___ Appreciate others' genuine strengths and contributions
___ Show respect
___ Show serious interest in others
___ Show true desire to understand culture in depth
___ Encourage others to share uniqueness
___ Ask for clarification when confused
___ Give sufficient time and patience when English is not first language
___ Notice nonverbal feedback
___ Change one's perspective with new information
___ Negotiate and create effective process parameters
___ Seek and recognize common ground
___ Encourage and ensure equal participation of all
___ Accurately identify most important underlying needs, including unspoken
___ Validate all talents present
___ Reframe toxic language
___ Do not react to perceived slights
___ Express own need and perspective assertively with "I statements"
___ Avoid "you statements"
___ Pose good open ended questions
___ Stimulate ideas

2. Students of negotiation, mediation, and other cross cultural collaboration view the above skills as constantly evolving and improving over a lifetime of serious practice. The good news is that the slightest improvement in any one reaps important rewards. Start to approach trusted others to help you identify your strongest skills. These will become the bedrock of your negotiation/mediation style and niche.

3. Once you start practicing these skills professionally, it will become important for you to develop the regular habit of seeking and securing honest feedback from your clients and colleagues, particularly those from other cultures. You may benefit from experimenting with the use of anonymous evaluations or other safe forums.

4. Pick three ideas from this section that you have been consistently practicing or are willing to begin consistently practicing in your group(s) activities for the remainder of the semester. Share and discuss the results.

## References and Recommended Reading

Barge, K. 2001. "Integrating Theory, Research and Practice in Select Conflict Contexts: Creating Healthy Communities through Affirmative Conflict Communication." *Conflict Resolution Quarterly* 19–1: 92-93.

Bevir, M. 2007. *Encyclopedia of Governance*. Thousand Oaks, Calif.: Sage, 333–34, 593–95.

Bordens, K., and B. Abbott. 1999. *Research Design and Methods*. Mountain View, Calif.: Mayfield Publishing, 20.

Bush, R., and J. Folger. (1994). *The Promise of Mediation.* San Francisco: Jossey Bass.

Cohen, J. 2001. "When People Are the Means: Negotiating with Respect." *Georgetown Journal of Legal Ethics* 14: 739–802.

Deutsch, M. and P. Coleman. 2000. *The Handbook of Conflict Resolution: Theory and Practice*. San Francisco, Calif.: Jossey-Bass, 345–65.

Deutsch, M. 1973. *The Resolution of Conflict: Constructive and Destructive Processes*. New Haven, Conn.: Yale University Press, 360–62.

Dundon, E. 2002. *The Seeds of Innovation: Cultivating the Synergy That Fosters New Ideas*. New York: AMACOM, 16.

Druckman, D. 2005. *Doing Research: Methods of Inquiry for Conflict Analysis.* Thousand Oaks, Calif.: Sage, 7–9.

Erbe, N. 2006. "Appreciating Mediation's Global Role in Promoting Good Governance." *Harvard Negotiation Law Review, 11*, 370–419.

———. 2004. The Global Popularity and Promise of Facilitative ADR. *Temple International and Comparative Law Journal* 18(2): 345–71.

———. 2003. *Holding These Truths: Empowerment and Recognition in Action (Interactive Case Study Curriculum for Multicultural Dispute Resolution* Berkeley: Berkeley Public Policy Press, 52–168.

Erbe, N., T. Sebok. 2008. "Shared Global Interest in Skillfully Applying IOA Standards of Practice." *Journal of the International Ombudsman 1:* 28–38.

Erbe, N., and R. Smith. 2008. *Falling in Love with Teaching and Learning: Proven Activities for Engaging Diverse Students in Collaborative Learning.* Paper presented at the annual meeting of the International Society for Teaching and Learning, Las Vegas, Nevada (October).

Fink, D. 2003. *Creating Significant Learning Experiences.* San Francisco: Jossey-Bass, 40-42.

Fisher, R. and W. Ury. 1991. *Getting to Yes: Negotiating Agreement without Giving in*. New York: Penguin Books, 1–80.

Gellene, D. 2008. "Study finds left-wing brain, right-wing brain." *Los Angeles Times,* September 10.

Goleman, D. 1995. *Emotional Intelligence*. New York: Bantam, 159–63.

Johannesen, R. 1996. *Ethics in Human Communication.* Prospect Heights, Ill.: Waveland Press, 67-68.

Johnson, D., and F. Johnson. 2000. *Joining Together.* Boston: Allyn and Bacon, 321–29).

Kennedy, D., and J. Barker. 2008. *Putting Our Differences to Work: The Fastest Way to Innovation, Leadership and High Performance.* San Francisco: Berrett-Koehler, 127–37.

LeBaron, M., and D. Welch. 2005. *Arts, Creativity and Intercultural Conflict Resolution.* University of British Columbia, 2–18.

Lewicki, R., B. Barry, and D. Saunders. 2007. *Essentials of Negotiation* McGraw-Hill, 243–49.

Lowry, C., and S. Littlejohn. 2006. "Dialogue and Discourse of Peacebuilding in Maluku, Indonesia." *Conflict Resolution Quarterly* 23-4: 409–26.

Lynn, Laurence E. 1999. *Teaching and Learning with Cases.* Illinois: University of Chicago.

Oetzel, J., and S. Ting-Toomey. 2006. *The Sage Handbook of Conflict Communication: Integrating Theory, Research and Practice.* Thousand Oaks: Sage, 395–415.

Reuben, R. 2005. "Democracy and Dispute Resolution: Systems Design and the New Workplace." *Harvard Negotiation Law Review* 10: 11–51.

Roht-Arriza, N. 2004. "Reparations Decisions and Dilemmas." *Hastings International and Comparative Law Journal* 27: 191.

Rowe, M. 1995. "Options, Functions, and Skills: What the Organizational Ombudsperson Might Want to Know," *Negotiation Journal* 11: 103–14.

Skarzynski, P., R. Gibson. 2008. *Innovation to the Core.* Boston: Harvard Business School Publishing, 61–75).

Snyder, N., and D. Duarte. 2008. *Unleashing Innovation: How Whirlpool Transformed an Industry.* San Francisco: Jossey Bass, 1–169.

Triandis, H. 2003. "The Future of Workforce Diversity in International Organizations: A Commentary." *Applied Psychology: An International Review* 52-3: 486–95.

Tubbs, S. 1995. *A Systems Approach to Small Group Interaction.* New York: McGraw-Hill, 196–98, 236–38.

Section IV

# Skillful Conflict Process Shows Promise in the Face of Violent Ethnic Conflict

When I despair, I remember that through history the way of truth and love has always won. There have been tyrants and murderers and for a time they seem invincible—but in the end they always fall—think of it—ALWAYS. Mahatma Gandhi

Empowerment must be induced by first creating consciousness. . . . To facilitate . . . is the role of external agents. Experience has demonstrated that empowerment takes place in different scenarios. . . . There are no magic formulas or infallible designs, no single recipe or prescriptive (evaluative) model. Empowerment is not a linear process with a well defined beginning and ending that is the same for all. . . . Empowerment is shaped for each individual or group by their lives, context, and history, as well as according to the location of subordination in the personal, familiar, communal, and higher levels (Deere and Leon 1993).

[I found helpful] the knowledge to resolve conflicts peacefully and restoratively in my community pregnant with conflicts, the development of my mind on the importance of peace in the development of the home and the community . . . the improvement of my social relationships with friends, neighbors and even long time enemies . . . the definition of peace as a continuous process of resolving conflicts without the use of violence (Erbe 2001).

As demonstrated throughout this book, alternative dispute resolution's (ADR)[1] growth within courts and governments around the world[2] forecasts a significant global trend with international potential. (Note: Within the United States alternative dispute resolution refers to all conflict process used as an alternative to litigation). Particularly intriguing, however, is ADR's popularity with grassroots peacebuilding. Professionals in conflicted parts of the world, including some of our most intractable and dangerous ethnic battles, are embracing the concepts and practices of ADR,[3] with its creative possibilities and pragmatic options for reducing tensions within their countries.[4] Thus they empower more inclusive peacebuilding.

As introduced earlier, peacebuilding is the development of culture and societal institutions that support reconciliation and peace over time.[5] This section emphasizes the popularity and potential of ADR with track two diplomacy, prevention and restorative efforts after war.[6] As a reminder to the reader, track two, or unofficial, citizen diplomacy involves international actors other than nation-states (e.g., leaders of United States and Iraq) or designated international organizations (e.g., the United Nations). Joseph Elder's informal efforts as a Quaker mediator working with India, Pakistan, and Sri Lanka demonstrate track two diplomacy in action.[7]

An informal process can, and does, play a role in preparing for, and motivating, formal, traditional diplomacy. Visionary initiative creates unexpected opportunities.[8] For example, months of third-party assisted meetings and negotiations, which resulted in "direct, honest" communication and "mutual trust and affinity," preceded the Oslo Accords.[9] Jan Egeland asserts that nongovernmental organizations, or international nonprofits, are best positioned for such an initiative.[10] Those who can operate flexibly, with access to people and networks that can be mobilized quickly, should take the lead.

Brian Ferguson, a leading anthropologist of war, views contemporary outbreaks of ethnic violence as the most pressing issue of war.[11] Though developing formal mechanisms for creating and enforcing public international law is an essential priority at this point in history, the majority of ethnic disputes fall outside the jurisdiction, authority, and range of international forums as intranational. At present, there are about 35 conflicts of war within nations rather than between them.[12] The United States can only handle three at one time—if it decides to respond.[13]

## Citizen Diplomacy Facilitates Inclusive Peace Building

Without prompting, the community members surveyed here, in four different parts of the world, exemplify the viability and popularity of intercultural dialogue. They enthusiastically report ADR's principles and practices guiding the challenges of creating multicultural communities:[14] deepening and informing analysis of complex conflict dynamics, building party capacity, providing helpful approaches at different levels of society,[15] and otherwise creating effective processes. They repeatedly describe the details of facilitative approaches to dispute resolution and applaud their contribution to peace building.

Facilitation, defined simply, means assistance.[16] Scholars of groups, organizations, and systems popularized and expanded the term and practice: Group facilitation is a process where a substantively neutral person, whose selection is acceptable to all members of a group and who has no substantive decision-making authority, diagnoses and intervenes to help a group improve how it identifies and solves problems and makes decisions for the purpose of increasing the group's effectiveness. The facilitator's main task is to help the group increase effectiveness by improving its process.[17]

Other definitions of facilitation include "managing group processes and dynamics [and] influencing how [participants] work together . . . [with] a focus on group needs."[18] Common facilitator (third-party) tasks encompass process observation and analysis, and positive process influence through, for example, giving participants feedback about their approaches to communication and ideas for improving communication.[19]

This section presents the results of qualitative research asking parties to cross-ethnic dispute resolution to evaluate, in their own words, the effectiveness of their leaders, or third-party facilitators. The data reported here is from four different parts of the world struggling with ethnic conflict: the Balkans, Cameroon, Nepal, and the Ukraine. The majority of respondents have known violent conflict—war, terrorism, and long-standing tensions.

The survey's foremost discovery is the consistent popularity of facilitative approaches to dispute resolution with cross-ethnic conflict in all four regions. First, processes that include all ethnic groups equally are lauded as the most important variable for effective cross-ethnic conflict resolution. Second, research responses portray the best cross-ethnic leadership as assertive and empathetic. Identified characteristics of ineffective leadership are the opposite: insensitive, closed-minded, negative, critical, prejudiced, indifferent, and aggressive to name some of the descriptions. Third, research data describes the overriding importance of skilled attentive listening. Fourth, community members and professionals elaborate the value of conflict resolution training, or learning how to resolve their own conflicts by modeling cross-ethnic dispute resolution to their communities.

## Lauded Cross-Cultural Process: Top Practices[20]

| Rank | Descriptors |
|---|---|
| 1 | Open honest disclosure |
| | Information sharing |
| | Expressing and hearing feelings |
| | Discussing opinions |
| | Dialogue |

| | |
|---|---|
| | Exploring diverse gender and ethnic experience |
| 2 | Paraphrasing |
| 3 | Empowerment (training participants to resolve own conflicts) |
| 4 | Open-ended questions |
| 5 | Perspective-taking |
| 6 | Identification of interests and commonalities (shared interests) |

This section begins by discussing the rationale behind the survey design and how it was administered, including known characteristics of the population surveyed. It then introduces and contrasts facilitative and evaluative approaches to dispute resolution for readers new to ADR. The international community may be unknowingly incurring destructive costs with its myopic focus on evaluative approaches and apparent ignorance of facilitation's value and popularity. The next section analyzes survey results. It describes respondents' requests for personal contact across ethnic, religious, and caste lines and briefly relates ADR to broad global needs. The author reviews data, highlighting its strongest themes: multicultural equivalence, a process where all participate and are treated equally, and strong facilitative leadership which promotes astute understanding and guides participants in practicing their own dispute resolution skills.

## Survey Design and Implementation (Methodology)

Results of exploratory qualitative research[21] evaluating facilitated intercultural dialogue, dispute resolution training, and mediation are presented here. In partnership with a diverse group of professionals,[22] including those who facilitated cross-ethnic dialogue[23] and trainings in Bosnia and Herzegovina, Montenegro and Serbia,[24] a conflict resolution trainer, and mediator[25] from Cameroon,[26] a lawyer-mediator working with court-mandated mediation in Nepal,[27] and a community mediator practicing in the Ukraine,[28] we surveyed the evaluations of participants of multicultural processes.[29] (Note: Readers interested in learning about these countries and regions are directed to the book's appendices).

Curiosity about the reasons why those embroiled in multicultural conflict processes ask certain third-party interveners, or facilitators, to assist them, rather than others, motivated the survey design. The research was anticipated and proposed within the United States. The enthusiasm of international research partners,[30] however, altered its direction and scope. One body of scholarship focuses on exporting the North American expert experience, for the purpose of developing transferable models and best practices.[31] The research introduced here has quite a different purpose. For these studies, the users themselves, rather than outside experts, evaluated the conflict intervention. Except for one North American trainer in Cameroon, all interveners are non-American.

Both North American researchers and the scholars here, however, share one concern: the lack of "sustainable conflict-handling institutions," or effective community capacity.[32] One reason users were asked to evaluate their own experience in the assisted conflict process was because "sustained capacity for conflict handling starts with a commitment to do so."[33] Why not build on existing commitment by having the users themselves identify the practices and concepts they evaluated most highly?

Studying multicultural processes is unavoidably complex. Researchers must be particularly sensitive to their own cultural assumptions and biases. For this reason, researchers used Michael Patton's approach to evaluative research.[34] Unlike quantitative research, Patton's qualitative approach begins without formulating researcher premises. Instead, those surveyed create their own evaluation criteria. A series of eliciting, open-ended, and incomplete statements are used to encourage respondents to identify and describe their priorities in the language and description of their choice. The overriding goals are to obtain descriptive data as free as possible from the researcher's perspective, bias, and language, and instead, to focus on the essential premises formulated and prioritized by the respondents themselves. In accordance with objectivist grounded theory, researchers did not force data into preconceived categories through the imposition of artificial questions.[35]

Readers are more likely to be familiar with quantitative research samples and statistical analysis than with qualitative research. Qualitative research aims to provide a focused and in-depth understanding of a particular psychology, life experience, or community through interpersonal methods, like interviews, and interpretative, rather than statistical analysis. Such ethnomethodological approaches to social inquiry are broadly concerned with how people construct their own definitions of social situations.[36]

Questionnaires and human subject informed consent forms were mailed to six research partners, which included three in the Balkans, one in Cameroon, West Africa, one in Nepal, South Asia, and one in the Ukraine. Research partners gave questionnaires to participants on completion of the multicultural conflict process.[37] Respondents were given the option of requesting a phone or electronic interview. None elected the latter option. Because the sensitive nature of the process being evaluated, particularly in the context of postwar reconstruction, could discourage open and honest disclosure, survey respondents were allowed to remain anonymous and were promised confidentiality. As a result of this anonymity and confidentiality, further exploration and elaboration of responses was prohibited.[38]

Respondents, themselves, determined whether their process was multicultural. Ninety percent of the surveys from Cameroon and the Balkans, 85 percent from Nepal, and 60 percent from the Ukraine identified and evaluated cross-cultural process and leadership. All respondents chose to describe their experience in English. Whenever possible, in sharing the results, respondents' own words are used. Interestingly, many used technical language from the field of dispute resolution, like paraphrasing, impartiality, and perspective-taking.

The study asked respondents:

**Question 1.** I would rate the cultural approach, rapport, awareness, sensitivity and competence of my trainer(s), group members, facilitators, negotiators and/or mediators (please circle which apply) as:

excellent average poor

Please explain: (Note: If your rating varies depending on behavior, please use a range.)

Respondents were also asked to evaluate their dispute resolution process in general, once again, with their own words:

**Question 2.** I found the following:

Helpful:

Unhelpful:

Overall, I would recommend or suggest:

Some readers may feel frustrated with response brevity, particularly when English is used as a second or third language. Research was conducted, however, with the stated purpose that its results be used to frame criteria for case-by-case evaluation of future outside, or third-party, multicultural effectiveness. It is hoped that the results will guide and inspire in-depth interviews, focus groups, field observation, analysis of published sources of information, and longitudinal quantitative research. Often the meanings emerging from qualitative data, like the process evaluation here, are tested in subsequent quantitative studies for plausibility, sturdiness, conformability, or validity.[39]

## Facilitative ADR Deserves Broader Credit and Consideration

International peace builders, conflict resolvers, and lawyers routinely face enormous questions of complexity and urgency. How do we facilitate recovery and resilience in the face of war and other conflicts that scar? Counter intractable cycles? Nurture critical steps forward? The author never anticipated that one of the answers might be the facilitative approach to dispute resolution.

The survey results reported here favor a facilitative response to cross-cultural conflict. The preference is impossible to ignore. The value of the facilitative response like careful listening and encouraging parties' self determination is repeatedly described in concrete detail. The heart of the debate between evaluative and facilitative approaches to disputes in the United States is within the alternative dispute community mediating litigation. Nevertheless, it is referenced here. The author is concerned when commercial and corporate arbitrators and mediators with evaluative approaches are quoted on issues of international significance as if their approach to ADR is comprehensive.[40] It is frightening to see commercial and corporate arbitrators speaking as authorities on mediation's value with complex political disputes and international relations when they are not educated in the type of mediation that may be most needed.

Before contrasting approaches to mediation, a description of the evaluative approaches to dispute resolution will provide a clearer framework.

> Judges, arbitrators, neutral experts and advisors are evaluators. . . . To [make decisions,] they use predetermined criteria to evaluate evidence and arguments presented by adverse parties. [Their tasks include] finding "the facts,' by properly weighing evidence, judging credibility, and allocating burden of proof, determining and applying relevant law, rule, or custom to the particular situation, and making an award or rendering an opinion. The adverse parties have expressly asked the evaluator—judge, arbitrator, or expert—to decide the issue or resolve the conflict.[41]

The following quotes preceding the U.S. war with Iraq indicate strong bias favoring the evaluative approach and the belief that it represents mediation's full potential. "If Hussein has contractual obligations [to disarm] that sets up a better case for mediation. . . . It gives the mediator something to work with. . . . [42] The next step, mediators say, would be to . . . [determine] where compromises can be made and how much flexibility both parties are bringing to the equation. . . . An especially tricky task for any mediator would be coming up with a solution. . . ."[43]

The mediator who evaluates often helps participants understand the strengths and weaknesses of their positions, assuming that the mediator has knowledge, expertise, and opinions that must be shared for optimal problem-solving. In contrast, the facilitative approach provides a framework that assists parties to discover and create options, even if they and third parties cannot envision any when they first meet.[44] "The mediator who facilitates assumes that the parties . . . can develop better solutions than any mediator might create."[45]

With the evaluative approach, participants' style of speech and behavior aim to convince their decision maker.[46] Because facilitators have no decision making authority, however, participants share information and relate to each other with the aim of reaching a mutually beneficial agreement. Participants may decide to consult with experts, but decisions are their own.[47]

The directive style can and does include suggestions, heavy-handed pressure, and pushes participants towards the third-party's conception.[48] The facilitative mediator assumes his principal mission is to clarify and enhance communication between parties so as to help them decide what to do.[49]

An Argentine lawyer studying ADR brought the issue of facilitative relevance to the author's attention. After hearing her presentation on multicultural conflict resolution, he asked if the facilitative approach is the most appropriate for cross-cultural mediation. The survey data reviewed here answers affirmatively, with a loud yes, while simultaneously validating the roles of expertise and direction within facilitation. The result may be seen as an optimal balance and blending of the best of both styles.

These results demonstrate how ADR's most important issues can influence and transcend diverse forums—international and domestic, public and community, as well as litigated disputes. Fundamental questions are raised about global dispute resolution while they are also being raised regarding the role of mediators, facilitators, trainers, lawyers, arbitrators,[50] and judges working with disputes involving several cultures, within and outside of legal systems. The need to knowledgably contrast facilitative and evaluative strengths and weaknesses before choosing the "best option" is universal. The results cannot be quickly or easily assessed as a clear-cut "either/or." Authority, expertise, and evaluation can, and do, play essential roles within cross-ethnic disputes. What is their optimal role? When is their contribution risky?[51]

The author introduced the need for a similar discussion among public health workers at an international conference in India a few years ago. Sponsored by professional groups from Canada and India, the gathering drew nurses, doctors, social workers, and academics that came from and worked in diverse countries including Bangladesh, Iran, Nigeria, Thailand, and Vietnam. Many resonated with the assertion that, despite acknowledging need for more public participation, critical blocks to international development include predominance of the evaluative, or expert, approach, along with failure to facilitate effective partnerships with concerned communities. At the same conference Burmese activists requested that the United Nations and development organizations initiate "inclusive dialogue" and local involvement in negotiations, along with community training (capacity building) in "negotiation, conflict resolution, and dialogue skills."[52]

Related requests are being made with regard to the emerging international courts of justice. When asked about the International Criminal Tribunal, Bosnian legal professionals expressed concern that the tribunal was pursuing its "own determined agenda, without meaningful input . . . [and thus] international organizations run the risk of undermining the very goals they are trying to achieve."[53] The report recommends that "additional interventions that are different from, but complementary to trials, such as facilitating culturally accepted mechanisms of justice should be considered. . . . Social reconstruction may not occur when people are faced with judicial decisions that do not correspond to their perceptions of what happened, i.e., their "truth."[54]

An essential consideration for the international community, particularly with transitional and emerging democracies where the rule of law and legal institutions require capacity building, is the distance between law, practice, and community norms. Many countries with exemplary constitutions and extensive formally stated laws have little or slow enforcement in daily life. Ideally, public process respects and reflects the law. Real practice, however, can be dramatically different.[55] In this context, ADR provides viable options for critical problem-solving and plays an essential role in empowering the participation necessary for good governance.[56]

A related question is whether equity[57] is truly possible without citizens' direct participation in decision making and other exercises of power. "Time and again we have seen these campaigns [promoting ethnic violence] to be conceived, planned, and coercively executed by centralized power elites seeking to maintain or expand their hold on power and wealth [with messages of hate internalized and horrifically advanced]."[58] Empowering communities in the face of corrupt and self-interested political leadership is many communities' best, perhaps only, option for building peace.[59]

## Part 1: Facilitation Is Praised

Crossing historic boundaries of ethnic, class, religious, and regional distance with simple human contact, and, even more so, with communication and relationship, is being embraced around the world through facilitated mediation and dialogue.[60] While strong critique exists of the risk that informal process allows participants to perpetuate, even hide, prejudice and discrimination,[61] its growing popularity reflects participants' desire to meet each other face-to-face, as human beings, rather than mythologized, and too often demonized, "others."[62] Participants wish to hear each other's stories and perspectives—often for the first time. In a city like Mostar, such dialogue presented a rare opportunity to cross imposed separation.[63]

Mostar was a city in southern Bosnia and Herzegovina strongly divided into two ethnically-driven communities. The division was the consequence of fierce armed conflicts during the war. Political structures were only deepening the gap between the two communities. Yet during these times, there were young people willing to cooperate and overcome the polarization.[64]

Those attempting to overcome their community's polarization through cross ethnic and caste conversation completed and returned 115 surveys here. Survey respondents, from Mostar and other world regions, lauded facilitative process and its fruits. Facilitating inclusive dispute resolution can effectively bridge difference. At its best, facilitation creates positive multicultural spirit and climate, emphasizes careful, respectful listening, and results in the empowered capacity necessary for tough, collaborative problem-solving.

Nepalese respondents explicitly mentioned the value of facilitative participatory process in reference to cultural diversity and conflict.[65] One Nepalese party esteemed mediation as a means for parties to enlighten each other about differences through cultural education.[66] Others spoke out against dividing into groups based on ethnic difference.[67]

The facilitative approach to mediation was likewise preferred in the Ukraine.[68] "[The mediator] has to help [us] to find resolution but not resolve it by himself."[69] This echoed an earlier Cameroon evaluation: "I suggest that many people should be trained so that they will solve their problems without looking for third parties to solve their problems. This will go a long way to reduce the number of problems that exist in society."[70] Some Ukrainian respondents appreciated, and even requested, impartiality: "not interfering [in] the process of discussion" or pushing for agreement.[71] At the same time, respondents applauded assisting parties recognize, admit, and take responsibility for the harms and consequences of their conflict.

Eighty respondents from the Balkans evaluated a range of facilitated practice. Ninety percent described their processes as multicultural. Several were more than enthusiastic, using exclamation points and words like "precious" and "brilliant."

## Advancing Inclusive Dispute Resolution

In all four regions surveyed, the opportunity to participate in,[72] and create, an inclusive process[73] was the most popular reason for highly rating mediation and other facilitated conflict process.[74] Use of words[75] like "equal treatment" and "participation" by respondents illustrate optimal multicultural conflict experience.[76] Even merely introducing all participants equally was applauded.[77] The partakers of conflict resolution training in Cameroon[78] affirmed the importance of active participation, with opportunity for community members to share and discuss real life experiences. One participant declared the importance of facilitating a community's resolution of their own conflict in nonviolent ways rather than directing parties to conflict.[79] Most responses from Nepal[80] promoted low power distance,[81] or power sharing, regardless of caste or ethnic difference.[82] When all people were not involved, uniform inclusion was requested more than once. Many expressed the belief that decisions made by "common consensus" were more acceptable and easier to implement than those made by a single person.[83]

Several respondents from the Balkans[84] prized inclusive participatory process. "Discussing . . . religion is so hard and I wanted . . . [everyone to have a voice]."[85] They rated highly their third parties' open-mind "for everyone," regardless of ethnic or gender difference.[86] Additionally, they relished opportunities for teamwork.[87]

The strongest preference, repeated again and again, was facilitation of equal treatment, with respect. Some asserted that prejudice and discrimination, including favoritism, should not be tolerated. Others suggested that minorities should be allowed to voice their opinions first. If necessary, processes should be private to prevent public harassment and abuse. Some believe that those not agreeing with democratic processes should be excluded, particularly if they are societal authorities perpetuating discrimination and other wrongs.

Balkan respondents not only valued the conflict process, but often expressed gratitude for its broader contribution to emerging democracy in their societies.[88]

## Top Recommendations for Cross Cultural Conflict Process

| Rank | Recommendations |
|---|---|
| 1 | Include all voices |
| | Encourage active participation |
| 2 | Tell the truth |
| 3 | Increase seriousness of participation |

Several respondents underscored learning the principles of democratic society and "new ideas for implementing democracy in our community."[89] One respondent stated, "I discovered that I'm not as democratic as I thought. . . . All of this showed me that I am not what I hoped . . . and how to become what I like . . . open-minded and democratic."[90] In praising the facilitator the respondent stated, "He did a great and important job. He directed our mind to think about democracy!"[91] (Note: This capacity for democracy building will be explored in more detail in the book's last section).

Once respect was established, the optimal multicultural spirit and climate described provides much needed relief from the seriousness and tension of escalating conflict. Balkan groups elucidated the spirit of ideal multicultural leadership as interesting, easy-going, funny, energizing, and friendly. Fun, or play, was applauded and requested.[92] One respondent from Nepal also stressed mediator humor, with an interesting statement about culture. "Only the same culture, religion or traits doesn't make the mediator perfect. The sense of humor, his personality . . . also counts."[93]

## Notes and Questions

1. Are you truly aware of how you treat others? Most human beings, if not all, including mediators, have blind spots. According to the theory of self-serving bias, we routinely see ourselves in a better light than others see us. For example, years ago, several teachers were videotaped in their United States classrooms. The taping revealed that the majority of these teachers were acknowledging the raised hands of boys more than the raised hands of girls. Thus they were encouraging boys to speak more than girls. At least one mediation article identifies the same dynamic in couple mediations. How many of these teachers and mediators would

you imagine are aware that they are encouraging boys and men to speak more than girls and women?

1. It is critical that facilitators and mediators find ways to fully see themselves and their treatment of group members and parties to mediation. With permission from all concerned, audio and videotaping are possibilities for advancing detailed awareness.

   A simple exercise is to begin observing oneself and evaluating equal treatment through asking questions like the following.

   Who do I greet and ask to speak first? A member of a group with whom I identify (e.g., gender, culture, color, religion, etc.)?

2. Another simple and recommended exercise for raising awareness of equal participation is observing process dynamics with a means of measurement. One can simply tally and count the number of times each participant speaks or use a watch to note the length of time each participant speaks.

3. Of course, once again, finding ways to receive regular honest feedback from dialogue participants, mediation parties, and others is also needed. How they perceive you is as important, if not more, than how you perceive yourself.

4. The best of facilitators are life-long students of facilitative skills. If you find yourself being evaluated as partial or evaluative, you will likely benefit from additional education, training, and connection; perhaps mentoring, with masterful professionals and their communities.

## Part 2: Balancing Deep Understanding with Assertive Leadership

How do we facilitate constructive contact and communication in the face of destructive realities, especially as they manifest themselves in communities like those surveyed, with generations of stubborn ethnic conflict, violent terrorism, abuse, mistreatment, and suppression?[94] The following as well as the remainder of the book is based on the premise that such a critically important question deserves a case-by-case answer.[95]

### Inspire Utmost Respect for Self and Others

Survey respondents from the Balkans, Cameroon, Nepal, and the Ukraine - four very different parts of the world—laud and illustrate some key themes for optimal multicultural leadership in circumstances like those described above.[96] Dispute resolution professionals from the United States may feel ill-qualified to respond. Unexpected and striking, however, are the parallels between the evaluation detailed here and a study of the best lawyer negotiators in the United States. The most effective in both studies are universally perceived as assertive and empathetic problem-solvers.[97] Skilled empathy, or deep recognition and understanding of the other's perspective, seems ideally suited for cross-cultural dispute resolution. Perspective-taking describes the popular "walking in another's shoes," or attempting to "see through another's eyes" and experience.

In Cameroon and throughout the Balkans, evaluators spoke out in gratitude for their third party's understanding:[98] "Leaders always tried to understand our point of view."[99] More than one recognized that this was a "very delicate situation regarding cultural and religious differences."[100] Americans may imagine the understanding being appreciated as intellectual or academic—what is required for evaluative expertise in arbitration or litigation. In the majority of cases here, the dispute resolution leadership being validated, however, as emphasized earlier, emulates facilitative, not evaluative, skills and attitudes.

For example, Balkan respondents disparaged a closed mind and "put-downs," the opposite of empathy.[101] Open-minded tolerance, or lack of prejudice, described the most popular climate and spirit with Balkan process. Positivity was stressed repeatedly in evaluating the most effective multicultural process in the Ukraine.[102] When third parties in the Ukraine failed to create a positive climate, for example, by forgetting to suspend judgment,[103] they were often criticized. One party felt scolded and saw the mediator emphasizing the negative aspects of their conflict.[104] Another criticized lack of sensitivity to the parties.[105] On a similar note, a Cameroon respondent stressed "transforming the existing negative attitudes and stereotypes."[106] In Nepal, patience was prized.[107]

## Worst Cross-Cultural Leaders: Reported Weaknesses[108]

| Rank | Descriptors |
|---|---|
| 1 | Do not listen carefully |
| | Lack deep understanding |
| 2 | Judgmental |
| | Disrespectful (e.g., put down parties) |
| | Bad tempered |
| 3 | Emphasize negative |

Once again, these survey results mirror research of lawyer negotiators in the United States. Words like stubborn, arrogant, egotistical, and unethical describe the least effective lawyer negotiators studied in the United States.[109]

## The Worst Cross-Cultural Process: Top Indicators

| Descriptors |
|---|
| Indifference |
| Prejudice dividing into ethnic and national groups |

Increased awareness perceived as leading to despair

A Jewish-Palestinian group studying peacemaking in the Middle East described what they need to engage in dialogue: suspension of judgment so that all can speak candidly without fear of being labeled. Respect and open-mindedness for all, without domination or attack, encourages voices seldom heard and testing out of thoughts without feared "eternal stigma." Passionate concern that allows open expression of deep feelings, without screaming and shouting, is requested. Mentioned most was the need for flexibility, or the willingness to change opinions with new understanding.

Why would empathy lead the skills mastered by the most highly rated dispute resolvers, in both tough U.S. litigation and cross-ethnic disputes around the world? Fierce advocacy popularly symbolizes legal contests. Police and military forces are the most visible international presence with cross-ethnic violence. Yet related research illuminates that, not surprisingly, misunderstanding results from the closed minds filled with prejudice and judgment. This same characteristic was criticized in the Balkans, Cameroon, Nepal, and the Ukraine. Prejudgment or quick judgment based on one's own worldview and experience, rather than broader realities, reinforces erroneous assumptions. Prejudice hinders and precludes actual experience with and understanding of the "other."[110] Those defending judgment only "see" and gather data supporting their preconceptions.

There has been a tendency to quite inaccurately characterize the cognitive perspective in psychology as viewing people as entirely conscious and rational. This erroneous characterization is deserved up to a point. It was quickly discovered, however, that if anything, people are better described as faulty computers—their natural cognitive functioning produces all kinds of biases and distortions.[111]

These cognitive challenges are not simply faced by those defending rigidly held beliefs, however. Research shows a human tendency to create more favorable versions of ourselves and less favorable versions of the "other" when in actual and perceived conflict.[112]

Empathetic negotiators, on the other hand, are more likely to interpret the behavior of others accurately.[113] What could be more important under the pressure of devastating conflict than the ability to objectively gather quality information? A practitioner who diffused ethnic crisis within the United States describes empathy's value with information gathering:[114]

The ability to listen with empathy may be the most important attribute of interveners who succeed in gaining the trust and cooperation of parties to intractable conflicts and other disputes with high emotional content. Empathic listening enables the skilled listener to receive and accurately interpret the speaker's message. It (1) builds trust and respect, (2) enables disputants to release their emotions, (3) reduces tensions, (4) encourages the surfacing of information, and (5) creates a safe environment that is conducive to collaborative problem-solving. Empathic listening is often what sets the mediator apart from others involved in the conflict.[115]

The ability to avoid cognitive distortion and facilitate understanding deserves special recognition across cultural differences, especially with intractable conflict. As introduced earlier, according to some theorists, people perceive what is against them, or outside, their core sense of identity as a threat. This can result in cognitive distortion in an attempt to "reduce," even eliminate the threat. An attempt to protect and defend identity may be made through ignoring, minimizing, or rationalizing what is threatening. Once again, by choosing to defend what is familiar and known, rather than focusing on learning more about what is new, less true information is received. As the reactor increases reliance on his or her own psychological interpretations to describe, dehumanize, and objectify "the other," misinformation increases. An escalating spiral of destructive conflict easily results.[116]

Third parties intervening in volatile conflict, however, cannot soar on one skill, no matter how important or strong. The most effective lawyer negotiators in the United States are described as both empathetic and assertive. This critical combination is also stressed in the regions surveyed here.

## Most Esteemed Cross-Cultural Facilitators[117]

| Rank | Descriptor |
|---|---|
| 1 | Knowledge and Experience |
| 2 | Tolerance |
| | No Prejudice |
| | Open-Mind |
| 3 | Skillful Facilitation |
| 4 | Engaging |
| | Interesting |
| 5 | Energetic/Dynamic |
| 6 | Cultural and Religious Understanding |
| 7 | Amusing |
| 8 | Influence/Charisma |
| 9 | In Charge While Guiding |
| 10 | Promotes Cooperation |
| 11 | Positive Spirit/Feeling |
| 12 | Patient |
| 13 | Impartial |

Throughout the Balkans, popular cross-cultural leadership was appreciated, first and foremost, for sharing valuable knowledge and experience.[118] Reported second in importance was influence, or "possessing skills to change our opinions."[119] Included in this category were the third party's values, personal and professional, communication skills, and ability to "be in charge of the topic and guide the audience."[120] The obvious challenge in cases like those reviewed here is that dispute resolution must somehow embrace, or at least find a way to work with, the opposite of the optimal climate described earlier: destructive, competitive systems permeated with corruption and nurturing violence. Parties to mediation in Nepal, for example, criticized and described bad faith on the part of other parties.[121] The bad faith described encompassed: (1) attempting to break the promised and signed agreement, (2) deceit and failure to share important information or "secrets," (3) not observing ground rules, (4) trying to overpower the other party and treat the party as inferior, (5) misusing the process for self-interest, and (6) rigid indifference. Indifference was also criticized in the Balkans.[122] Aggression and expression of anger were criticized several times.[123]

How do skillful dispute resolvers proceed in the face of such power abuse and corruption? As introduced in earlier sections, the practice of conflict resolution does offer several tools for facilitating small (micro) steps forward with such challenges. The ground rules introduced in section two and reviewed in section three,[124] for example, are one concrete response esteemed by Ukrainian evaluators.[125] As a review for the reader, all those concerned negotiate detailed agreements about what is necessary to proceed constructively, step-by-step, interaction-by-interaction. Such process parameters serve several purposes. They offer an option for balancing power. Reflecting on work with multicultural communities and violence and crisis, critical themes are consciousness and power. Self-determination "crosses cultural barriers" and allows parties to structure the process appropriate for them. Creating ground rules, or shared agreements and understandings, with everyone's input, respects individual and group, or cultural, norms equally to build a solid multicultural foundation.

Ground rules can establish moral boundaries, such as good faith. Words like "respectful and humane," "working hard for us," and "support of the individual in the group" were used to illustrate optimal multicultural facilitation throughout the Balkans.[126]

Mediators and facilitators also model respectful behavior. They treat the parties with dignity, listen with care, and project their interest in and concern for what each party says. Their example, at its best, sets the tone for how the parties can listen to and treat one another.[127]

The best of cross-cultural facilitators are described here as having enough charisma and influence to gracefully assert ground rules so that all feel safe, respected, and welcome to speak. The same time, these facilitators are the exceptional listeners and nurturers described throughout this book. They emulate exquisite balance between assertiveness and receptivity.

## Find Gold in Every Difference

All surveyed championed careful listening.[128] It is hard to imagine skilled empathy and understanding without careful listening. Respondents from the Ukraine stress its importance and value again and again.[129] A few of the parties to mediation in Nepal, along with at least one respondent from Cameroon, found paraphrasing helpful.[130] "Listening and rephrasing of what parties are saying builds confidence in the parties."[131] The picture that emerges from the survey results regarding the importance of careful listening is twofold. First, the third party encourages increasing disclosure of vital information across culture, heightening understanding between and within the parties to the conflict; even personal transformation. Second, by modeling open-minded empathy and understanding, the third party inspires the parties to more careful listening of each other.

Once again, the most popular leaders of cross-cultural processes are portrayed as balancing receptivity and rapport with assertive direction. Respondents from several regions mention direct, detailed questioning as important to careful listening.[132] Open, honest disclosure must result.[133] This was particularly true in Nepal, where questions and open discussion led the most compelling multicultural process.[134] One of the parties to mediation in the Ukraine appreciated "allowing people to talk freely about their feelings, perceptions, needs, and suggestions."[135] "I'm glad that I had the opportunity to talk to people with different views. It is good that we all could say what we think . . . was wrong and what is still wrong."[136] Another was disappointed with being unable to discuss what was happening between parties.[137]

If numbers alone are considered, the Balkan evaluations led all surveys in appreciation of open, honest sharing.[138] Respondents frequently mentioned hearing, understanding, and discussion of different feelings, opinions, and experiences, including ethnic and gender difference, and requested that all participation be serious.[139] Several in the Balkans, as well as at least one participant from Cameroon, valued learning to be a better listener. Balkans evaluators spotlighted understanding the causes of conflict and "other's feelings, needs, and perspective."[140] Participants throughout the Balkans repeatedly elaborated on the value of perspective-taking. One appreciated becoming more open-minded and tolerant.[141] A few mentioned actually changing their points of view, seeing conflict "more deeply . . . with [the] thinking of all parties involved." A participant, from "Dialogue and Cultural Identity" in Mostar, found the truth "meeting peoples who live . . . in my town on west and east side . . . and that changed me."[142]

Ukrainian evaluators credited identification of commonalities, or shared interests, as building a foundation and possibility for positive change.[143] William Ury, of the Harvard Negotiation Project, agrees. He envisions mobilizing "the power of peer . . . from a perspective of common ground."[144] Most recommended more: "especially for [the] Balkan region, where we have strong emotions and a lot of unsolved problems."[145]

### Top Benefits Reported From Participation in the Cross Cultural Conflict Process[146]

| Rank | Descriptors |
|---|---|
| 1 | Practical tools for change |
| | Techniques for peaceful resolution of conflict |
| 2 | Increased understanding (of conflict and thinking of those involved) |
| 3 | Skills for better communications (e.g., listening) |
| 4 | New ideas for building democracy |
| 5 | Increased self-awareness and understanding |
| 6 | Widened perspective-taking |
| | Increased tolerance |
| | Improved open-mindedness |

## Empowering Party Capacity

The theme of individual empowerment runs throughout this survey. "Conflict resolution training helped me see things on the micro, or individual, level and . . . connect this with the global structure." [147] "[I found helpful learning the positive aspects of conflict]—a sign that we are living. . . . Conflicts build our identity, help us to mature, oblige . . . us to recognize the existence of others, and reveal what is hidden in us. . . . It works!"[148] Empowerment can be defined as "the restoration to individuals of a sense of their own value and strength and their own capacity to handle life's problems."[149]

Many respondents reported a heightened understanding of themselves,[150] their needs, and their feelings, with practical ideas and tools for self-improvement and satisfaction of needs.[151] Repeatedly chronicled was the usefulness of conflict resolution in their daily lives.[152]Respondents felt empowered to make a broader difference in their societies, stressing the power of the people in a democracy.[153] "I thought that democracy comes from government. I realized that we [individuals] have to create healthy democratic society by ourselves. . . . Conflict seminars . . . are very helpful for increasing the well-being of our society."[154]

Many international students, particularly those acting as social leaders, mention the potential they see in facilitative dispute resolution for addressing intragroup tensions. Groups that fight and are fragmented from within are ill-positioned to negotiate with the outside world.

At their best, facilitative tools increase intragroup understanding and unity. These tools result in stronger party capacity, including the ability to advocate and negotiate, with enhanced credibility and a more effective strategy.[155] To be truly strong in self-determination, internal conflicts must be addressed. Slow, steady steps forward are likely to frustrate those who want dramatic revolutionary change. False unity, however, created by attempting to unite against the "other"[156] through displacing tensions from within,[157] is fragile and hollow.

Many of the most conflicted groups are not addressing their own needs. Their haunting question is: Can this region in its desperation (e.g., poverty) afford to feed on each other's animosity? Widespread apathy and lack of response to basic community needs are some of the most common challenges heard from peacebuilders around the world. How can we engage an unresponsive bureaucrat? How can we motivate our community to care? Facilitative practices, like reframing tensions into collaborative questions, (e.g., How do we preserve our cultural identity while openly engaging with others?) have the potential to illuminate desperately needed transcendent possibilities.

Several respondents stress that peace begins with the individual:[158] Another imagined that changing oneself provided an example for others.[159] Gathering with others who were also in the process of examining how to make a positive difference with their actions encouraged another respondent.[160] "[This made] me realize that people can be more creative . . . work hard on peace and that there are many things we can do to avoid the escalation of conflict."[161]

Respondents specially valued information about problems of communication and conflict and rated conflict analysis highly more than once.[162] Participants specifically mentioned the conflict resolution tools of interest analysis[163] and option generation.[164] "It also helped me direct my acquired knowledge, related to different social matters, towards a direction which brings about positive solutions."[165]

A misconception, among those who have not studied facilitative approaches to dispute resolution, is that the conflicting parties must first "both . . . [be] willing to . . . discuss other options . . . [and/or] must want to resolve [their conflict] . . . otherwise, there's no reason to begin talks."[166] In complex intractable conflicts, however, parties frequently despair. Facilitative tools, like option creation and interest analysis, are designed to help parties discover new possibilities in the midst of entrenched perspectives.

Roger Fisher, founder of the Harvard Negotiation Project, popularized interest analysis as an alternative to positional, or power, bargaining with international relations.[167] Rather than expecting political leaders to abandon threats and political posturing, or waiting for diplomatic openings, positions are analyzed and collaborative alternatives generated through identifying all sides' underlying needs, concerns, and fears, or interests.[168] The principals' interests provide an explicit framework for generating options and otherwise stimulating creative problem-solving.[169]

A survivor of torture and exile, Ezat Mossallanejad, powerfully described how seemingly simple tools can make a powerful difference when used with passion and determination. Mossallanejad expressed how important his search for alternatives was in his efforts to survive: "Throughout my life, when I felt hopeless and desperate, several things helped to sustain me and give me hope . . . no matter what happens we must always look for alternatives."[170] In addition to the search for alternatives, Mossallanejad credits other familiar steps of the facilitation process for his survival: task setting, information exchange, "sharing common goals and understanding," acknowledgment of interdependency, and reflective practice.[171]

## Cross Cultural Experience and Potential

Even though historically peace studies and related fields like international relations have prioritized the study of war or conflict between nation states, the most troubling conflict has never limited itself to war but predictably includes cross-ethnic conflict within a single nation state. The most tragic pattern shows itself in horrific genocide. This is one of the reasons the book includes this chapter. Stimulating critically needed discussion about how conflict resolution techniques are showing potential with reducing, containing and preventing violent conflict is essential. In the book's next and last chapters, this potential will be demonstrated by a mediator working in Cameroon for the last decade with cross cultural conflict between previously warring tribes. While government and church intervention were needed to stop violence, mediator Ndi's reported success with subsequently building cross-cultural rapport, recruiting mediators from all communities and thus preventing relapse into violence is worth studying closely.

Western scholars and practitioners must be careful not to spread generalizations and conclusions about other cultures that might unintentionally serve as false, inaccurate barriers to exploring conflict resolution's real potential with communication and understanding. Frankly, the author's experience indicates that while cultural research and frameworks can help open minds to cultural difference and provide insight, they fall far short of the intimate case-by-case and individual-by-individual exploration and relationship building required to effectively bridge culture and promote trust.

For example, reading popular scholarship asserting that face to face interpersonal discussion and interest-based analysis may worsen conflict with certain Asian cultures, the author reflects on her years facilitating cultural understanding tours with Japanese middle managers from prominent corporations, mediating with Korean employees from SK Telecom, teaching Thai, Nepali, and Vietnamese students, and helping to facilitate Indian-Pakistani dialogue. She participated in several rich interpersonal discussions with all groups. While she could not expect disclosure to conform to American expectations, open discussion unquestionably occurred. In the evaluative research reported in earlier chapters, Nepalis valued open honest disclosure as the most important part of their court mandated mediation experience.

The author did observe a white male American engineer from a prominent corporation become frustrated with the Japanese managerial practice of carefully discussing an issue. He became quickly impatient and was ill prepared to respect their cultural approach. Was this because he was male? White? An engineer? The answer requires careful study.

In the author's experience facilitating and mediating cross-ethnic discussion, cultural guides, consultants, and co-mediators from the cultures concerned have proven invaluable. This is true in reference to gender, sexual preference, religion, and all important difference.

On the other hand, even conflict resolution and peacebuilding scholars who are members of conflicted groups, or insiders, report challenges. Communities who know war and violent conflict struggle with trusting members of their own groups and communities as well as outsiders. One Greek Cypriot scholar, as an instance, found such lack of trust and open disclosure inhibiting her research in Cyprus, even when interviewing members of her own Greek Cypriot community. Case-by-case inquiry and practice is also needed here to problem solve and progress.

## Notes and Questions

1. A common misconception found in the general public, at least in the United States, associated with traditional gender socialization, is that empathy, or compassion, weakens the one offering it. There is a related fear that deep understanding disables one's ability to assert and respect oneself. Skilled mediators, however, know that in practice the opposite is more likely. Only the most secure of negotiators and mediators have the self confidence necessary to focus on deeply and accurately understanding another's perspective.

   In my experience, most students of mediation and negotiation have a harder time identifying their personal or professional boundaries and learning how to quickly and effectively assert them whenever needed. Empathetic listening comes relatively easy, at least when extended to friends and classmates.

   It may take years of concerted practice to learn how to balance simultaneous respect for self and respect for others through assertion of boundaries, sincere interest, suspension of judgment, and perspective taking. Recommended is that students start with each as a separate skill: (1) identification-brainstorming of boundaries, whether mediation, dialogue, or personal, (2) effective assertion of boundaries through I statements* whenever needed, (3) empathetic and other attentive listening skills, along with suspension of judgment, to encourage increasing disclosure and ensure accurate deep understanding.

*Assertive and receptive communication skills are regularly taught in interpersonal communication classes. Recommended as one highly popular text is Robert Bolton's People Skills.

Students aspiring to negotiate and mediate will need to eventually practice all skills simultaneously. To begin, though, students are encouraged to pick one of these skills and focus on it for an extended period of time, e.g. perhaps daily reflection or practice for a week. Share and discuss the results with others doing the same.

2. Personal or process boundaries can be explored by simply asking:
   How do I and others expect to be treated?

   What does respect look and sound like in concrete specifics:
   Fairly equal time talking?

   Attentive listening?

   Paraphrasing that shows accurate understanding?

   Etc.

   Optimally, what behavior encourages:
   My best authentic self?

   Open, honest disclosure?

   Increasing trust?

   Deep understanding?

   Etc.

3. Exploring and brainstorming multicultural process parameters requires extraordinary awareness of one's own cultural norms and expectations. Simply asking oneself the question "What does my culture(s) expect in conversation?" one begins to discover the complexity of this process. It is necessarily

an evolving dynamic process which must be approached with sensitivity and an inquisitive and observant mind.

Try asking yourself the above question as well as asking the same question to a few friends who belong to your cultural group. Do you have the same or different answers?

4. Most mediation, at least in the United States, has a process ground rule that prohibits personal attack. Related is the recommended practice of suspending judgment to open one's mind to accurate and full understanding.

   Try watching yourself for 10 to 15 minute intervals listening to or observing others. How often do you see your mind judging another?

   Try reducing the above number. Share and discuss your experience, including any discoveries you are making about what helps you suspend judgment.

   How often do you observe yourself saying something that sounds critical or judgmental to others?

   Try reducing the above number. Share and discuss your experience, once again including any discoveries you are making about what helps you contain criticism and reframe comments so they do not sound judgmental.

5. This section has reviewed several skills introduced in section two and elaborated in section three.

   ___Explore differences with an open mind

   ___Listen actively with paraphrasing to ensure accurate understanding

   ___Suspend judgment

   ___Understand others' perspectives

   ___Encourage others' communication

   ___Create positive, comfortable, safe environment

___Show respect

___Show serious interest in others

___Negotiate and create effective process parameters

___Seek and recognize common ground

___Encourage and ensure equal participation of all

___Express own need and perspective with "I statements"

It has also added:

___ Open honest disclosure

___Information sharing

___Expressing and hearing feelings

___Empathetic listening and understanding

___Serious participation

___Charismatic influence

___Leadership

___Sense of humour

As you did in the last section, note your strengths; perhaps rank ordering all the skills listed above.

## Notes

[1] This section assumes that readers are new to alternative dispute resolution, or appropriate dispute resolution, [hereinafter ADR], its terminology and approaches, and the concrete details of facilitative approaches. ADR encompasses a broad continuum of responses to conflict that fall between avoidance and escalation. Linda R. Singer, *Settling Disputes: Conflict Resolution in Business, Families, and the Legal System* (Westview Press, 1994). It includes community and public dispute resolution as well as alternatives

within legal systems. See, e.g., E. Franklin Dukes, *Resolving Public Conflict: Transforming Community and Governance* (Manchester University Press, 1996, 7). The research reviewed in this chapter strongly promotes facilitative ADR, which is described and explained throughout. See, e.g., Leonard Riskin, "Decisionmaking in Mediation: The New Old Grid and the New New Grid System," 79 *Notre Dame L. Rev.* 1 (2003).

[2] An increasing number of governments use ADR in their bureaucracies. See, e.g., William J. Klausner, *Reflections on Thai Culture* (1993); Christopher W. Moore, *The Mediation Process: Practical Strategies for Resolving Conflict* (2d ed. 1996, 32-40) (introducing the People's Conciliation Committees in China, court-based mediation in Australia, Japan, and Korea, and the Barangay Justice System in the Philippines); Ngoh-Tiong Tan, "Community Mediation in Singapore for Community Conflict Resolution," 19 *Conflict Resol. Q.* 289 (2002). However, the reasons behind this bureaucratic trend may differ from the author's research findings regarding the use of ADR: "being time-limited and problem-focused in approach, the limitation . . . in dealing with deep-seated issues needs to be recognized. Conflict is often resolved superficially, and the transformative potential of mediation, in imparting skills and engaging in structural change, is neglected. . . . Mediation centers . . . are often perceived as government agencies." Tan at 292, 299; see also Vivian Wiseman and Jean Poitras, "Mediation within a Hierarchical Structure: How Can It Be Done Successfully?" 20 *Conflict Resol. Q.* 51 (2002).

[3] The label, "Americanization of international dispute resolution," risks doing damage unless it is acknowledged that the conscious choices of international dispute resolvers to adopt (and import) practices are helpful. Otherwise, critique flatters the American ego, reinforcing and magnifying the image of American importance and dominance, while denying and minimizing international actors' self-determination, autonomy, and power.

[4] Indigenous practices also play a foundational role in community-initiated conflict management. See, e.g., Klausner, *supra* note 2, at 162-63 (describing bhikkhus and Cao Khote, the revered village elders acting as arbiters). Some communities develop hybrid processes that combine traditional approaches with the practices praised in this article. Dr. Sukla Deb Kanango explains that the traditional village panchayat justice system currently addresses the majority of community disputes throughout India. However, the facilitative approach to mediation is becoming more popular with divorces, particularly those that involve children. Such disputes require the time that facilitative mediation can provide. Interview with Dr. Sukla Deb Kanango, Professor of Social Work, Visva-Bharati, Sriniketan, West Bengal, India, in Bangkok, Thailand (Feb. 17, 2003).

[5] Elise Boulding, *Cultures of Peace: The Hidden Side of History* (Syracuse University Press, 2000).

[6] Louis Kriesberg, "Conflict Resolution," in *Peace and World Security Studies: A Curriculum Guide*, ed. Michael T. Klare 6th ed. (St. Martin's Press, 1994).

[7] Thomas Princen, Joseph Elder, "Quiet Peacemaking in a Civil War," in *When Talk Works: Profiles of Mediators*, ed. Deborah M. Kolb (Jossey-Bass, 1994). Jimmy Carter's formal diplomacy also incorporated mediation. Eileen F. Babbitt, "Jimmy Carter: The Power of Moral Persuasion in International Mediation," in *When Talk Works: Profiles of Mediators,* ed. Deborah M. Kolb (Jossey-Bass, 1994). Informal diplomacy deserves extended scholarly documentation and evaluation, as is currently being seen with institutionalized diplomacy using international mediation. See, e.g., Jacob Bercovitch, "Understanding Mediation's Role in Preventive Diplomacy," 12 *Negotiation J.* 241 (1996) (studying the conditions for effective mediation and naming the critical context variables to be the nature of the parties' dispute and mediation, the process used, and the relationship between the mediation strategies and outcomes).

[8] Jan Egeland, "The Oslo Accord: Multiparty Facilitation Through the Norwegian Channel," in *Herding Cats: Multiparty Mediation in a Complex World*, ed. Chester A. Crocker et al. (United States Institute of Peace Press, 1999, 358).

[9] *Id.*

[10] *Id.*

[11] Brian Ferguson, "The History of War: Fact vs. Fiction," in *Must We Fight? From the Battlefield to the Schoolyard: A New Perspective on Violent Conflict and Its Prevention*, ed. William L. Ury (Jossey-Bass, 2002).

[12] Former Ambassador John MacDonald, Ethnic Conflict in Today's World, Presentation at Weaving the Future of Peacemaking (April 7, 2003).

[13] *Id.*

[14] Readers interested in exploring culture, ethics, and conflict resolution through an interactive case study format (workbook) are directed to Nancy Erbe, *Holding These Truths: Empowerment and Recognition in Action* (an interactive case study workbook for multicultural conflict resolution) (Berkeley Public Policy Press, 2003). The author welcomes feedback and is available to assist with classroom delivery and other uses. Direct questions to: nerbe@csudh.edu.

[15] Conflict involves layers of dynamics; or social, intellectual, and moral forces that produce and change conflict (*The American Heritage Dictionary*, 4th ed. 2001, 268). These layers are often not expressly acknowledged, but they are a part of every international and domestic process. These layers include: (1) intrapersonal dynamics, or what occurs within the individuals that is relevant to the conflict in question, such as cultural bias; (2) interpersonal dynamics, or what occurs between the individuals that is relevant to the conflict, such as interpretation of conversations; (3) intragroup dynamics, or what occurs within the groups, such as authoritarian or "top-down" leadership; (4) intergroup dynamics, or what occurs between the groups, such as historic blaming and power imbalances; and (5) system dynamics, or what occurs within and between "interacting variables creating complex wholes." *Id.* at 832. Systemic examples relevant to conflict include societal discrimination and denial of wrongdoing. See, e.g., Boulding, *supra* note 5; John Feffer, "Conflict Resolution in Korea: A Workshop for Korean Activists," 18 *Conflict Resol. Notes* 30 (2001).

[16] *The American Heritage Dictionary* (Dell, 4th ed. 2001).

[17] Roger Schwarz, *The Skilled Facilitator* (Jossey-Bass, 2002, 5).

[18] Thomas Justice and David W. Jamieson, *The Facilitator's Fieldbook: Step-by-Step Procedures, checklists and Guidelines, Samples and Templates* (AMACOM, 1999, 4).

[19] *Id.* at 6-7.

[20] Nancy Erbe, *Cultural Competence: Surveying Party Perception* (Univ. of California, Berkeley, 2001).

[21] Thanks to the Flora and Wallace Hewlett Foundation for its support of this inquiry.

[22] The professionals include an engineer, a former military officer, a psychologist, and several journalists, teachers, and lawyers. The latter group was the largest.

[23] Facilitated dialogue and public participation in government decision-making and policy creation have grown more popular with public dispute resolution in recent years. Several overlap. As in the facilitative approach to mediation, listening and understanding, embracing differences while seeking common ground, being open to change, and problem-solving are valued features. See, e.g., Dukes, *supra* note 1, at 62-75; Study Circles Resource Ctr., Facing the Future: How Should We Move Forward After September 11?:

A Guide for Public Dialogue and Problem Solving (July 2002), available at <http://www.studycircles.org/pdf/singlesess.pdf>. Dialogue became widely publicized as various sponsors brought Israelis and Palestinians together for the first time. The Nansen Network, sponsored by Norway and one of the efforts evaluated in this article, is an example of facilitated dialogue in the Balkans. See, e.g., The Collaborative for Development Action, Reflecting on Peace Practice Project: Prio/ Nansen Case Study: The Balkan Dialogue Project, available at <http://www.cdainc.com/rpp/publications/casestudies/ Case19PRIO.pdf> (2001).

[24] See Laura Silber and Allan Little, *Yugoslavia: Death of a Nation* (Penguin Books, 1997); Susan L. Woodward, *Balkan Tragedy: Chaos and Dissolution after the Cold War* (The Brookings Institution, 1995); Conference, The Past as Prelude: The Cultural, Social, and Political Roots of Identity in the Caucasus, Center for Slavic and East European Studies, (University of California, Berkeley, May 17, 1996) (materials from an outreach conference, Institute of Slavic, East European and Eurasian Studies, University of California, Berkeley (1996) are available at <http://socrates.berkeley. edu/<diff>csees/out reach2.html>). See discussion *infra* App. I for an introduction to the social, economic, and political conditions in the Balkan region during the time surveyed.

[25] In simple terms, mediation is a popular form of ADR where a third party facilitates or assists negotiations. See, e.g., John Lande, "How Will Lawyering and Mediation Practices Transform One Another?" 24 *Fla. St. U. L. Rev.* 839 (1997) (citing Moore, *supra* note 2).

[26] *Introduction to the History of Cameroon: Nineteenth & Twentieth Centuries*, ed. Martin Njeuma (Macmillan, 1989); Ambe J. Njoh, "The Political Economy of Urban Land Reforms in a Post-Colonial State," 22 *Int'l. J. Urb. & Reg'l Res.* 408 (1998); Francis B. Nyamnjoh, "Cameroon: A Country United by Ethnic Ambition and Difference," 98 *Afr. Aff.* 101 (1999); see discussion *infra* App. II for an introduction to Cameroon's context.

[27] At the time of the survey's design, the research partner in Nepal sought training in mediation for educators throughout Nepal. In the face of escalating violence, he hoped that widespread training would help the government's negotiations with terrorists. Former ambassador John McDonald and his Institute for Multi-Track Diplomacy proceeded to provide such training. This research partner was not available to provide contextual perspective. See discussion *infra* App. III (for an introduction to Nepal's social and political background).

[28] See Roman Szporluk, *Russia, Ukraine, and the Breakup of the Soviet Union* (Hoover Institution Press, 2000); Andrew Wilson, *The Ukrainians: Unexpected Nation* (Yale Nota Bene, 2002); Michael M. Naydan, "Teaching Post-Independence Ukrainian Culture in Western Cultural Space," 43 *NewsNet: Newsletter of the Am. Ass'n for the Advancement of Slavic Studies* 7 (2003); discussion *infra* App. IV (all discussing the Ukraine's social, economic, and political conditions during the time of this research).

[29] Thanks to Director Barbara Voytek, Program Coordinator Stella Bourgoin, and Jennifer Johnson, University of California, Berkeley, for their assistance. More evaluative research is needed regarding participant satisfaction, characteristics of an effective mediator, and the essential qualities of a successful mediation. See, e.g., Frank E. A. Sander, "Some Concluding Thoughts," 17 *Ohio St. J. on Disp. Resol.* 705 (2002).

[30] I met some of the research partners while teaching conflict resolution at the University of Oslo International Summer School. I was invited to do so by my Norwegian colleagues at the International Peace Research Institute of Oslo. I was also introduced to Dan Smith, the Institute director at that time. He invited me to meet his Balkan col-

leagues in the Nansen project, several of whom joined my research team. I acknowledge and thank them all.

[31] See, e.g., Douglas H. Yarn, "Transnational Conflict Resolution Practice: A Brief Introduction to the Context, Issues, and Search for Best Practices in Exporting Conflict Resolution," 19 *Conflict Resol. Q.* 303 (2002).

[32] *Id.* at 306.

[33] *Id.* at 315.

[34] Michael Quinn Patton, *Qualitative Research and Evaluation Methods,* 3d ed. (Sage Publications, 2002).

[35] See Barney G. Glaser, *The Grounded Theory Perspective II* (Sociology Press, 2003).

[36] See Chris Mann and Fiona Stewart, *Internet Communication And Qualitative Research* (Sage Publications, 2000).

[37] This research assumed that most respondents are unfamiliar with the conflict process under evaluation. Thus, they are not asked to explain or describe the conflict process. They are simply asked to evaluate the effectiveness of their third-party facilitator, or assistant, in their own words and from their own perspective.

[38] Research regarding cross-ethnic conflict requires balancing a desire for extensive, in-depth data against respondents' reluctance to participate unless they can maintain anonymity with regard to responses to sensitive issues. At the very least, this should result in some presumably honest data.

[39] Matthew B. Miles and A. Michael Huberman, *An Expanded Sourcebook: Qualitative Data Analysis*, 2d ed. (Sage Publications, 1994).

[40] David Lazarus, "A Dispute Beyond Mediation," *San Fran. Chron.*, Mar. 19, 2003, at B1 (exploring mediation's potential with respect to the war in Iraq).

[41] Lela P. Love, "The Top Ten Reasons Why Mediators Should Not Evaluate," 24 *Fla. St. U. L. Rev.* 937, 938 (1997). However, not all scholars of ADR agree with this framework. Professor Antonio Mendoza believes that the evaluative approach does not necessarily amount to mediator decisionmaking. Evaluative mediators may share their expertise while leaving decisions to the parties. Conversations with Professor Antonio Mendoza (Sept. and Oct. 2003).

[42] Lazarus, *supra* note 40.

[43] *Id.*

[44] Parties in conflict only need to show a willingness to learn more about mediation in order to begin talks.

[45] Joseph B. Stulberg, "Facilitative Versus Evaluative Mediator Orientations: Piercing the 'Grid' Lock," 24 *Fla. St. U. L. Rev.* 985, 995 (1997) (quoting Leonard L. Riskin, "Understanding Mediators' Orientations, Strategies, and Techniques: A Grid for the Perplexed," 1 *Harv. Negot. L. Rev.* 7, 24 (1996)).

[46] Joseph B. Stulberg, "Questions," 17 *Ohio St. J. on Disp. Resol.* 531, 532 (2002).

[47] *Id.*

[48] "Mediators using a facilitative style focus on eliciting principals' own opinions and refrain from pressing their own. . . . I believe that the term 'evaluative' often refers to the level of directiveness or coercion that a mediator employs." Stulberg, *supra* note 45, at 997-98.

[49] Many mediators advocating the facilitative approach believe that the evaluative approach should be called "nonbinding arbitration," meaning the parties are free to reject the third party's decision and evaluation, or neutral case evaluation, where the third party is acknowledged as an ethical expert with no personal interest in the evaluation. Another

option is "private settlement conferencing," where the third party's legal experience is used to advise parties of the costs and benefits of negotiating a decision compared to proceeding with a lawsuit. Lande, *supra* note 25, at 850, 855, 864. For those who prefer or need the evaluative approach, "ombuds neutral factfinding" provides an alternative to facilitated mediation and dialogue, as well as litigation and arbitration. The United Nations views ombudsing as an important tool to help and protect international human rights, and as a result, many ombuds offices have been established in the governments of third world countries. In the United States and Canada, ombuds agencies have been created to assist citizens, consumers, and employees who wish to address concerns about administrative actions or lack of action (government, nursing home, prison, etc.). University and College Ombuds, A Brief History of Ombudsing, at <http://www.colorado.edu/Ombuds/UCOA/history.html>. Adequate information is necessary for the ombuds process to work. Klausner, *supra* note 2, at 243.

[50] In civil law the key word is "mediation,' derived from vermittlung, which means medium, or the middle. A mediator stands in the middle between two disputing parties. . . . This has nothing to do with a private arbitrator. . . . The difference is considerable . . .since the arbitrator decides just like a court. . . . The mediator however does not decide, but rather attempts to guide the disputing parties to a mutual agreement . . . the parties themselves . . . decide the dispute." *The Negotiating State, Die Ziet* (Zeitverlag Gerd Buceris, 1999). Thanks to Anja Zuckmantel for her translation and contribution.

[51] See Murray S. Levin, "The Propriety of Evaluative Mediation: Concerns about the Nature and the Quality of an Evaluative Opinion," 16 *Ohio St. J. on Disp. Resol.* 267 (2001) (reviewing the risk of inaccurate information).

[52] Alternative Asean Network on Burman, Special Report: A Peace of Pie?: Burma's Humanitarian Aid Debate 57 (2002), available at <http://www.ibiblio.org/obl/docs/peaceofpie.htm>.

[53] The Human Rights Center et al., "Justice, Accountability and Social Reconstruction: An Interview Study of Bosnian Judges and Prosecutors," Human Rights Center, 18 *Berkeley J. Int'l L.* 102, 145 (2000).

[54] *Id.* at 149, 155 (emphasis added).

[55] Carmen Diana Deere and Magdalena Leon, *Empowering Women: Land and Property Rights in Latin America* (University of Pittsburgh Press, 2001); Klausner, *supra* note 2, at 234-42; "Transition to Democracy" in *Latin America: The Role of the Judiciary*, ed. Irwin P. Stotzky (Westview Press, 1993).

[56] See, e.g., Klausner, *supra* note 2; Jennifer A. Widner, *Building the Rule of Law* (W. W. Norton, 2001, 35, 282) (judging ADR to be the most effective option for confronting corruption in Tanzanian courts unless the dispute involved the government).

[57] In this article, equity will be defined as "justice administered according to fairness." *Black's Law Dictionary* (5th ed. 1979, 484).

[58] Ferguson, *supra* note 11, at 36.

[59] "Power from within or internal power . . . has to do with generating strength from within oneself . . . and is apparent when someone is able to resist the power of others by rejecting undesired demands." Deere and Leon, *supra* note 55, at 25.

[60] In the United States, "research reveals that three elements—participation, dignity and trust—play a large role in people's assessment of procedural fairness." Ellen A. Waldman, "The Evaluative-Facilitative Debate in Mediation: Applying the Lens of Therapeutic Jurisprudence," 82 *Marq. L. Rev.* 155, 161 (1998) (emphasis added).

[61] See, e.g., Richard Delgado et al., "Fairness and Formality: Minimizing the Risk of Prejudice in Alternative Dispute Resolution," *Wis. L. Rev.* 1359, 1387-91 (1985); Trina

Grillo, "The Mediation Alternative: Process Dangers for Women," 100 *Yale L.J.* 1545 (1991); Isabelle R. Gunning, "Diversity Issues in Mediation: Controlling Negative Cultural Myths," 1 *J. Disp. Resol.* 55 (1995). Mediation and other popular informal conflict intervention are criticized for pacifying, avoiding important conflicts with essential social issues, and circumventing legal proceedings. Laura Nader asserts that "disputing without the force of law . . . [is] doomed to fail." Jerold S. Auerbach, *Justice without Law?* 145 (Oxford University Press, 1983). A legal ethical perspective equates enforcement of democratically developed law with collective conscience and morality. A lawsuit, with its protections of public record, scrutiny, and precedent, is arguably more ethical than private and informal negotiation, or mediation, which can conceivably push for conformity and omit critical legal and constitutional rights. At the beginning of mediation's growth in popularity in U.S. legal systems, Auerbach saw mediation as being "most enthusiastically prescribed for disadvantaged citizens who only recently had begun to litigate successfully to protect and extend their rights," and believed that "without legal power, the imbalance between aggrieved individuals and corporations or government agencies cannot be redressed." *Id.*

[62] The social identity theory asserts the tendency to see the world in an "us-versus-them" framework. There is an in-group-out-group bias in which we hold less favorable opinions about groups to which we do not belong. . . . According to social identity theory . . . we use group membership as a source of pride and self-worth. . . . To feel such pride, however, we must assume that our group is, in fact, superior[,] . . . [leading] us to inflate the positive aspects [of our group] and belittle [others]. David W. Johnson and Frank P. Johnson, *Joining Together: Group Theory and Group Skills*, 6th ed. (Allyn and Bacon, 1997). With scapegoating, a group or individual is habitually blamed, often irrationally, through displacing tensions from another conflict. At scapegoating's worst, the vilified "other" is described as "evil." Dehumanization and resultant prejudice rationalize and encourage attack. *Id.* "All my life I have lived in a small community united only by its insensitivity for another people." Interview with anonymous international student, Berkeley, Calif. (Summer 2000) (complete anonymity was a condition of the interview, hence, certain information is withheld to protect that guarantee); see also Ernst Gunter Beier, "The Effect of Induced Anxiety on Flexibility of Intellectual Functioning," in *Psychological Monographs: General And Applied* 65 (Herbert S. Conrad ed., 1951); Ernest R. Hilgard and Gordon H. Bower, *Theories of Learning,* 3rd ed. (Meredith Publishing Co., 1966) (1948); Irving L. Janis and Leon Mann, *Decision Making: A Psychological Analysis of Conflict, Choice, and Commitment* (Free Press, 1977); C. F. Smart et al., "Diagnosing Corporate Effectiveness and Susceptibility to Crises," in *Studies on Crisis Management* ed. C. F. Smart and W. T. Stanbury (Institute for Research on Public Policy, 1978).

[63] Nansen Network, Democracy, Human Rights, and Peaceful Conflict Resolution, at <http://www.ndc.net.mk/angliski/activities_10-14.05.2000.asp> (last accessed Nov. 9, 2004).

[64] *Id.*

[65] *Id.*

[66] *Id.*

[67] *Id.*

[68] Eleven surveys evaluating community mediation and conflict resolution training were completed in the Ukraine. Sixty-three percent evaluated multicultural process and leadership. *Id.*

[69] Erbe, *supra* note 20.

[70] *Id.* See also James H. Stark, "The Ethics of Mediation Evaluation: Some Troublesome Questions and Tentative Proposals from an Evaluative Lawyer Mediator," 38 *S. Tex. L. Rev.* 769 (1997). "Mediation recognizes human intelligence. Mediation assumes that the parties are competent to resolve their own disputes. Often, people who have been socialized to feel powerless rise to the occasion during mediation. . . ." Salem and Davis, *supra* note 76.

[71] Erbe, *supra* note 20.

[72] Waldman, *supra* note 60.

[73] Erbe, *supra* note 20.

[74] *Id.* "There are countless examples of symbiotic coexistence between people who are dramatically different. . . . Collective violence along cultural and other lines of identity does not bubble up in the populace itself." Ferguson, *supra* note 11, at 36.

[75] All participants evaluated their experience in English, so no translation was needed. Whenever possible, respondents' own words were used. Interestingly, many respondents used technical language such as "paraphrasing," "impartiality," and "perspective-taking."

[76] Ferguson, *supra* note 11, at 36. Richard Salem headed the U.S. Community Relations Service in Chicago for 14 years. In that capacity, he mediated politically renowned ethnic disputes such as Wounded Knee and the Nazi protests in Skokie, Illinois. Salem describes the impartiality of mediation: "Throughout the process, the mediator conveys the message that the parties are treated equally by controlling the way in which they are greeted, seated, addressed, listened to, and responded to. This treatment is a strong stimulus for the parties to treat each other as equals." Richard A. Salem and Albie Davis, "Dealing with Power Imbalances in Mediating Interpersonal Disputes," 6 *Mediation Q.* 19 (1984).

[77] Burmese (Burma has become Myanmar) activists promote process "where all stakeholders are equals," elaborating that this "would be the first time in many decades that all political stakeholders can engage in dialogue on an equal playing field, hence contributing to the development of pluralism and democratic governance" (emphasis added). Alternative ASEAN Network on Burma, *supra* note 52, at 57.

[78] Ten respondents evaluated conflict resolution conducted by an ecumenical religious institute in Cameroon, comprised of facilitators from Cameroon and the United States. Nine respondents described their experience as "multicultural." All respondents evaluated their experience highly, with requests for more.

[79] Erbe, *supra* note 20.

[80] Fourteen surveys were completed after court-mandated mediation in Nepal, with 85 percent of respondents describing their experience as multicultural.

[81] Geert Hofstede labels societies that confer superior and inferior status, based on age, class, and other differences, as "high power distance." Geert Hofstede, *Cultures and Organizations: Software of the Mind* (McGraw-Hill, 1991, 23-48). Bosnian legal professionals report feeling inferior and not "co-equal partners in the design and implementation of many of the programs intended to rebuild their legal system and their country." The Human Rights Center et al., *supra* note 53.

[82] Erbe, *supra* note 20.

[83] *Id.* "When the Department of Justice dispatches a team of mediators to service racial conflicts . . . the last thing parties will embrace is someone trying to tell them how to live their lives." Stulberg, *supra* note 45.

[84] About two-thirds of surveys were from different parts of the Balkans, including Podgorica, Montenegro, Mostar, Bosnia-Herzegovina, and Belgrade, Serbia.

[85] Erbe, *supra* note 20.

[86] *Id.* "In my experience [mediating in Northern Ireland], I have found that retaining a mentality of impartiality, of being "open-minded' in my work has often made me 'other centered. . . .'" McAllister, *supra* note 172, at 26.

[87] Erbe, *supra* note 20.

[88] Their acknowledgment is echoed in many quarters. For example, the Third U.N. World Conference on Women in Nairobi in 1985 deemed democratic participation necessary to empowering women. "Using mediation to facilitate conflict resolution and encourage self-determination . . . strengthens democratic values and enhances the dignity of those in conflict." Jay Folberg and Alison Taylor, *Mediation: A Comprehensive Guide to Resolving Conflicts without Litigation* (Jossey-Bass, 1984, 35).

[89] Erbe, *supra* note 20.

[90] *Id.*

[91] *Id.*

[92] This type of leadership may facilitate open-mindedness and understanding.

[93] Erbe, *supra* note 20.

[94] Like the dispute resolution field but unlike traditional academic research, peace research advances an obligatory link between theory and practice. Theory must apply to the solution of actual problems and prove itself in combating violence while championing peace. See Helge Hveem and Svree Lodgaard, "An Editorial," *15 J. Peace Res.* 1, 1-2 (1978). Proving and measuring contribution, however, is extremely challenging. There are many complex social, political, cultural, and economic variables. As one example of the gauntlet, a popular movement within peace studies posits that emerging democratic practice reduces societal violence. See, e.g., Nils Petter Gleditsch, "Peace and Democracy," in *Encyclopedia of Violence, Peace & Conflict,* Vol. 2 (Academic Press, 1999). Yet without established theory, critics challenge. See, e.g., Scott Gates et al., "Democracy and Peace: A More Skeptical View," 33 *J. Peace Res.* 1, 1-10 (1996).

[95] "Peacemaking is marked by experimentation. There is no right way to go about creating peaceful communities and a peaceful world. Working for peace will differ according to context." Judy Zimmerman Herr and Robert Herr, Transforming Violence: Linking Local and Global Peacemaking (Herald Press, 1998, 19).

[96] Erbe, *supra* note 20.

[97] The most effective lawyer negotiators are also described as "trustful," "sincere," and "facilitative." Andrea Kupfer Schneider, "Shattering Negotiation Myths: Empirical Evidence on the Effectiveness of Negotiation Style," 7 *Harv. Negot. L. Rev.* 143, 147-48, 153 (2002).

[98] Understanding denotes the facilitative approach. See Love, *supra* note 41, at 939; Riskin, *supra* note 1, at 33.

[99] Erbe, *supra* note 20. The degree to which a disputant is treated with respect and dignity also influences perceptions of procedural justice in the United States. People feel as if they are treated fairly when they trust that the "authorities with whom they are dealing are concerned about their welfare and want to treat them fairly." Waldman, *supra* note 70 (citing Tom R. Tyler and E. Allan Lind, "A Rational Model of Authority in Groups," 25 *Advances in Experimental Soc. Psychol.* 115, 137-66 (1992)).

[100] Erbe, *supra* note 20.

[101] *Id.*

[102] "Productive" and "constructive" were also used. *Id.* Responses continue to highlight the facilitative approach, especially when the evaluative approach includes "disparaging participant's positions." Lande, *supra* note 25, at 864.

[103] Related to suspending judgment is the principle and practice from interest-based negotiations of separating people from the problem. See Roger Fisher and William Ury, *Getting to Yes: Negotiating Agreement without Giving In*, 2d ed. (Penguin Books, 1991).

[104] Erbe, *supra* note 20.

[105] "Never tell people what they did wrong." *Id.* Groups with defensive climates waste more time with ego-protecting discussions and accomplish less than those with supportive environments. Jack R. Gibb, "Defensive Communication," 11 *J. Comm.* 141, 141-48 (1961).

[106] Erbe, *supra* note 20.

[107] *Id.*

[108] Erbe, supra note 20.

[109] Schneider, supra note 97, at 147.

[110] See, e.g., Walter H. Crockett, "Schemas, Affect, and Communication," in *Communication, Social Cognition, and Affect*, ed. Lewis Donohew et al.(L. Erlbaum Associates, 1988, 33); Matthew McKay et al., *When Anger Hurts: Quieting the Storm Within* (Raincoast,1989); Carol Tavris, *Anger: The Misunderstood Emotion*, 2d ed. (Simon and Schuster 1989); Heindrie Weisinger, *The Anger Work-Out Book* (William Morrow, 1985); see also Federal Emergency Management Agency, *Behavior and Attitudes Under Crisis Conditions: Selected Issues and Findings* (1984).

[111] John A. Bargh, "Automatic Information Processing: Implications for Communication and Affect," in *Communication, Social Cognition, and Affect*, ed. Lewis Donohew et al. (L. Erlbaum Associates, 1988, 9).

[112] See, e.g., Roy Cameron and Don Meichenbaum, "The Nature of Effective Coping and the Treatment of Stress Related Problems: A Cognitive-Behavioral Perspective," in *Handbook of Stress: Theoretical and Clinical Aspects,* ed. Leo Goldberger and Shlomo Breznitz (Collier Macmillan, 1982, 695); see also Beverly Davenport Sypher and Howard E. Sypher, "Affect and Message Generation," in *Communication, Social Cognition, and Affect,* ed. Lewis Donohew et al. (L. Erlbaum Associates, 1988, 81). Such distortions do not simply damage the other. Distorted reaction increases the probability of conflict or issue avoidance and hinders effective diagnosis of reality. Distortion prohibits the comprehensive, in-depth information gathering necessary for optimal formulation of strategy to advocate one's own needs.

[113] Schneider, *supra* note 41, at 147.

[114] Richard A. Salem, "The Importance of Empathetic Listening in Mediation" (2003) (Working Draft).

[115] *Id.*

[116] See, e.g., Terrell A. Northrup, "The Dynamic of Identity in Personal and Social Conflict," in *Intractable Conflicts and Their Transformation*, ed. Louis Kriesberg et al. (Syracuse University Press, 1989, 55); Stuart J. Thorson, "Introduction: Conceptual Issues," in *Intractable Conflicts and Their Transformation*, ed. Louis Kriesberg et al. (Syracuse University Press, 1989, 1).

[117] Nancy Erbe, *Cultural Competence: Surveying Party Perception* (Univ. of California, Berkeley 2001).

[118] *Id.*

[119] *Id.* Students find the following characteristics persuasive: (1) rapport and trust, (2) strong perspective-taking, or knowing the audience well, (3) recognizing commonal-

ties, or what is shared amongst those to be persuaded, (4) genuine concern, partially demonstrated through presenting information relevant to the audience's needs, (5) "custom-designed" presentations that interest and engage, (6) considerate framing of language, and (7) adequate space and time. They are not persuaded by personal attack or blame, attempts at domination, and failure to anticipate their perspective.

[120] *Id.* See also Klausner, *supra* note 2 (recognizing the importance of a leader's character or "vibes" in Thai villages).

[121] Erbe, *supra* note 117. Words like "middle way" were used to describe effective process. *Id.*

[122] *Id.*

[123] *Id.*

[124] *Id.*

[125] Erbe, *supra* note 117.

[126] *Id.*

[127] Salem and Davis, *supra* note 76.

[128] Erbe, *supra* note 117.

[129] *Id.*

[130] *Id.* Optimal listening accurately interprets the speaker's meaning or perspective, with a focus on what matters most. When culturally welcome, paraphrasing, or rephrasing key words, emotions, and meaning, is a skill used by listeners to verify understanding. In response, the speaker will ideally correct, clarify, elaborate, and otherwise verify accuracy and completeness of listener understanding. Accurate paraphrasing necessarily relies heavily on corrective feedback from the speaker, since a listener will naturally interpret through the listener's experience and perspective. Taking the time to complete this dialogue until the speaker verifies listener understanding is essential. Otherwise, the listener may appear to understand by repeating words and emotions, yet never actually understand the speaker's most important message.

[131] *Id.*

[132] *Id.* Skilled negotiators use questions more than twice as much as average negotiators. See Neil Rackham, "The Behavior of Successful Negotiators," reprinted in *Negotiation: Readings, Exercises and Cases*, ed. R.J. Lewicki et al. (McGraw-Hill Book Company Ltd, 1999).

[133] Erbe, *supra* note 117. How to encourage disclosure of important information across culture is a fundamental question. Astute parties, particularly minority groups who are cautious and alert with majority groups, observe behavior rather than listen to words in deciding whether to trust and speak openly. Asserting ground rules so that parties are assured of good faith is also key.

[134] Erbe, *supra* note 117.

[135] "Mediation is an open process. It has none of the mystique usually associated with the adjudicative process. Mediators describe the philosophy, the process, and the ground rules, and they encourage questions. By their openness, mediators convey the message that information is to be shared." Salem and Davis, *supra* note 76.

[136] Erbe, *supra* note 117.

[137] *Id.* Again, the facilitative approach is preferred because it prioritizes direct communication. Lela P. Love, "The Top Ten Reasons Why Mediators Should Not Evaluate," 24 *Fla. St. U. L. Rev.* 937, 938 (1997). However, not all scholars of ADR agree with this framework. Professor Antonio Mendoza believes that the evaluative approach does not necessarily amount to mediator decision-making. Evaluative mediators may share their expertise while leaving decisions to the parties. Conversations with Professor Antonio

Mendoza (Sept. and Oct. 2003). The evaluative and directive approach can and does limit direct communication between participants. Stulberg, *supra* note 44.

[138] Erbe, *supra* note 117.

[139] *Id.* Urging participants to weigh their own values and priorities also reflects the facilitative approach. Love, *supra* note 137, at 939.

[140] Erbe, *supra* note 117. This sounds in part, like the interest analysis valued and described earlier. See Fisher and Ury, *supra* note 103.

[141] Erbe, *supra* note 117.

[142] *Id.* The fruits of perspective taking, perhaps because so difficult and rare, can be life-changing. Clayton Robarcheck and Carole Robarcheck, *Waorani: The Contexts of Violence and War* (Harcourt Brace College Pub., 1998).

[143] Erbe, *supra* note 117. In simple terms, commonalities are the interests, needs, and hopes shared by the parties to conflict. See, e.g., Fisher and Ury, *supra* note 103. In one study of negotiators, the most effective negotiator spent over three times as much attention to identifying commonalities. Stewart L. Tubbs, *A Systems Approach to Small Group Interaction*, 5th ed. (McGraw-Hill, 1995, 271). Danilo Dolci has been called the "Gandhi of Sicily.". His maieutic method of creating communities embraced empathy as the means to raise consciousness of shared concern and prepare communities to confront government neglect and Mafia domination. Danilo Dolci, *The Man who Plays Alone* (Atonia Cowan trans., MacGibbon and Kee eds., 1968).

[144] William L. Ury, "The Power of the 'Third Side': Community Roles in Conflict Resolution," in *Must We Fight? From the Battlefield to the Schoolyard: A New Perspective on Violent Conflict and Its Prevention*, ed. William L. Ury (Jossey-Bass 2002, 43) (viewing strong relationships with related attitudes and skills as a basis for preventing conflict and containing escalation, through noticing early warning signs and addressing latent tensions) (emphasis added).

[145] Erbe, *supra* note 117.

[146] *Id.*

[147] *Id.*

[148] *Id.*

[149] Robert A. Baruch Bush and Joseph P. Folger, *The Promise of Mediation* (Jossey-Bass, 1994, 89-91); see also Love, *supra* note 137, at 939. Reframing is a facilitative skill that enhances perspective-taking. Third parties are trained to reframe, or restate, what they hear to emphasize the most important underlying message in ways that do not distort the speaker's message and simultaneously encourage a constructive proceeding. Moore, *supra* note 2. Understanding, or perspective-taking, is necessary for accurate reframing.

[150] Erbe, *supra* note 117.

[151] *Id.*

[152] *Id.*

[153] *Id.*

[154] Many facilitative-broad mediators will help participants find opportunities to educate or change themselves, their institutions, or their communities. *Id.*; Riskin, *supra* note 1, at 32.

[155] Erbe, *supra* note 117; see Deere and Leon, *supra* note 55, at 24.

[156] Self-fulfilling prophecy describes those times when parties are truly "their own worst enemy." For example, one party assumes the other is belligerent and proceeds to treat the other party in a hostile way. The first party through its own belligerence thereby provokes actual belligerence from the second party. The first party then uses the bellige-

rence they provoked to confirm or prove their original assumption that the other party is belligerent. Johnson and Johnson, *supra* note 62.

[157] Displacement can also be consciously used to preserve intragroup harmony and intended for conflict management. For example, prachot is the Thai word for directing one's own anger towards a third party, with the purpose of indirectly communicating with the actual party to conflict. Klausner, *supra* note 2.

[158] Erbe, *supra* note 117.

[159] "[An] interesting area . . . is . . . the identification of the "indigenous" problem-solvers who are found within various . . . domains. Within any community, one can usually find individuals who, based on their interpersonal skills or social position, are frequently approached by people seeking problem-solving assistance." Bill Warters, Researching Campus Conflict Management Management Culture(s): A Role For Ombuds?, at <http://www.ombuds.uci.edu/JOURNALS/1995/researching. html> (last updated Feb. 21, 1997).

[160] Resignation learned under oppression must be reversed in any way possible. Erbe, *supra* note 117. The term power can be defined as the ability to influence or control others. . . . Power is relative. Outward appearances notwithstanding, everyone has some power. An indigent tenant with few apparent resources may have the ability to organize an entire apartment building. It is equally important to consider how willing people are to use their power and the conditions that might discourage them from using it to the fullest extent. For example, a person might be physically strong and never resort to threats of violence, or a corporation with access to the best legal advice might wish to avoid the bad publicity involved in a lawsuit. Salem and Davis, *supra* note 76.

[161] Deere and Leon, *supra* note 55, at 24 (describing the Fourth Latin American Feminist Meeting in Taxco, Mexico, in 1987).

[162] *Id.*

[163] See, e.g., Fisher and Ury, *supra* note 103, at 40-55.

[164] See, e.g., Deere and Leon, *supra* note 55, at 23 (referencing Gita Sen's and Caren's Grown's manuscript for the Third U.N. Conference on Women in Nairobi in 1985 called Development, Crises, and Alternative Visions: "Empowerment is . . . the basis for generating alternative visions. . . ."); Salem and Davis, *supra* note 74 (stating that "the mediation process is designed to surface the issues underlying a dispute and to encourage open exploration of options. This quality in itself can lead to settlements that transcend solutions that arise from the sheer use of power."); Everitt K. Wilson, in Moral Education xii (The Free Press of Glencoe, Inc., Everett K. Wilson trans. and ed., 1961) (1925) (stating that "the difference between self-determination and witless submission lies in the ability to predict accurately the consequences of alternative courses of action. Autonomy involves a personal decision in full knowledge of different courses of action" (emphasis added)).

[165] Erbe, *supra* note 117.

[166] David Lazarus, "A Dispute Beyond Mediation," *San Fran. Chron.*, Mar. 19, 2003, at B1 (exploring mediation's potential with respect to the war in Iraq). (quoting Steve Rosenberg, a Mill Valley mediation lawyer who was commenting on the Iraq standoff).

[167] Fisher and Ury, *supra* note 103, at 40-55.

[168] *Id.*

[169] *Id.*; Deere and Leon, *supra* note 55, at 23.

[170] Ezat Mossallenejad, Surviving Torture Through Self-Rehabilitation and Love, in First Light, at <http://www.ccvt.org/ezat.html> (last accessed Nov. 9, 2004) (emphasis added).

[171] The Arabic word t'aamol describes "the action of seeing something, pausing and considering it very carefully before taking action." Survivors also embrace forums, story-telling, creative expression, and validation of "small but critical" movement forward. *Id.*; see also Judith Lewis Herman, M.D., Trauma and Recovery (Basic Books, 1992).

Section V

# African Leaders Look to Conflict Resolution for Progress.

> He developed a capacity for putting himself in the shoes of the enemy and thinking through a situation from the perspective of the enemy. . . . He taught the underground that it must respect rather than simply hate the enemy. If you hated the enemy, you dismissed him, depersonalized him; and as a result, you would always underestimate his ability to destroy you. On the other hand, if you respected your enemy, you never forgot how formidable he was. . . . Hatred would kill you, not the enemy (Mandela, 2007).

Last year, a law review solicited thoughts about, in their words, pushing the envelope with social justice and negotiating peace in a world dominated by power and violence.[1] Taking their language literally, one must ask how to effectively address contemporary obstacles to ensure that the message and, most importantly, the means of justice are truly delivered to those in need.[2] One answer—which may seem obvious to readers but is actually much too rare in practice—is to work with, empower, and support the conflict work of the community members themselves. This section introduces the plans of five African professionals, demonstrating their skill and leadership as members of diaspora and domestic circles. All five African professionals are intent on serving their communities through offering the best of conflict resolution practice, including integrative bargaining[3] and restorative[4] victim-offender mediation.[5]

Renowned leaders like Nelson Mandela deservedly receive much attention and acclaim. What matters most, though, is that their hard-earned wisdom is actually practiced and spread. This section attempts to introduce a few lesser known inspirations working within—emerging voices with innovative and practical plans. The Africans highlighted here are in turn inspired by the emerging discipline of conflict resolution, a field that directly resonates with Mandela's quote above, teaching that the best negotiators know the power of thoroughly understanding their adversaries.[6] All are accomplished scholars from Cameroon, Kenya, Nigeria, and Zambia. They will describe how to use restorative and facilitative mediation and integrative bargaining to address some of the toughest, most troubling, and costly conflicts facing their communities, nations, and continent. They address violent tribal conflict in Cameroon, the crippling intragroup and intergroup wounds and tensions from Britain's colonization of Kenya, the challenges of reintegrating child soldiers into viable, life sustaining communities, and the debt crisis drowning the continent.

These African voices see and describe contemporary conflict techniques as facilitating critical societal development in many ways. In-depth conflict analysis motivates resolution, raising awareness regarding the costs of continuing conflict, and guiding conscious exploration and creation of alternatives. Equivalent conflict training for all concerned parties balances power and builds the capacity needed to proceed with collaborative problem solving. Truly impartial and skillful facilitation of interest-based negotiation builds essential trust and confidence conflict by conflict, with every conflict solved to the parties' satisfaction. Thus, the foundation for bringing together conflicting parties is built.

Once a majority of a community stands for peaceful conflict resolution and coexistence, political leaders and elders are more likely to follow their community's lead. These visionary Africans agree that political and governmental stakeholders represent their greatest challenge, along with the multinational corporations who partner with these leaders and exploit community resources. They do not pretend that these are simple challenges with easy solutions. Instead, they strongly concur that their societies are better prepared to confront these challenges with empowered mobilization of nongovernmental and faith-based networks and communities. Each also sees much potential for grassroots community to mediate daily conflict and build "unity and diversity" through joint ventures, like the economic cooperative described in Cameroon, while rallying for responsive state institutions and leadership.

The African collective is inherently strengthened by its restorative conflict traditions as publicized to the world through South Africa's Truth and Reconciliation Commission.[7] Victim-offender mediation that includes extended family and community and negotiates amends represents a long-standing African practice.[8] Daniel Karanja and Neba Mbonifor call for harnessing this resource and proceeding with truth and reconciliation in response to erupting tensions in Kenya, as well as the difficult task of reintegrating child soldiers.

Introduced and described later by Ndi Richard Tanto, each vision exemplifies requisite reflective practice—that conflict techniques are tested and retested in the context of each particular conflict, challenge, and community to ensure optimal effectiveness. Impartial leadership must be prepared to persist over time in the face of political pressure.

Chinedu Ezeh, Neba Mbonifor, and Daniel Karanja represent the contemporary voice, influence, and power of the African diaspora. They are the natural leaders for bringing the West's attention to and garnering Western support for what matters most.

This section provides a rare opportunity for Western academics and practitioners in the fields of conflict and dispute resolution to learn how Africans interpret the concepts and the techniques of these fields. Rather than ask the West to guide or even to assist them, these scholars lead readers through their own analysis of what is needed, from their African perspective.

Part 1 of this chapter presents attorney Chinedu Ezeh's brief introduction to the history and present status of African conflict. He calls for a continent-wide infusion of conflict, negotiation, and mediation skills training for the grassroots citizenry and professionals within conflict zones.

Part 2 is a decade-long case study example showing that grassroots and professional training in skills, inclusion in conflict processes, and participation in day-to-day decision making can transform violent tribal conflict into a sustainable coexistence by prioritizing economic needs when empowered by an Non-Governmental Organization (NGO), such as Ecumenical Service for Peace, and mediators like coauthor Ndi Richard Tanto. Tanto describes what he views as best practices as well as ongoing political challenges in step-by-step detail.

Part 3 describes the working vision of Pastor Daniel Karanja in response to present-day political tensions in Kenya—the most visible evidence of the destructive wounds and tensions remaining from the atrocities of British colonialism. Aspiring to learn from South Africa's experience (a process in which coauthor Mubanga was intimately involved), Pastor Karanja has already taken a lead in proposing truth and reconciliation with the legislative bill he describes.

Part 4 likewise stresses the importance of restorative rather than retributive justice in Africa. Activist and historian Mbonifor explains how integrating African restorative traditions into existing family and community mediations would help reintegrate child soldiers throughout the African continent.

Part 5 is perhaps the section where the western world needs to start. Sound, good-faith negotiation and mediation of the African debt crisis may be the only alternative the West has once it admits that its imposed solutions have continually failed and that it repeatedly participates in bad faith and exploitative processes when African interests are involved.

## Part 1: A Call for Widespread Collaborative Conflict[9] Resolution Training to Rebirth Peace

Most scholars and informed observers would agree that European colonialism had a devastating impact on Africa.[10] Developed countries freely adjusted boundaries in treaties between one another to suit their administrative conveniences without regard to the disparity between some of the groups that were being lumped casually together.[11] It is not farfetched to say that when the ruling colonialists left, their colonies were inadvertently rigged for failure from the very start.[12] The artificial boundaries created within Africa brought together ethnic people without providing for cultural diversities.[13] Nations were lumped together without regard to the fact that they were divergent and sometimes incompatible neighbors.[14] The Human Rights Violations Investigation Commission—the Nigeria equivalent of the South African Truth and Reconciliation Commission, called Oputa Panel, stated in its report submitted to the then president Olusegun Obasanjo that "the various ethno-communal groups in the country, including the major ones, complain of marginalization in the scheme of things."[15]

Marginalization is one of the results of a tit-for-tat response to the nasty tactics of destructive power games, polarizing the parties and ensuring that they work at opposite ends rather than from constructive common interest-oriented principled bargaining approach to conflict. It finds justification in reciprocity of response, but ultimately generates a continued hostility and at best a stalemate that refuses to take actions based on objectivity and consideration for the other's point of view. Most conflicts in former colonies, especially those in Africa, have struggled to rebuild themselves and find new identities.[16] In the process, Africa has seen millions of its people slaughtered and millions more as refugees.[17]

## Nigerian Legal Perspective on Contemporary Conflict in Africa

The simplistic approach to Africa's problem is to blame colonization for all Africa's woes, but that would be wrong. In attorney Ezeh's opinion, African nations, despite the wrongs of colonization, have acquired a history that can be harnessed to cultivate a culture of "unity in diversity." While the various factions wrangle for control, the fact that stands out is that they do not desire secession from the whole, but rather justice within the system. The solution lies in Africans beginning to ask each other why the events started. In the words of W. B. Yeats in the poem, "The Second Coming": "Turning and turning in the widening gyre; The falcon cannot hear the falconer; Things fall apart; The centre cannot hold; Mere anarchy is loosed upon the world."[18]

Fortunately, Africa has shown resilience in its ability to withstand the various conflicts that have beset it. Scholar Ezeh[19] is of the school of thought that in order for Africa to deal with its various conflicts, it must begin to look inwards and start developing conflict resolution mechanisms that address its peculiar conflict problems. While commending the African Union for its efforts in bringing peace to Africa, scholar Ezeh does not think it has done enough. The Union has not shown tenacity or resoluteness in addressing its various conflicts with the view of bringing them to an end immediately, or at least reducing them to a level of positive conflict that could be exploited for development.

Conflicts have always divided communities. Not all conflicts are bad, however, because some level of conflict is required to instigate growth and development.[20] The deep moral conflict that contemporary situations generate present opportunities for rich "interpersonal learning, improved relationships, and creative collaboration."[21]

Much of the conflict in Africa today is caused by power games[22] engaged in by leaders who want to hold on to their political power for as long as they can. The national question for most African countries in dispute involves the issue of power and power sharing. In Sudan, Nigeria, Rwanda, and the Congo, the same recurring question always intrudes into the political, social, and human development of the various states.[23] The question is inevitably: Who wields the political authority and controls the economic, natural, and human resources?[24] All other conflicts, ethnic, economic, and even environmental, subsume under that power frame.

The power game is a political manipulation game engaged in by political leaders who seek to dominate their opponents, and in turn, the opponents feel that they have no choice but to join in the confrontation. The game of dominance progresses to the detriment of the populace, who become the pawns in the power game. The negative result, however, is that unless one party has a decisive power advantage, the other party usually fights back, reverting to anger and hostility, clinging more stubbornly to positions, and becoming increasingly resistant to reaching an agreement.

Each side views the power struggle in terms of short-term simplistic loss or gain frames: We are in power, so we must be gaining, or we are out of power, so we must be losing.[25] This becomes an identity framing by the parties—a winner takes all identity frame.[26] This leads to the mad desire to accumulate wealth by corrupt means while in power; thus creating a further economic crisis. Predictably, the factions polarize and begin to characterize each other by reference to who they are or what they have done that has affected the other adversely.[27] Relationally, struggles to ascend to power at all costs and to sabotage those already in power lead to the use of force and violence to achieve the desired goal.[28] To achieve their ends, the political players have always relied on group, ethnic, religious, and sometimes military class affiliations. They seek a voice for their group, using any means possible: force, threats, moral and religious persuasion, and appeals to the sympathy of the populace in identifying with them in one way or another. As the focus and goals of the leaders and the opposition become distorted, both the leaders and their opposition lose sight of the whole frame, the succinct issue of what a nationality is in the true sense of the word. National development is lost to personal or sectional development.

Author Ezeh successfully practiced "generous tit for tat" in the face of these nasty tactics. Instead of reciprocating in kind and escalating destructive conflict, he committed to principled negotiations, gently and firmly taking care of himself in the face of attack, and nevertheless showing respect for the person of the attacker; thus, improving his relationship with the attacker. Even more importantly, he established his community profile and reputation as a person of moral integrity.

Jeffrey Sachs, an economist and author of *The End of Poverty: Economic Possibilities for Our Time*, is another contemporary example of a spokesperson promoting the negotiation strategy of generous tit for tat as key to avoiding disastrous confrontation. As introduced earlier, in traditional tit for tat strategy, a negotiator adopts the position of cooperation as long as the other negotiators do. With generous tit for tat, though, if a party begins to cheat, attack, or otherwise not cooperate, the first negotiator only stops cooperating to let the other know the consequence of noncooperation. At the same time, that same negotiator generously forgives by not reciprocating in a nasty way. Instead, the door for cooperation is left open. The first negotiator may even generously "extend" the olive branch of renewed cooperation in the hope of enticing others to resume cooperation.[29]

## Face-to-Face Communication Has Been Fruitful in the Worst of Scenarios

Scholar Ezeh wonders if much of the world may be ignoring humanity's greatest gifts: the gifts of communication and reason. He believes that the only way out of the destructive power game described above is not to play it at all. He calls to change the trained incapacity of face-to-face confrontation described above, through empowering side-by-side joint problem solving throughout African communities.[30] He believes strongly that the destiny of people depends on individual decisions and actions—that one individual can truly make a difference in social conflict. As chief legal officer for the Anglican Church Diocese of Niger state, Ezeh was able to build critical and reliable alliances that allowed him to navigate the treacherous tensions of negotiating between Muslims and Christians.

Improved cooperative communication helps reduce the incidence of conflict in the body polity.[31] Communication can be a constructive instrument that socially defines conflicts, enabling parties to be positively engaged in the meaningful exchange of information and understanding.[32] The breadth and intensity of a conflict is bound in communication. A proper understanding and use of communication skills may help soothe a rather painful conflict situation and resolution process. Effective communication creates attentiveness among members of a group, one to another, enabling them to be willing to be influenced by the ideas of the other group members;[33] thus creating a bridge of proper perspective in conflicts.

As scholar Mubanga witnessed, there are other situations in Africa where these practices have been applied with success, such as the South African Truth and Reconciliation Commission and the Nigerian Human Rights Violations Investigation Committee (Oputa Panel). In the Nigerian case, the reconciliation of the factions of the Ogoni four and Ogoni nine was a high point in the commission's assignment. They were able to moderate a dialogue that enabled the warring factions to sign an accord that has held up until the present time.[34] Moreover, the outcome helped empower the Ogonis who, after the peace accord, were able to speak with a more united voice.[35]

## Widespread Empowerment of Citizenry Is Critical

For the African nation to come out of its current myriad of conflict there is a need to bridge the theory practice gap in conflict and peace studies. While there are skilled conflict transformation professionals in Africa and in the international agencies working in Africa, there has been too little gain in translating their experiences into practice. The skilled professionals are usually outside the zones of conflict. Their current practice involves only coming into the zone to deal with specific conflicts. The people that need their skills are found directly within the zones of conflict, with little or no valuable skills to enable them to deal with the situations that they face daily. The few gains made in nationally and individually induced conflict resolution processes are soon lost in sectarian wrangling and power plays within the governments' systems, as well as lack of bureaucratic follow-through.

There is inevitably a negative emotion associated with negotiations when the negotiation is based on positional bargaining.[36] Consequently, people in conflicts have often avoided negotiations as they tax the energy of the participants.[37] If people are taught that there is an alternative, a collaborative style of bargaining that is "hard on the problem, [and] soft on the people,"[38] it will help in enabling parties to overcome their phobia of conflict resolution and management. Promoting interest-based bargaining may, in scholar Ezeh's view, further the emergence of factors necessary for the positive socio-economic growth in Africa again.

Human rights, environmental protections, and conflict transformation policies are not achieved by accident, but through well thought out planning processes, rigorously achieved by the consistent monitoring and enforcement of laws, policies, and agreements reached after collaborative discussions aimed at such purposes. Collaborative efforts should be aimed at training people at the grassroots levels, empowering them through skills training.[39] As the saying goes, it is time to teach the people to fish rather than give the people fish when they are hungry.[40] As just one example, parties can be empowered through encouragement to actively create "best alternatives." Awareness of "BATNAs" ("best alternatives to negotiated agreements") can further motivate parties to be more responsive to needs and interests and maximize assets while negotiating.

African citizenry and professionals need special training in effectively confronting and transforming relationships with their most powerful stakeholders, including their own political leaders, governments, and most, if not all, multinational corporations (MNCs). For years, MNCs have been making huge profits from the natural resources of Africa. Beginning with human goods in the form of slavery, then agricultural produce, timber, precious metals and stones, and finally oil and gas, the economic exploitation has been considerable. When people feel the direct natural and environmental impacts of destructive MNC operations but lack the requisite communication and negotiation skills, they have resorted to using the age old method of brawn, like seen with the Ogoni and Shell BP conflict in Nigeria,[41] to express their frustrations and disaffection with long-standing systemic abuses. While mobilizing has helped the African people achieve unity and brought the world's attention to their problems, it has still not advanced their critically needed economic development. Recently, Dr. Bernard Lafayette, one of Dr. Martin Luther King's colleagues in birthing the civil rights movement, has recognized this need and flown to Nigeria and South Africa to further train the citizenry in nonviolent resistance for use in their struggle against outside control of African resources.[42]

In Cameroon, as a result of the conflict arising between the Bafanji and Balikumbat villages, Ndi Richard Tanto and his team of Ecumenical Services for Peace (SeP) pioneered a novel process of training the parties in mediation and negotiation skills rather than mediating the problem for them. They thus created a pool of people who not only aspire to peace, but who are also are skilled in the process of achieving peace. This resulted in the achievement of lasting peace in an area that otherwise was known for its recurring conflicts. This is similar to the process Ezeh is designing and implementing in Nigeria through the training of Anglican priests for the purpose of being agents of grassroots peace processes and initiatives. The scheme is called the Anglican Peace Initiative. Since the priests have ministry services all over Nigeria, touching most grassroots areas of the country, their training is intended to create much needed peace ambassadors at the grassroots in Nigeria. They are capable of having their thumbs on the conflict pulse of the country. Hopefully, their training will help reduce incidents of violent conflict from erupting periodically as is constantly the case at present.

As things currently stand, most of the skills required are only taught in the classrooms or conference venues, while those who need this knowledge drown in ignorance. Quoting W. B. Yeats again, "The best lack all conviction, while the worst are full of passionate intensity. Surely, some revelation is at hand; Surely the Second Coming is at hand."[43] If only the best of our learning can be merged with the passionate intensity of the innocent dying in ignorance and frustration, then surely the second coming will be at hand, the second coming of the reign of peace in Africa, the rebirth of the land of innocence.

## Part 2: A Real World Case Study of Empowered Conflict Resolution and Democratic Peacebuilding

The conflicts between Balikumbat/Bafanji and Bagam/Bamenyam center on land. These conflicts started during the colonial period and persist due to the inability of the state to address them to the satisfaction of all parties. Multiplicities of maps define village boundaries. Each village holds tenaciously to the map that gives it a comparative advantage. The National Institute of Cartography, in trying to draw new administrative maps, most often reawakens some of the old conflicts as new administrative boundaries do not always respect the old ones. In situations of open clashes between communities, the government is reluctant to demarcate boundaries. When it does, it gives scant attention to the traditional chiefs who only have observer status in the demarcation commissions.

## Civil Society[44] Provides Requisite Strategic Oversight through Reflective Practice

Effective conflict resolution is not spontaneous and sporadic. It takes time to prepare with the parties in conflict and to monitor every intervention, to give feedback, and to modify strategy when the need arises.[45] Principal challenges include bringing and engaging key leaders in a long-term process, which first requires reducing mistrust and building capacities of conflicting parties so they can effectively participate in the process.[46]

Before the Ecumenical Services for Peace (SeP) took the challenge to mediate the conflicts between Balikumbat/Bafanji and Bagam/Bamenyam in 1999, sporadic attempts to mediate had been made by the government and the churches. The intervention of the state was focused on enlisting leaders to end violence and destruction. The church appealed to their members to forgive each other and to follow the example of Christ. These approaches were good in that they ended the violence. They were not sustainable and democratic, however, because the interests of the parties were not identified and addressed. Furthermore, the process did not involve all the stakeholders.

SeP started its intervention with data collection and analysis of the conflicts. During the process of data collection and analysis, the major stakeholders, the interests of the parties, and the beneficiaries of the status quo were all identified. Information from this premediation stage helped to shape the intervention strategy. The strategy consisted of training, creating space for dialogue, and direct mediation. It took six years of actions and reflections[47] for a sustained peace to be achieved. During these six years, many lessons were learned about the process, which can be useful in similar conflict situations in other communities and will be shared here.

## Case-by-Case Success in Resolving Conflict Builds Necessary Community Confidence

Just as democracy depends on majority participation, conflict resolution and transformation depends on enjoying the confidence and participation of the majority.[48] In the Balikumbat/Bafanji and Bagam/Bamenyam conflicts, the purpose of the first trainings organized by the Ecumenical Service for Peace was to empower participants with knowledge of the concepts of conflict and peace[49] and nonviolent strategies in resolving conflicts.[50] The objectives were to provide participants with a forum to vent their trauma from conflict and simultaneously win their support for the process.[51] These first trainings were organized with the conflicting parties separately.[52]

At the end of these trainings in the separate communities, structures referred to as Peace Committees were formed.[53] The objectives of the Peace Committees were many, but most importantly they acted as forums for the sharing of experiences and relay units in the field for sensitization of their community members on issues of conflict and peace and resolution of conflicts within the community.[54] There were more than one Peace Committee in some communities depending on the population and the geographical size of the community. Bagam had five committees while Bamenyam only had one.

These committees became reflection centers, par excellence in issues of conflict resolution, and were co-opted by village chiefs to settle conflicts brought to the traditional councils for resolution.[55] Community members identified committees as structures that settled community conflicts impartially, and many community members brought their conflicts to the committees rather than the traditional councils.[56]

SeP monitored the process through monthly reports of the committees and organized field visits to discuss challenges.[57] The successes registered by the committees, in handling conflicts within and without the family, made them very popular. Many community members wanted to join them. Since membership of the committees was conditioned by participation in a workshop in conflict resolution strategies, other workshops were then organized with the support of SeP to increase the membership of the Peace Committees in each village. In the Bagam village, more than five hundred people were trained, including quarter heads, social group leaders, members of the traditional councils, and church leaders. After a year, the communities were sufficiently mobilized for peace.

## Sustainable Conflict Resolution Depends on Equal Empowerment of All Parties and Eventually Bringing Them Together with an Inclusive Process

Adequate empowerment of all concerned was crucial to the success of the conflict resolution process described here.[58] Equal empowerment of conflicting parties, or power balancing, puts them at the same level of knowledge on issues of conflict and resolution and facilitated rational and informed discussions regarding their conflict situation.[59]

Once parties were sufficiently empowered, they were skillfully brought together. While the first workshops were organized for the community, the second series of workshops were organized for Peace Committee members of the conflicting communities.[60] The organization of the second workshops with conflicting parties was a serious challenge. Victims of violence saw their property destroyed and lost dear ones. After boycotting roads and services in each other's community, to be able to come together for three to five days to attend a workshop was a major step in the process.

The focus during these second workshops was on continuing empowerment through training in mediation skills, facilitating peace-building through analysis of the conflict by the parties, and developing scenarios for resolution. The cost-benefit analysis tool proved very effective. After analyzing their conflict's impact, participants became acutely aware of what they were losing because of their conflict. This motivated them to work for resolution.

These second workshops brought together conflicting parties to reflect on their problems, to commit themselves to a peace process, and to make proposals for possible solutions.[61] This working together and analyzing their situation together helped to clear misunderstandings between them, reduce stereotypes,[62] and reestablish relations. The facilitated processes helped build a common understanding and vision for the conflict. That vision focused essentially on the future of their relationship rather than the past and its tribulations. It was during the second workshops, which took place in Balikumbat, with the participation of Balikumbat and Bafanji, that the idea of exchange visits between conflicting communities was proposed and accepted as a good strategy to rebuild relationships and communication between conflicting parties.

After this series of second workshops, the participants were sufficiently empowered to monitor and to mediate most of their conflict without assistance. SeP continued to monitor from a distance, but waited for parties to initiate consultation when difficulties arose.

## Exchange Visits Reestablished Relationships and Began Rebuilding Trust

The second workshops described above stimulated large-scale mobilization for exchange visits between conflicting communities.[63] In the Balikumbat and Bafanji conflict, the first visit was organized in Bafanji.[64] The Peace Committee mobilized the entire village to prepare to receive the Balikumbat people at its market square. Committees were formed to take care of the reception, feed guests, and provide program activities during the visit. This first exchange visit brought together over five hundred people. The Peace Committees presented reports of their activities, successes, challenges, and orientations for the future. The administrative authority, SeP, and the Church all made commitments to the process. The exchange visit was further characterized by singing, making sketches, and feasting. This communion of people, who were enemies for years, opened a new chapter in the peace process. Those who were initially skeptical about the outcome of the peace process joined the crusade for peace.

One of the events that marked the first exchange visit in Bafanji was the testimony of a mother, Mary Lum, who saw the nurse that helped her birth twins at the Balikumbat Health Center on the eve of the 1995 war. She gripped the nurse with tears of joy, hurried to her house, and brought out her twins who were already seven years old.

This testimony was followed by that of many others. Participants were free to talk about the war without pain, indicating that they had forgiven the past.

This exchange visit marked the beginning of informal visitations between the people of the conflicting communities. Other exchange visits were organized with the same popularity.

In addition to playing a great role in mobilizing people for the peace process, the exchange visits helped rebuild broken relationships, commit community leaders and administrators to the peace process, and reestablish communication, as well as promote communal use of social services like schools, hospitals, and roads in each other's community.[65] The exchange visits further permitted SeP to evaluate the progress made by the parties and to identify issues needing attention to facilitate the process further.

## Direct Mediation with Chiefs Has Been Necessary to Move from Positions to Interests

Mediation is a very delicate balance. If the mediator is identified as taking sides with one of the parties, the process is frustrated; instead the mediator must be impartial.[66] As introduced earlier, impartiality encompasses a lack of bias and an inclusive treatment of all voices concerned with a particular conflict. When done appropriately, mediation responds to the needs and interests of all stakeholders,[67] including the most marginalized and contentious, in equivalent ways, balancing power so that all have an equal opportunity to be heard.[68] In contrast, ineffectual conflict processes around the world routinely exclude one or more significant interests, often mirroring the political tactics that incite ethnic conflict.[69] Without impartiality, mediation and other conflict processes easily become pawns for powerful interests.

Mediating with leaders who hold steadfastly to their positions is a serious challenge. Working with community members has been much easier than working with their chiefs. Direct mediation is important because the interests of chiefs often differ from the interests of their populations. A chief might need political power, for example. The communities usually seek their interests, or underlying needs, while their leaders are prone to taking entrenched positions, seeking power rather than environments conducive to running farms without fear of destruction, as one common example. His people are held hostage in conflict unless ways are found to persuade the chief that serving his people's interests also secures and builds political power.

One of the achievements of exchange visits, described earlier, was the fact that it made the chiefs, who considered themselves all-powerful, follow in the steps of their people. The chief of the Balikumbat village, Doh Gah Gwayin, who was not prepared for the peace process, discovered that his quarter heads and traditional council members were very involved in the process and had to join the bandwagon. In the Bagam/Bamenyam conflict, it was during an exchange visit that the chief of Bagam, Simo Tankeu Jean Marie, declared before hundreds of people from the conflicting villages that, "People can make mistakes and can repent when they are made to recognize the mistake." He made it clear that he was ready to change and to promote peace in the subdivision.

Direct mediation between the chiefs themselves has also been an important stage in the conflict resolution process in the Bagam/Bamenyam conflict. SeP facilitated several mediation efforts. SeP used the office of the Divisional Officers, who are the direct administrative heads of the chiefs, to convene the meetings. During these meetings SeP facilitated discussions. The meetings and discussions were very hostile in the beginning, with the Fon of Bamenyam refusing to take part in the entertainment after the meeting with the excuse that "The pot is still on the fire." By this he meant that there was still tension between the parties, making it difficult for any form of sharing to take place. During the last meeting that was held, the two chiefs accepted concessions.[70] The chief of Bamenyam, Moko Moko Pierre, could now participate in the entertainment. He even remarked, "If you carry a basket of maize on your head and fall, you cannot recover all the grains." This was an indication that with the concessions made, the tension between the two parties had been reduced. He was ready to share in the feasting since according to him, "The food is now ready and can be eaten." This is a classic example of how extending an olive branch can work in the generous tit for tat negotiation strategy.

## Community Consensus Has Prioritized the Importance of Establishing Communal Projects for Socio-Economic Empowerment—Going Further Will Require State Collaboration

In the situation of the Balikumbat and Bafanji communities, when the Peace Committee members saw that relations between them had normalized, they brought up an idea to form a farmer's federation, bringing the parties together. After a series of reflections on the structure of the federation, the Balikumbat Subdivisional Integrated Farmer's Federation was formed to promote agriculture and to seek funding and markets for the members' produce. The leadership of the federation, as well as the hosting of the meetings of the federation, rotates between the two communities. This has helped to reinforce relationships and to build a common vision for the villages.

Within the last five years, the peace committees are still very vibrant in villages. Peace forums that bring together peace committees are still operational. No incidences of conflict have been reported. However, all the issues that led to the conflicts have not been addressed. The roles of the administration, the chiefs, and the elite remain major challenges.[71] Nonviolent strategies have proved effective in transforming negative conflict interactions into cooperative and positive interactions,[72] but much stills needs to be done for this approach to be endorsed and supported by the government. Additionally, the government has to revisit its land tenure systems and exercise authority over land rather than leave land issues in the hands of traditional rulers. The future of peace in Africa lies in the recognition of the role of the civil society in conflict transformation and the collaboration of the state.

## Part 1 and 2 Notes and Questions

1. Pick a conflict that passionately concerns you where outside commentators have despaired and painted an overwhelmingly negative and pessimistic picture. Using this section's ideas and case study examples, identify one or more conflict tools that could make a critical difference if implemented and evaluated by devoted community and leadership. Explain how "your case study" could be influenced and changed for the good by concerted conflict effort. Share and discuss.

2. Pick a conflict that concerns you—the one picked earlier or another. Consider whether conflict practitioner Ezeh's observation regarding the lack of conflict resolution training for those intimately involved with and affected by conflict is also true with your conflict. How might you empower all concerned with your conflict to proceed in more constructive ways? Share and discuss.

3. In Cameroon, the state and church leaders effectively stopped violence. What, in your experience, is needed to stop violence?

4. The type of strategic oversight and reflective practice described by mediator Tanto as necessary to democratic and sustainable resolution are still rarely seen in conflict resolution and peacebuilding. If they are fundamental to the success described in Cameroon, they deserve to be studied and promoted. Using this case study, design strategic oversight and reflective practice for a group in your life. Include observation for and evaluation of constructive and destructive behavior and a process for effective improvement. A simple process evaluation can be done by simply observing and noting exactly what is helpful and what is not. Start, as mediator Tanto did, by identifying the interests of each group member. Continue interest analysis as you observe any behavior that you perceive as possibly or actually harmful to the group. Share and discuss.

Once you have polished your strategic oversight and reflective process, implement and note the results.

5. Schools within the United States have experimented with peace committees like the ones described in this section. Santos High School of Los Angeles, California, introduced in section 2, included a peace committee or council in its successful reduction of school violence.

6. Do you know of any forums provided for groups and communities to vent their trauma from conflict? Simultaneously learn about nonviolent strategies for resolving conflict?

   List several groups-communities you know who might benefit from the above forum. Identify one entity (e.g., community mediation center, church, nonprofit, social worker, government agency, etc.) who could provide such a forum.

7. What percentage of people in your country or community are skilled and knowledgeable in nonviolent conflict strategy? What can/will you do to help change this?

   Note: You might start by analyzing and identifying costs of one conflict, or continuing the status quo, as was done in Cameroon, and starting to share your cost analysis with those concerned.

8. Identify one or more of your political leaders or representatives (including religious). Can you find evidence that this/these leader(s) is/are truly serving the needs and interests of their community?

Brainstorm additional ways one of these religious or political leaders could act to serve their community, e.g., sponsor a community forum or conflict resolution training.

9. Design a collaborative project involving two or more groups in conflict like the Farmers' Federation in Cameroon or Seeds for Peace. Share and discuss.

10. Impartiality is the active commitment of a third-party mediator to transcend or stay detached from partiality, or "the sides" of parties to conflict. Some organizational ombuds have reframed impartiality as multipartiality, or the ability to hear and understand every party's perspective equally, without bias or preference.

Americans often talk about the risks of peer pressure, especially among young people and others eager to belong. In contrast are practices like impartiality, which demand rare independence from political and popular pressure as well as self interest. As you prepare to act as a mediation impartial, consider ways you have found to effectively resist peer and political pressure, even cruel bullying and attempts to manipulate you through flattery and promises. Reflecting on your life to date, what else might you have done to "stay true to" and respect yourself. Share and discuss.

Note: Many successful people have intimately faced the risks and costs of success: nasty, false gossip, personal attacks. . . . Numerous human beings, at least in the United States, expect others to take their side, agree with them, and not show any evidence of superiority or distance. If you dare to not agree with them, you risk being viewed as a traitor and even becoming a scapegoat target. This is one of the reasons mediators from a cultural group may hesitate in mediating with those from their own cultural group. Effective mediators find ways to diplomatically walk this tricky dangerous middle; somehow maintaining rapport and trust with all concerned. Ask a seasoned mediator who you respect and admire to describe their impartiality in action.

## Part 3: Victim Offender Mediation Can Immediately Help with Intratribal and Intertribal Conflict in Kenya.

As a Kenyan theologian, Reverend Karanja[73] has a vision for restorative justice in Kenya. Specifically he envisions a truth and reconciliation commission mirroring the South African experience. It would incorporate integrative negotiation as well as victim-offender mediation, utilizing lessons learned from similar commissions as resources. He has assessed truth and reconciliation as the best way to deal with atrocities committed by British colonialists against the Gikuyu people in Kenya and the resultant intragroup and intertribal tensions within the third and fourth generations.[74] Pastor Karanja sees truth and reconciliation as providing an "appropriate forum to process deeply hidden anger to prevent future violent retaliation."[75] Like attorney Ezeh, Pastor Karanja encourages working with stakeholders to realistically assess their BATNAs.[76] Violence can be prevented if parties are empowered by being made aware of their BATNA early enough before the conflict explodes to uncontrollable proportions. They must be encouraged to create stronger, more desirable alternatives—if at all possible.

### Kenya's Conflict

In December 2007, Kenya held a fiercely contested general election followed by unbelievable intertribal violence.[77] Intense negotiations, led by former U.N. Secretary General Kofi Annan and backed up by international pressure, saved the country from disintegrating into the likes of the Rwandan genocide.[78] The postelection violence was just the tip of a hidden iceberg of unfair, postcolonial land ownership policies, tribalism based political and economic control of resources, and escalating intertribal, campaign rhetoric rivalry between political camps.[79] The president appointed a commission of inquiry headed by a former South African judge. The team conducted open fact finding hearings across Kenya.[80] The commission's report concluded that overall the votes were not stolen in favor of one side. Negative civil society activism through the mass media planted the first seeds of violence. Civil society members prior to the elections alleged that the government had already planned to steal the elections and had planned official violence to cover up their sinister motives. The debate of whether these conclusions were trustworthy continues. With such a questionable ethical stance, the civil society has some work to do to prove its integrity to all. Unfortunately, the truth and justice reconciliation process promised during the negotiations has not yet been formed.[81] Fighting politicians formed a government of national unity to protect their selfish interests (while the masses wallow in despair, disease, poverty, and remain estranged from the very government their parents and family members died for). There were still some internally displaced people (IDPs) eight months after the chaos ended.[82]

The seeds of suspicion and mistrust planted during this period of violence can only be uprooted by a long-term process of direct engagement between the affected tribes and by addressing the root causes of intertribal mistrust and violence.[83] Leaders must be challenged to persuade their followers, before, during, and after the elections, that no one wins in violent conflict.

## A Vision for Truth and Reconciliation Beginning with Intratribal Tensions

Pastor Karanja plans to first educate and rally clergy to build the capacity for negotiations from within before seeking regional and international support.[84] Indigenous, traditional methods of negotiation[85] provide foundational support. There are known African methods of reconciliation and healing that could immensely help in this process. Cultural awareness of tribal and ethnic underlying interests cannot be ignored if conflicts are to be resolved. The role of formally recognized elders and their time-tested expertise in bringing warring sides together, especially among pastoralists competing for dwindling water and grazing areas, must be embraced. Pastor Karanja's father was village chief. Every Monday he gathered with recognized elders to hear grievances from various parties and to decide accountability and punishment. This system worked since the village concept of justice recognized that the complainant and the offender belong to the village before and after the punishment. Thus, rehabilitation was deeply ingrained in this village judicial process. John Mbiti, an African philosopher, explains the necessity of communal understanding even in conflict resolution: "[I] am because we are . . . because we are therefore I am." Parties understand that life is intricately held together and interlinked between families, villages, and regions and hence conflicts must be resolved through the involvement of the entire community.

Once a Kenyan Truth Reconciliation Commission (TRC) is convened, it will begin by addressing intragroup conflicts resulting from Britain's divide and rule policies. Colonial related wounds that have never been addressed must be the starting points in order to acknowledge the immense nature of tribal-based bias and prejudice that leads to generational violence. Face-to-face negotiations are encouraged between the Gikuyu and loyalist Gikuyus and other tribes. The Gikuyu believe that they bore the heaviest burden in leading the Mau Mau war against Britain and assume a sense of entitlement and privilege ahead of the loyalist Gikuyus and other tribes. Other tribes do not take this assumption lightly and hence dislike Gikuyu domination in the country

Pastor Karanja stresses the importance of impartial and sincere dialogue where pain is acknowledged and heard and losses are deeply honored. Victims need a safe place to tell their stories, grieve their losses, and hear offenders take responsibility for the harm they have committed for healing to commence.[86] Ideally, new perspectives form. Perhaps the victim is able to see the perpetrator as vulnerable and in need of care and compassion for the first time. Optimally, individual and group identities are transformed through redemption.[87] While care must be taken not to rush the process of forgiveness, parties would do well to remember the words of Archbishop Tutu: "Without forgiveness, there is no future."[88]

Mandela truly expressed care for his enemies. He invited them to social events, called them during their birthdays, and attended family funerals. Building trust must be the foundation to quelling strong feelings of revenge. In violence there is no winner. All sides lose. Learning as much as possible about the other side, likes, dislikes, and favorite routines, can move relationships to new and healthy levels where the communication barrier is broken.

One conflict resolution tool necessary for creating the safe space described above is the inclusive selection of impartial facilitators, investigators, and mediators like Tutu and Mandela for the truth and reconciliation process. All concerned must be satisfied and willing to proceed with some degree of trust.[89] Pastor Karanja is satisfied with the approach South Africa took here, convening a qualified panel of commissioners who openly shared the process and resultant information with their publics.[90]

Another conflict resolution tool Pastor Karanja recommends for creating the safe space described above is negotiation of process parameters, or ground rules, such as respect for others and detailed responses to anticipated outbursts of anger.[91] As introduced earlier, ground rules are process principles and boundaries agreed to by parties involved in a conflict process.[92] They can be negotiated to effectively respond to angry outbursts and other conflict escalation.[93] They can also craft a uniquely effective multicultural process.[94]

The preparation process of all key participants will be critical to the success of the TRC. For example, understanding Mandela's eight secrets of leadership introduced and exemplified above[95] will empower the participants as well as motivate a win-win outcome. The eight lessons of leadership stated by President Nelson Mandela during an interview marking his 90th birthday celebration are: (1) "Courage is not the absence of fear—it's inspiring others to move beyond it, (2) Lead from the front—but don't leave your base behind, (3) Lead from the back—and let others believe they are in front, (4) Know your enemy—and learn about his favorite sport, (5) Keep your friends close—and your rivals even closer, (6) Appearance matters—and remember to smile, (7) Nothing is black or white, and (8) Quitting is leading too." These enduring principles of leadership especially at the negotiation table will eliminate positional and inefficient negotiation ushering integrative win-win outcomes for all.

This conversation is necessary as all sides dig deeper to slowly rebuild trust through small agreements that genuinely address the needs of those present, followed by the consistent implementation needed to demonstrate trustworthiness.[96] After shared acknowledgment of victimhood (underlying their intra-group conflict) and trust-building, the Gikuyu people would then begin exploring the victim-offender mediation process. Victims need an opportunity to examine and to evaluate which options are realistically available to them.[97] If they consequently determine that a meeting with their offender is of value to them, they are then able to negotiate on behalf of their needs and interests.[98] An offender may agree to responsibility for the harm caused, even some form of punishment, or offer to repair physical, emotional, and psychological harm in ways that are unexpectedly attractive and healing to victims.[99]

## Repair of Harm Must Prioritize Community Development

Pastor Karanja further elaborates his thoughts about the lessons learned from South Africa's experience and other more recent truth and reconciliations. Most importantly, he promotes community, rather than individual, reparations—repairing harm in ways that advance the educational and economic status of the communities injured; thus avoiding complex disputes and ongoing tensions over amounts of individual reparations.[100] He is quite critical of how western perpetrators, often co-conspirators and beneficiaries of international crimes, have not been held accountable for repairing harm.[101] He also hopes to avoid a small elite group of well-connected Gikuyu people benefiting to the detriment of many, which happened in Kenya following independence. In Kenya, families of former Gikuyu loyalist politicians, who were supporting the colonialists, carved out thousands of acres of land at the expense of the majority—poor Mau Mau warriors and their families who had fought for independence.

A recent report on development assistance aimed at ending ethnic conflicts found that while there are no formulas for resolving ethnic conflict, natives must be engaged fully in deciding what they consider fair and equal distribution of resources.[102] Identifying mutual interests and building consensus goes a long way in building sustainable community. Furthermore, the empowerment of local institutions must be prioritized in capacity building. Local authorities and distribution infrastructures under reasonable accountability supervision can get the job done. Some foreign donors' "Santa Claus" mentality, where they magically drop from nowhere to "administer aid" and then disappear, destroys these communities more than they help salvage them over time. Oxfam international has been successful in this area and others would do well emulating Oxfam.

## Learning from and Building on Past Truth and Reconciliation

The unanswered question to be explored is how to avoid retraumatizing victims during the TRC process. Employing the skills of professional pastoral caregivers during the TRC process could provide necessary emotional and psychological counseling that was absent during the South African TRC.

Pastor Karanja is further searching for ways to avoid a repeat of the isolation and harassment that occurred to women who participated in Rwanda's Gacaca courts when they came forward to testify against their perpetrators. All participants could be requested to sign an agreement guaranteeing the safety of all participants and freedom from all forms of intimidation before, during, and after the process.

## Civil and Faith-Based Communities Must Hold Government Accountable for Transformation of Relationships

The situation in Kenya is similar to what has been described by the other co-authors of this chapter regarding their governments. The government of Kenya is likewise a tough stakeholder. Kenya's past track record with commissions of any kind is foggy and shrouded with secrecy. Unless faith-based communities and civil society members take full responsibility and hold the government accountable, this TRC process will be just another empty drill without meaningful results.[103] Vigilance, after TJRC submits its reports, is critical, given the fact that previous commissions have not addressed issues of impunity. Many reports are still gathering dust in government offices. How do you compel a government to ensure that the recommendations are followed to the letter? How do you ensure that victims get justice? There are major questions and skepticism towards the roles of TJRCs in meeting their goals. Huge differences in understanding and expectations of the process exist between elites and communities. TJRCs across the world are notorious in their failure to implement their recommendations. This has led to rare attainment of the expected moral regeneration of society.

The ethnic and political divisions look even more set to make the work of TJRC more difficult in Kenya. The government and its agencies as well as the citizens must behave in a manner to further the ideals of such a process. As long as previous injustices continue being replicated in Kenya, such as gross human rights violations like extra-judicial killings and torture, then TJRC may not succeed. It would easily turn into another token conflict resolution mechanism. The truth-seeking process is unfinished business that provides a foundation for the transformation of the state. It is only a step in the process of addressing long-term and short-term issues.

The lessons learned from South Africa are vital and should be considered each step of the way in order for the Kenyan process to succeed. Reconciliation must move past the mechanics of conflict resolution and literally focus on healing and repairing broken relationships. Understanding the wounds of each participant, as well as the shared desire for wholeness and restoration, could overcome all barriers and roadblocks of self-interest. The chapter of violence, death, and destruction may never be permanently closed, but this process would provide a new vocabulary for telling the story to succeeding generations in a way that would hopefully prevent future fractures from occurring and taking these communities through the same cycle of violence over and over again.

# Part 4: Reintegrating Child Soldiers through Engaging Communities in Victim-Offender Mediation That Embraces Indigenous African Tradition

In co-author Neba Mbonifor's[104] experience, one of the greatest challenges in postwar recovery and reconstruction is effectively rehabilitating and reintegrating former child soldiers into productive sectors of society. Since the end of Liberia's civil war in 1998, both local and international NGOs have been running a series of programs to rehabilitate thousands of former child combatants. Scholars describe and evaluate their work as combining family reunification, access to education, skill training, health service, and psychological recovery.[105] Family and community mediation have been instrumental to these rehabilitation and reintegration efforts,[106] bringing whole families, traditional authorities, and the church into the rehabilitation process. While much has been achieved, there is an overall feeling that progress has been slow.[107]

Research concluding that inadequate social institutions hinder reintegration of child soldiers mirrors the condition initially attributed as responsible for child soldiers: lack of political will on the part of regional governments and the international community to enforce and respect legal instruments governing the involvement of noncombatants, especially children in warfare. International legislation regulates the protection of children in conflicts.[108] Yet, law alone has not been enough to prevent the involvement of children in war in the face of present day trends in weapon manufacture.[109] Modern weapons are light to carry and are easily operated by children as young as 10 years old.[110] Children with little or no education, poor economic backgrounds, and broken homes are the most vulnerable to forceful enlistment, especially those children who are refugees.[111] These same children struggle with rehabilitation.

Yet, once again, as stressed repeatedly by earlier co-authors, African communities have informal options for addressing their needs that can be exercised while waiting for and working on the strengthening of social institutions. This is particularly true when discussing the reintegration of offenders into families or broader communities (when viable families no longer exist).[112]

## Victim-Offender Mediation Embraces Long-Standing African Conflict Practice

Co-author Mbonifor concurs with scholars who attribute the slow pace of rehabilitation to an overemphasis on economic rather than psychological recovery.[113] He believes that while providing livelihood for these children is indispensable, repairing their "damaged self" can do more for effective reintegration. He proposes that victim-offender mediation, incorporating African restorative traditions, be added to the family and community mediation processes currently in use. Mbonifor sees the contemporary restorative justice processes of victim-offender encounter, public forgiveness, restitution, and community service as ripe for blending with native African forms of restitution, forgiveness, and ritualistic cleansing.

Restitution and public forms of forgiveness are not new to most traditional African communities.[114] The only new thing being promoted here is that these forms of restoration be used with child soldiers. Traditional societies have reserved such methods for notorious adult criminals, like murderers, thieves, adulterers, sorcerers, and others, who have terribly gone against public norms and then sought repentance and forgiveness from their societies.

It is important to first explain the relevance, process, and consequence of the traditional form of public repentance, forgiveness, and restitution in the form of community service within an African context. African offenders are expected to actively seek forgiveness and restitution. They are strongly motivated to do so because they understand the consequences that will befall them should they choose to stay in the community with the blood of innocent people on their hands. It is safer and cheaper to offer to do community service than to wait and be ostracized or exiled from their community. Even in moderate cases, no one will marry from a family whose father, mother, or sibling has once spilled human blood or been involved in a crime of similar magnitude.

In most of North West Cameroon, traditional and ritualistic ceremonies are organized mostly in public squares where whole families and communities turn out to witness the purification and readmission of previously "bad birds" of the society. At these events, all family members are cleansed from the humiliation brought by the evil acts of their loved ones. Most important to understand is the community-centered approach. The collective system in most African traditional societies stipulates that though crime may be the direct blame of the individual offender, the community within which the offender was born and nurtured shares in the complexity of the offense. Consequently, child-soldiering is a crime against the entire community by an important segment of the same community.

The offending and offended community can even go beyond the family. Just like other traditional systems in many parts of the world, traditions in North West Cameroon revere children as the collective wealth and even the engine of society. In return, teenagers are expected to give the same respect to neighboring parents or seniors as they would accord to their own parents. This same reverence further means that a juvenile offender not only humiliates the offender's immediate family but also the offender's neighbors and entire community.

This African belief is distinct from the conclusion of some pro-children's rights authors who largely attribute child-soldiering to failed societal responsibility.[115] Western scholars generally see young ex-combatants as victims of neglect by their families and societies.[116] The African family system belief, however, is that children are supposed to be good, respectful, and hardworking. There is no justification for crime, no matter the circumstances. Thus, irresponsibility—like choosing to fight in war and kill—must be forgiven for children to be accepted back by their families and society in general. The western and international worlds may not agree with giving children the blame for infant soldiering.

Yet understanding the African perspective helps in understanding the importance of giving the children the opportunity to regain their lost image of goodness by offering to pay a price for it, appearing in public, and doing community service.

At the same time, as explained above, children's families, immediate and extended, share in some degree of culpability. Thus, they too, must be prepared to seek forgiveness and make amends. Including these traditions in current efforts at mediation would likely facilitate integration of child soldiers.

## Part 5: Negotiating and Mediating Africa's Debt Crisis

Most of the world now understands that Africa's debt and health crises have escalated to breaking points.[117] Out of the 41 heavily indebted poor countries in the world 33 are in Africa.[118] Many African countries are paying more for debts than for health care and other essential domestic services.[119] On average, African countries are spending eight times more repaying foreign debts than funding domestic social services.[120] For every one dollar poor African countries get in grant aid, they pay back 15 dollars on debts.[121]

In response, Mubanga hopes to use his negotiation and mediation skills and personal knowledge to persuade international leaders and lenders to consider several options for debt relief rather than simply insist on current requirements.[122] The options he promotes here include: (1) a bankruptcy like option for African countries; (2) tracing and freezing the accounts of corrupt African leaders outside of Africa by the Group of Eight (G8), International Monetary Fund (IMF), Paris Club, and World Bank when these accounts contain loan money stolen from African people; and (3) flexibility in the conditions that poor countries in Africa must meet to qualify for debt relief, including the waiver of conditions under certain circumstances.[123]

### Mediating a Bankruptcy-Like Approach

Living in the U.S. has given Mubanga an opportunity to observe big companies in the U.S. survive total collapse by filing for bankruptcy. To be eligible to file, companies must first reach a critical stage, similar to the one seen in Africa, accumulating overwhelming debts. A considerable number of American companies learn from their mistakes and do very well after reorganizing themselves under the protection of bankruptcy law. Mubanga is not a lawyer. He envisions, however, that African leaders might make it clear that they have reached bankruptcy-like status and are prepared to negotiate debt repayment.[124] This is similar to Columbia economist Jeffrey Sachs' work with countries like Bolivia and other countries at the point of bankruptcy.[125]

## Negotiating Help in Effectively Tracing Funds Stolen by Corrupt African Leaders

Another issue ripe for negotiation with lenders would be support for effectively tracing funds that have been absconded by corrupt African leaders.[126] Most of the money loaned to African countries, a reported $ 140 billion since independence, has been taken by such leaders and hidden in foreign accounts.[127] Those who hide their money abroad are given impunity. For example, for over two hundred years, Switzerland has not allowed the disclosure of banker information, providing an ideal location to conceal funds.[128]

Despite obstacles, African governments are finding creative approaches to trace such funds that promise some success. Support from international lenders would likely heighten progress here. For example, the Kenyan government led by President Kibaki, who succeeded Arap Moi, hired an American company, Kroll of New York, to trace these funds. To date, the company has made shocking revelations and forced many high ranking judges to resign.

Once corrupt leaders die, money is even harder to trace.[129] Mobutu Seseseko, the former president of Zaire, which is now the Congo Democratic Republic (DRC), is an African leader who absconded billions of dollars in foreign accounts. After his death, the government of DRC failed to trace the funds.[130] Likewise, Sani Abacha, the former president of Nigeria, took billions of dollars that he kept in separate accounts abroad. When he died in office in 1998, the Nigerian government initially could not trace the money. Yet, amazingly, after constant pressure from the new president, Olusegun Obasanjo, Switzerland returned $1 billion of the stolen money to Nigeria.

## Mediating and Negotiating Options to the Debt Crisis That Truly Work

As mentioned earlier, excessive reliance on outside experts who attempt to act for the parties rather than empower the parties to act on their own behalf has not worked.[131] This is typical of what is happening in Africa. Instead of negotiating mutually beneficial ways to resolve the debt crisis with African leaders,[132] the World Bank and the IMF set up the standards to be followed. The World Bank and the IMF, for example, implemented a policy that cancelled debts of heavily indebted African countries that registered growth and reduced poverty.[133] This did not work. Even though cancellation of debts was done in good faith, in April 2001, the IMF and the International Development Association (IDA) issued a joint paper conceding for the first time that debt cancellation was not benefiting poor African countries.[134] The policies that the countries were required to meet to qualify for debt cancellation resulted in negative growth and a sudden increase in poverty.[135]

Yet another program was introduced in spring 2005, which allowed IMF and World Bank to guide poor African countries in how to remain above the

150% debt-to-export ratio for 10 years or more. Out of the 33 heavily indebted countries in Africa, only Malawi and Niger are on course. The other 31 countries have failed to reach the goals.

Mubanga concurs with the World Bank and IMF idea of cancelling Africa's debts. The results would have been different, however, if officials from the World Bank and the IMF had sat down with representatives from Africa to explore common grounds and interests, to share and create mutually agreeable reasoning, and to build future relationships.[136]

Facilitative mediation could clearly guide good faith collaborative problem-solving.[137] At its best, it facilitates broad participation among diverse interests for consensus building and sustainable resolution.[138] As will be demonstrated in the next section, the IMF is already intimately acquainted with such mediation.[139] Years ago it created an ombuds-mediator office in response to harsh civil society criticism of its support for mining operations in Peru.[140] That office has already mediated community processes similar to those being proposed here.[141]

Mediation would give African leaders an important opportunity to educate their lenders about the specific reasons why they are defaulting on their debts. African countries are failing to repay their debts on time for a variety of reasons.[142] The major one is drought.[143] Countries like Uganda, Kenya, Tanzania, and the Ivory Coast, just to name a few, depend on agricultural exports.[144] Once they are ravaged by drought, their major source of earning much needed dollars for debt repayment is crippled.[145] The countries end up defaulting on their loans, resulting in the devaluation of their currencies. When the local currency is devalued, the price of imports increases, and the price of exports decreases to very low prices, resulting in stagnant domestic growth.[146] Negotiation would facilitate troubleshooting of this mutually harmful cycle and brainstorming of options so that both African and lender interests are satisfied.

Negotiating through face-to-face mediation would also give African nations and lenders a chance to discuss the challenges involved with meeting conditions that qualify African nations as heavily indebted poor countries (HIPC), and thus make them eligible for debt forgiveness. To qualify for HIPC status, poor nations must drop subsidies for basic commodities, eliminate trade tariffs, and open their markets to free trade.[147] As Gerald Lenoir, writing for American Friends Service Committee, notes: "With unrestricted access to African economies, foreign companies flood their markets with cheap goods that wipe out local industries. Instead of supporting independence and development, too many African HIPCs appear to foster increased dependence and perpetual underdevelopment."[148]

Due to the problems with corrupt African leaders described earlier, Mubanga proposes creation of an impartial oversight panel that would screen loans, negotiation terms, and agreements, and otherwise provide transparency and accountability to ensure good faith. This would be an independent body with representatives from all African countries and done in consultation with the African Union, which is the mother body of all African countries. The officials will be accorded responsibilities that range from screening loans given to African countries to implementing proper usage and coming up with affordable payment plans with lenders.

Mubanga hopes to produce a television documentary that will examine what is required for a poor country to qualify for debt cancellation and the effect of delaying debt cancellation until a country reaches heavily indebted poor country status to qualify for debt cancellation. The documentary will compare conditions prevailing before countries qualified for debt relief and ask: Has the situation changed for better or for worse? A portion of the documentary will look at the possibility of unifying the countries of Africa into one entity, the United Nations of Africa (UNA). Uniting the countries of Africa into one dominant force may have many advantages. This is evident in the United States of America (USA) where most poor states, like Louisiana, survive major catastrophe after receiving funding from the federal government.

Some politicians in Africa may feel uncomfortable with people discussing openly the current situation in their countries and may persecute them. However, before the start of recordings, this researcher will spend time educating local political and religious leaders on the importance of this documentary. Moreover, this researcher will make it clear to the local politicians that allowing people to speak freely in this documentary may be the key to sharing the vital information needed to guide officials from various lending institutions to change their stance on Africa's debts.

## Conclusion

The coauthors in this section remind us of the resilience of the African spirit, as they see and strategize practical paths for hope in the face of violent ethnic eruption and repeated betrayal. As seasoned practitioners of many years representing law, medicine, theology, education, and community development, and as students of conflict and peace, they are able to guide the international community with specific ideas that they see bearing fruit.

All agree that truly impartial oversight and direction are critical to confidence building, through the inclusive conflict mechanisms necessary to create "unity in diversity" for sustainable problem solving, transparency, and accountability in the use of funds. Several recommend the conscientious reflective practice exemplified by Tanto's work in Cameroon. Like economist Sachs' diagnostic economics, African conflict and peace must be analyzed and evaluated case by case, relationship by relationship, and practice by practice.[149]

Most commend integrative rather than positional negotiation tactics. They ask that the communities in conflict be empowered themselves in conflict analysis and skills rather than being asked to rely on the sporadic intervention of skilled outsiders. Training in sophisticated evaluation, creation of alternatives, and identification of underlying interests can make a critical difference. At times, of course, skilled mediators may still prove necessary to moving forward, as once again exemplified by Tanto's decade of mediation in Cameroon and

Kofi Annan's recent mediation in Kenya. Leaders and communities must somehow be persuaded to participate in collaborative conflict work.

Africa has a long and revered tradition of restorative justice, or victim-offender mediation, introduced to the world through South Africa's TRC. Reflective practice allows for imperfections—new lessons can be learned and tested with each new attempt. Progress occurs through the inner strength to honestly reflect and the collective determination to keep building on what works.

None of the coauthors is proposing an easy answer or panacea. They acknowledge that they need international support in confronting elites, political leaders, governments, and MNCs whose self-interest holds communities hostage. At the same time, they see contemporary conflict techniques empowering and mobilizing communities to do what they can to meet their interests. Joined by skillful and devoted civil societies and faith-based networks, Tanto reports that even political leaders can be moved to serve community interest.

## Parts 3 -5 Notes and Questions

1. At this point the reader should have a strong and growing sense of their strengths in negotiation, conflict resolution and peacebuilding. This section added the following empowerment techniques:

   ___generous tit-for-tat negotiation strategy

   ___evaluating and creating best alternatives to a negotiated agreement

   (Note: Ury and Fisher and the Harvard Negotiation Project are credited for this concept as well as the one below: separating people from the problem.)

   ___empowerment strategy

   ___nonviolent resistance.

   It also shared the importance of:

   ___ motivating parties to conflict through cost/benefit analysis of the status quo.

   It then added the following:

   ___building trust

   ___separating people from problems

   ___conflict resolution monitoring, evaluation, and troubleshooting ___victim offender mediation.

Last, but not least, it reemphasized the importance of the following:

___examining threatening information, ideas, and opinions for insight and benefit

___imagining new possibilities

___generating several options or alternatives

___envisioning futures

___understanding others' perspectives

___encouraging others' communication

___creating positive, comfortable, low-risk climate

___showing serious interest in others

___changing one's perspective with new information

___negotiating and creating effective process parameters

___seeking and recognizing common ground

___encouraging and ensuring equal participation of all (impartiality)

___accurately identifying most important underlying needs, including unspoken

___not reacting to perceived slights

___learning that conflict can have positive benefits when approached constructively

___empathetic listening (acknowledging pain and honoring loss)

___conflict analysis that identifies all stakeholders and beneficiaries of status quo

___allowing parties to vent their trauma.

Review all compliments you have received during your study and practice of these skills. Rather than ranking the above skills according to your self perception, rank them as praised with your greatest strength as #1.

If you have not yet asked trusted others (friends and family) for feedback regarding these skills, ask several to identify and describe your top skill.

Note: Be careful that you do not solicit or receive overly "nice" or less than candid feedback, especially flattery. It does not help mastery to have your mother, for example, say you are already a master in all NCRP skills when most strangers would say that they perceive you as consistently demonstrating an open mind and suspension of judgment but you need to work on being a more careful listener and accurate reframer.

2. Identify one or more global concerns that truly matter to you. Envision several ways that the skills you are studying here could be used in responding to your concern(s). Share and discuss.

3. What is your highest or greatest vision for using and contributing these skills yourself? Describe in as much detail as you can.

Optional: Many students enjoy studying a timeline of their life to-date created through asking themselves to identify their most significant life events at five-year intervals. They then study all events to identify life patterns and narrative. Some do appreciative inquiry of their lives, creating a list of their greatest assets.

Try outlining an action plan for implementing your vision with 1-, 5-, and 10-year goals, along with a few actions you can take towards each goal.

Recommended: Focus on what is most important to you. Rather than write several yearly goals, try three goals for each year with three action steps under each goal (that you rigorously commit to do no matter what)!

4. What will help you achieve your vision and goals? Daniel Karanja, for example, went on to obtain his masters in theology and build additional alliances with pastors in Kenya to achieve his dream. George Mubanga obtained financial backing to film his documentary to educate those he hopes to influence.

## Notes

[1] Thanks to my colleague, Col. Swaranjit Singh, for his assistance with this and the following chapters.

[2] Any pragmatic reader is likely to be moved to ask how seeds of peace can ever grow in the face of glorified violence and resultant destruction through unending attempts to dominate. Tension and contradiction are ever present. Those desiring peace for their families and communities are eternally called to meet these challenges with every action and choice, despite unanswered questions and doubts. Peacebuilders must be as vigilant, if not more, as those intent on intimidation and manipulation. United Nations Educational, Scientific, and Cultural Organization (UNESCO) defines peace culture as:[A] culture that promotes peaceable diversity. . . . The ceaseless culture-creating activity that characterizes the social body involves interaction at every level, from the intrapersonal. . . to the interpersonal—in house-hold, neighborhood, and community, on through successive levels of civic organization through city to the United Nations. . . . Because there is constant inte-rpenetration of levels, the societal capacity for aggression or peacebuilding depends on patterns developed in every domain. . . . Elise Boulding, *Cultures of Peace: The Hidden Side of History* (Syracuse University Press, 2000, 1) (emphasis added).

[3] See Howard Raiffa et al., *Negotiation Analysis: The Science and Art of Collaborative Decision-Making* (Belknap Press of Harvard University Press, 2003, 191). Integrative, or interest-based, negotiation was made popular by Roger Fisher and William Ury in their book, *Getting to Yes*. See generally Roger Fisher & William Ury, *Getting to Yes: Negotiating Agreement Without Giving In*, ed. Bruce Patton, 2d ed. (Penguin Books, 1991). Rather than the more common distributive bargaining where parties simply divide what is being negotiated, usually through a series of concessions, an integrative process leads parties in "expanding the pie" through conflict analysis of underlying interests and

creative options evaluated with principled criteria to optimize outcomes for all concerned. See Nancy D. Erbe, "Appreciating Mediation's Global Role in Promoting Good Governance," 11 *Harv. Negot. L. Rev.* 355, 386-89 (2006) ("Parties might ask, for example: "How can we [both] generate ore and protect infants simultaneously?'").

[4] Restoration represents a completely different approach to criminal justice than the better known retribution approach. It is defined by one leader in the field as: [A] systematic response to wrongdoing that emphasizes healing the wounds of victims, offenders, and communities caused or revealed by crime. [Restorative practices] . . . respond to crime by: (1) identifying and taking steps to repair harm, (2) involving all stakeholders, and (3) transforming the traditional relationship between communities and their governments in responding to crime.

Lynette Parker, "Restorative Justice: A Vehicle for Reform?" Paper presented at the annual meeting of Latin American Studies Association, Las Vegas, Nevada (2004) (citing Daniel W. Van Ness, "Justice that Restores: From Impersonal to Personal Justice," 23 *J. of Religion in Soc. Work*, 93-109 (2004)). Truth and reconciliation commissions are the most widely known example of restorative justice. *Contra* Nancy Erbe, "Appraising Surge in Legal Scholarship Regarding Restorative Justice and Discovering Lenses to the South: Is Global Criminal Justice Necessarily Different Than United States Ideal?", (bepress Legal Series, Working Paper No. 560, 2005), available at <http://law.bepress.com/cgi/viewcontent.cgi?article=2750&context=ex presso> (arguing that truth and reconciliation commissions represent hybrid justice, combining retributive and restorative approaches to justice for highly pragmatic reasons, such as the need to force the most powerful offenders, like the Catholic Church, to dialogue through cost-prohibitive lawsuits and embarrassing publicity).

[5] As earlier defined, mediation is any force outside of a conflict that helps with the negotiation, resolution, and transformation of that conflict. For this book, mediation is defined as "facilitated face-to-face dialogue . . . allowing communication, understanding, rehumanization of the enemy, reframing of the conflict as a shared problem to be solved[,] . . . moving towards inclusive processes of mutual empowerment . . . in a way that respects the interests, needs, and values of all." Erbe, *supra* note 3, at 371 (citing John Davies and Edward Kaufman, *Second Track/Citizens' Diplomacy* (Rowman & Littlefield, 2002, 3)).

[6] Padraig O'Malley, *Shades of Difference* (Viking, 2007, 1-2). See Nancy Erbe, "Negotiation," in *Encyclopedia of Governance 1,* ed. Mark Bevir (Sage Publications, 2006, 333-34). Conversely, in multiple studies, the worst negotiators and facilitators of cross-cultural processes are described as poor and judgmental listeners lacking deep understanding. Nancy Erbe, "The Global Popularity and Promise of Facilitative ADR," 18 *Temp. Int'l & Comp. L.J.* 343, 343-89 (2004) [hereinafter Erbe, "The Global Popularity"]; Andrea Kupfer Schneider, "Shattering Negotiation Myths: Empirical Evidence on the Effectiveness of Negotiation Style," 7 *Harv. Negot. L. Rev.* 143 162-84 (2002).

[7] See, e.g., Boulding, *supra* note 2, at 83.

[8] See generally Erbe, *supra* note 4.

[9] Conflict is defined here as: "Any perceived divergence of interest." Dean G. Pruitt and Sung He Kim, *Social Conflict: Escalation, Stalemate and Settlement*, 3d ed. (McGraw-Hill, 2004, 7-8).

[10] See generally GlobalIssues.org, Conflicts in Africa <http://www.globalissues.org/Geopolitics/Africa?Intro.asp#TheLegacyofEuropeanColonialism (last visited March 20, 2009).

[11] Richard H. Robbins, *Global Problems and the Culture of Capitalism* (Allyn & Bacon, 2002); Bob Geldof, "Why Africa?", Straight.com, Nov. 10, 2004, <http://straight.com/article/why-africa?#>.

[12] Geldof, *supra* note 11.

[13] GlobalIssues.org, *supra* note 10.

[14] Id.

[15] Human Rights Violations Investigation Commission, "Synoptic Overview of HRVIC Report: Conclusions and Recommendations" (2002, 10), available at <http://www.nigerianmuse.com/nigeriawatch/oputa/OputaSummaryRecommendations.pdf> (emphasis added).

[16] Boundaries of the African countries were arbitrarily set by the colonial masters without regard to tribal and cultural affinities or differences. See GlobalIssues.org, *supra* note 10. Persons of the same affinities found themselves in different administrative locations, while persons of dissimilar affinities were lumped together, thus creating conflicts through quests for familial mergers and nonfamilial separations, leading to expected intraboundary and interboundary agitations. See *id.*

[17] The acknowledged international responsibility to protect countries whose governments fail to protect post-Rwanda is critical to future peacebuilding throughout Africa and will be mentioned in this chapter as relevant to specific plans (e.g., Kofi Annan's recent mediation in Kenya).

[18] William Butler Yeats, "The Second Coming," *The Dial*, Nov. 1, 1920, available at <http://www.poetry-online.org/yeats the second coming.htm>.

[19] Chinedu Bob Ezeh is an attorney of over 20 years whose practice in Nigeria included acting as an ombuds.

[20] The SAGE Handbook of Conflict Communication: Integrating Theory, Research, and Practice, ed. John G. Oetzel and Stella Ting Toomey eds., (Sage Publications, 2006, 391).

[21] *Id.* at 395.

[22] William Ury postulates that the game works by a threat to the other side through force or coercion, with the hope they will back down. William Ury, *Getting Past No: Negotiating Your Way from Confrontation to Cooperation* (Bantam Books, 1993, 6-14).

[23] See R. T. Akinyele, "Power Sharing and Conflict Management in Africa: Nigeria, Sudan, and Rwanda," 25 *Afr. Dev.* 209 (2000) (arguing that ethnic differences played a key role in the countries' power struggles).

[24] See generally Making Sense of Intractable Environmental Conflicts: Concepts and Cases, ed. Roy Lewicki et al. (Island Press, 2003).

[25] See *id.* at 31.

[26] See *id.* at 21.

[27] See *id.* at 23-24.

[28] See *id.* at 26.

[29] The power game, a dangerous psychological game of nasty tactics engaged in by most arbitrary leaders in the opinion of William Ury, has as its first victim the objectivity, in the face of a conflict, which is needed to negotiate effectively. Ury, *supra* note 22, at 37-39. This power game depends on your reaction to the threat or pressure from the other side. Your most powerful weapon in this circumstance is not reacting, but rather, responding by "going to the balcony," taking a dispassionate and objective bird's eye view of the problem and responding by the use of generous tit for tat in defusing the toxicity of nasty tactics in a conflict situation.

[30] See, e.g., Nancy Erbe, "Game Theory," in *Encyclopedia of Governance*, *supra* note 6, at 333-34.

[31] Morton Deutsch, "Cooperation and Competition," in *The Handbook of Conflict Resolution*, ed. Morton Deutsch et al. (John Wiley & Sons, 2006, 22, 30) (discussing how in constructive competition both the winner and the loser gain through their communication during the competition and "winners see to it that losers are better off, or at least not worse off" than at the start of the competition).

[32] *Id.* at 22, 27 (listing the benefits of cooperative communication versus competitive communication as: (1) effective communication is exhibited; (2) friendliness, helpfulness, and lessened obstructiveness are expressed in the discussions; and (3) coordination of effort, division of labor, orientation to task achievement, orderliness in discussion, and high productivity are manifested in the groups).

[33] See *id.* at 30.

[34] See Human Rights Violations Investigation Commission, *supra* note 15, at 9.

[35] In 1995, the government of Nigeria, under the military dictatorship of General Sani Abacha, executed nine young men from the Ogoni tribe of Nigeria for the alleged killing of four elders of Ogoniland. The Ogoni nine had been protesting the activities of the multinational oil companies (especially of Shell BP) on their land, the marginalization of the Ogoni people, whose land produced close to 35 percent of the total crude production of Nigeria, in the sharing of the revenue by the government, and also the negative and environmentally destructive procedures adopted by Shell BP in oil exploitation and production in the region. The Ogoni crisis ended with the murder of the four elders by irate youths, a lopsided trial, and judicial murder of the nine by the federal government. It is instructive that full oil exploration has not been restored in the Ogoni land since the incidents. It is indeed a tragedy that could have definitely been avoided if the parties had agreed to go to a negotiation, where they would have applied all the skills relating to principled negotiation, such as reframing, listening, fight and flight control, and possible inclusion of third-party impartial structures in the process. If these skills are filtered down to the people in such conflicts who really need them, it would help in no small measure in arresting similar conflicts taking place all over the region now.

[36] See Fisher and Ury, *supra* note 3, at 20 (discussing the difficulties with positional bargaining, as the relationship tends to become entangled with the problem, and relying on positional bargaining puts the relationship in conflict with the substance of the problem).

[37] Again, relying on the theories of positional bargaining, if people are in conflict and believe that their negotiation will end up being a bargaining over positions, they will be reluctant to enter the negotiation for fear that the negative emotions in the relationships will taint the negotiation. See generally, Fisher and Ury, *supra* note 3, at 20-21.

[38] *Id.* at 54 (in focusing on interests instead of positions, the authors suggest instead of committing as a negotiator to a position, rather firmly commit to an interest and spend the aggressive energies there).

[39] BATNA and WATNA are two examples of empowering negotiation tactics. The first is a party's empowered walk away alternative at a negotiation table and should not be confused with options, which are the possible routes parties generate and could take within the ambits of the negotiation process. See Ury and Fisher, *supra* note 3, at 99-100. BATNA and WATNA are the alternatives to the negotiation process itself. *Id.* BATNA is the acronym for Best Alternative To a Negotiated Agreement. It is the party's bottom line that is better than the agreement proposed at the negotiation table. *Id.* WATNA on the other hand is the acronym for Worst Alternative To a Negotiated Agreement, and is a

walk away alternative that is worse than a proposed negotiated agreement in a process. *Id.* at 97-106.

[40] Ezeh, *supra* note 19.

[41] See *supra* note 35 (discussing conflict between Ogoni and Shell BP).

[42] Richard C. Dujardin, "R.I. Students Bound for Belize," *Providence J. Bulletin*, May 31, 2000 at 1 (noting the success of a 10-day conference on "peace and non-violence in South Africa, arranged in part with Rhode Island's Bernard Lafayette.")

[43] Yeats, *supra* note 18.

[44] Ndi Richard Tanto is a mediator in Northwest Cameroon who has worked with the SeP for many years. Peace and Collaborative Development Network, Ndi Richard Tanto's Page, <http://www.internationalpeaceandconflict.org/profile/nditanto> (last visited Mar. 20, 2009).

[45] The author of this section, Tanto, is describing reflective practice—the fundamental conflict technique for evaluating and ensuring case-by-case effectiveness.

[46] See Howard Wolpe and Steve McDonald, "Democracy and Peace-Building, Rethinking the Conventional Wisdom," *The Round Table* 137, 138 (2008, 97), available at <http://www.wilsoncenter.org/topics/docs/Democracy%20and%20Peace building.pdf>.

[47] See *id.* (referencing reflective practice).

[48] See Erbe, "The Global Popularity," *supra* note 6, at 381.

[49] See generally *id.*

[50] See *id.* at 380-81.

[51] See *id.* at 380.

[52] See *id.* at 381.

[53] *Id.* at 380.

[54] See Erbe, "The Global Popularity," *supra* note 3, at 380-83.

[55] *Id.* at 380.

[56] *Id.*

[57] *Id.* at 380-81.

[58] See Wolpe and McDonald, *supra* note 46, at 140-41. The authors argue that there has been a missing link in the traditional approaches to peace-building. *Id.* That key link is building the capacities of key leaders to facilitate the peace process. In our effort to resolve the conflicts in West Cameroon, capacity building was a key component. *Id.* Leaders were trained to carry the process forward by analyzing the conflict and developing possible scenarios for peace.

[59] See *id.* at 140-42.

[60] See Erbe, "The Global Popularity," *supra* note 3, at 380.

[61] See *id.*

[62] *Id.*

[63] See *id.* at 381.

[64] See *id.*

[65] According to Susan Mckay and Dyan Mazurana, exchange visits bring opposing factions together to build a culture of peace based on the development of esteem and dialogue. Susan Mckay and Dyan Mazurana, "Raising Women's Voices: Peacebuilding," International Federation of University Women, 1999, <www.ifuw. org/peace/peace building/raising-womens-voices.html>.

[66] Erbe, *supra* note 3, at 357.

[67] Id. at 358-60. See id. at 398 for questions to evaluate inclusivity and authentic impartiality. In one study of cross-cultural conflict process in four regions of the world, inclusive process facilitated by an open-minded and encouraging, or engaging and con-

cerned, third-party facilitator was the top recommendation for a quality experience. Id. at 398.

[68] *Id.* at 381.

[69] See *id.* at 380-81. The external evaluation team of the International Monetary Fund ombuds mediators found that nongovernmental organization watchdogs are often necessary to safeguard third-party impartiality and independence when powerful stakeholders participate. *Id.* at 386.

[70] See *supra* note 30 (outlining tit-for-tat approach).

[71] Questions about ownership of land in Cameroon are very complex. The land tenure system designates all land in Cameroon as state land. Land is managed by the ministry of Territorial Administration through its decentralized structures. The closest administrator of land to the population is the Divisional Officer popularly called "Chef Terre," or "the Leader in charge of land." He works closely with village chiefs, referred to as Axillaries of the administration in the management of the land. By law, there is a hierarchy of power from the Minister of Territorial Administration to the village chief. While the first three categories of actors—Minister, Senior Divisional Officer, and Divisional Officer—have the authority to use their power to demarcate land, the chiefs have only consultative powers.

The situation described above is what happens in principle. In practice, however, the chiefs are the real owners of the land and can go as far as waging a war on whoever threatens their authority over land. All of the conflicts that have occurred in Western Cameroon within the last 15 years have been over land, due to the chiefs' disregard for state authority. The Balikumbat/Bafanji, Bagam/Bamenyam, Bali/ Bawock, and Mbessa/Oku conflicts are all due to the insubordination of traditional chiefs to constituted authority. In the Oku/Mbessa conflict, for example, the state planted pillars to demarcate the land, and the chief of Oku ordered the pillars to be removed. In the Bali/Bawock conflict, the administrative authority of Mezam wanted to solve the problem by demarcating the frontier between the two villages. The Second Assistant, SDO Muma Charles, who went to the field to examine the possibilities for the demarcation, was chased from the area on the instructions of the chief of Bali, Fon Galega. The Bali people went as far as taking the senior administrator to court for infringing on his land.

Insubordination can be understood against the background of the democratic practice in Cameroon. Democracy in Cameroon means rule of the majority at all costs. For that reason, political parties, in their struggle to win political power or stay in power, put in place mechanisms to ensure a majority vote at all costs in every election. Village chiefs have therefore been hotly sought by political parties because they have the power to mobilize and influence their subjects at the local level to vote for one party or the other.

Victory in an election could well be as a result of the ability of a political party to win the support of the village chiefs. As such, these chiefs stand in a vantage point to bargain for facilities from political parties, and the party that wins, due to their support, gives them a free hand in issues of land as compensation for votes. That was the case with the Balikumbat/Bafanji conflict, wherein Fon Doh Gah Gwayin rigged elections, secured the only CPDM party seat of the 20 seats in parliament for the North West Province, and invaded Bafanji, which largely voted for the opposition SDF party.

[72] See Erbe, "The Global Popularity," *supra* note 3, at 382.

[73] Daniel Karanja is a theologian from Kenya who has published works on oppressive tribal and cultural practices like female genital mutilation and the needs of women living in communities of oppression. He is currently engaged in developing a faith-based

conflict resolution curriculum for Kenya—laying the foundation for truth and reconciliation, first within his own community.

Charles O. Lerche III offers this definition of reconciliation: Reconciliation is currently essential to the construction of sustainable peace. It can be defined as a profound process of dialogue between conflicting parties, leading to the recognition of the "other," and respect for his or her differences, interests, and values. Reconciliation is "the action of restoring broken relations. . . . [It is] the acknowledgment of the dignity of victims long ignored. It restores the individual's capacity to take hold of herself and to manage the future and herself in that future. It restores the capacity to live with or alongside the other. It allows us, while remembering, to bring closure to a chapter in our past. It enables us to live in the present, making our life as a nation and our lives as individuals in a shared future. It always remains a never-ending process."

Charles O. Lerche III, "Truth Commissions and National Reconciliation: Some Reflections on Theory and Practice," 7 *Peace & Conflicts Studies* 3 (2000), available at <http://shss.nova.edu/pcs/journalsPDF/V7N1.pdf#page=2> (internal citations omitted).

[74] For one of the best-detailed historical accounts of the British atrocities in Kenya, see Caroline Elkins' award winning book entitled, Imperial *Reckoning: The Untold Story of Britain's Gulag in Kenya* (Henry Holt and Co., 2006). In 2006, Elkins was awarded the Pulitzer Prize for general nonfiction for her work in Kenya. She eloquently detailed how the British imperialists mistreated the Gikuyu people of Central Kenya. She is currently working at Harvard University as an associate professor in history in the Kennedy School of Government. Her focus is human rights issues.

[75] Daniel Karanja, *Final Portfolio.*

[76] See earlier discussion of BATNAs.

[77] See Associated Press, "At Least 94 killed in Kenya Election Protests," Int'l Herald Trib., Dec. 31, 2007, available at <http://www.iht.com/articles/ap/2007/12/31/ africa/AF-POL-Kenya-Elections.php>.

[78] AlJazeera.net, "Kenyan Leader Signs Power-Share Law," <http://english. aljazeera.net/news/africa/2008/03/200852514721316663.html> (last visited Mar. 20, 2009). Kofi Annan, former U.N. Secretary General, successfully negotiated a power sharing deal between the current Kenyan president and the then opponent who is now the prime minister under the new agreement. The ability to discern the immediate and long-term interests of the parties, plus the rising violence and destruction of life and property, resulted in high stakes. See Associated Press, "Kofi Annan Takes Over Kenya Mediation," CBSnews.com, Jan. 10, 2008, <http://www.cbsnews.com/stories/ 2008/01/10/world/ main3695650.shtml>. The Kenyan public seemed quite comfortable with Annan's team of qualified and experienced expert negotiators. Unfortunately, the root causes of these postelection violent acts are yet to be addressed and hence the urgent need for a full fledged truth and reconciliation commission. Michelle D. Gavin, Adjunct Fellow for Africa, Council on Foreign Relations Press, Policy Options Paper—Kenya (2008), <http://www.cfr.org/content/publications/attachments/ Kenya POP.pdf>.

[79] Njoki S. Ndungo, "Kenya: The December 2007 Election Crisis," *Mediterranean Q.*, Fall 2007, at 113, available at <http://mq.dukejournals.org/cgi/ reprint/19/4/111.pdf>. Ndungo states that: The simmering anger was the result of a combination of historical injustices from the time of Kenya's colonial past and the failure of successive governments . . . to address the problems of the inequality of its citizens. Inequality is seen in landlessness, gender status, youth unemployment, the widening gap between extremely wealthy and extremely poor citizens, and the marginalization of some ethnic communities. *Id.*

[80] See Dave Opiyo, "Kenya: South African Judge to Lead Polls Inquiry Arrives," *Daily Nation*, Mar. 20, 2008, available at <http://allafrica.com/stories/20080320 0075.html>.

[81] The recommended bill for a TRC appeared before parliament in a 42-page draft and had a very focused mission statement if only there was political will to follow. See RescueKenya.org, Draft Truth, Justice, and Reconciliation Bill—TJRC Draft Bill, <http://rescuekenya.wordpress.com/2008/04/24/draft-truth-justice-and-reconciliation-bill-tjrc-draft-bill/> (last visited Mar. 20, 2009). Unless faith-based communities take charge of this issue in an united interfaith approach, the TRC will likely remain where it is right now. The mission stated, "AN ACT of Parliament to establish a Commission to seek and promote justice, national unity, reconciliation and peace among the people of Kenya by inquiring into the human rights violations in Kenya and recommending appropriate redress. . . ." *Id.*

[82] International Committee of the Red Cross, "Kenya: Red Cross Counselors Provide Needed Help for the Displaced," Jan. 23, 2008, <http://www.icrc.org/Web/ Eng/siteeng0. nsf/html/kenya-feature-230108>.

[83] Ideally, present day generations of former British perpetrators will be moved by Gikuyu stories, feeling empathy and a genuine desire to make amends.

[84] Faith-based communities have both grassroots, regional, and national networks in place. For example, the Anglican Church of Kenya has an established justice and peace department including a research unit that has published on problem solving. The Catholic Church of Kenya too has a robust justice and peace unit staffed by professional experts familiar with local, national, and international issues. Building liaison with these and other interfaith networked organizations will add to the efforts going on in Kenya.

[85] Josiah Osamba, "Peace Building and Transformation from Below: Indigenous Approaches to Conflict Resolution and Reconciliation among the Pastoral Societies in the Borderlands of Eastern Africa," 2 *Afr. Ctr. for the Constructive Resol. of Disp.* 33, 42 (2001), available at <http://www.accord.org.za/downloads/ajcr/ajcr20011.pdf> (Osamba is a lecturer in the Department of History at Egerton University, Njoro, Kenya, studying towards a Ph.D. in Dispute Resolution as a Fulbright Junior Scholar at Nova Southeastern University, Fort Lauderdale, Florida).

[86] See Elizabeth M. Evenson, "Truth and Justice in Sierra Leone: Coordination Between Commission and Court," 104 *Colum. L. Rev.* 730, 737 (2004).

[87] See Richard Stengel, "Mandela: His 8 Lessons of Leadership," *Time*, July 9, 2008, available at <http://www.time.com/time/world/article/0,8599,1821467,00.html>. Rule 5 states, "Keep your friends close—and your rivals even closer." (Rule 4, "know your enemy—and learn his favorite sport," describes how Mandela came to understand Afrikaner's by learning their language and helping imprisoned ones as an attorney).

[88] Archbishop Desmond Tutu, "Foreword: Without Forgiveness There Is No Future," in *Exploring Forgivenes,* ed. Robert D. Enright and Joanna North (University of Wisconsin Press, 1998).

[89] See Erbe *supra* note 3 (describing the inclusive selective process).

[90] See Erbe, *supra* note 3, at 407-10 (an example of another authentically impartial panel with suggestions for creation).

[91] Nancy Erbe, *Holding These Truths: Empowerment and Recognition in Action* (Berkeley Public Policy Press, 2003, 166).

[92] See *id.*

[93] *Id.* at 166-71.

[94] See Erbe, *supra* note 3, at 403.

[95] See Stengel, *supra* note 87.

[96] See Erbe, *supra* note 3, at 408 (discussing how unkept promises and lack of transparency erode trust).

[97] See Fisher and Ury, *supra* note 3.

[98] See *id.*

[99] See *id.* Making amends will benefit by applying the four principles of negotiation offered by Fisher and Ury: (1) separate the people from the problem; (2) focus on interests rather than positions; (3) generate a variety of options before settling on an agreement; and (4) insist that the agreement be based on objective criteria. *Id.* at 18, 40. Such a sense of balance and fairness between third and fourth generations who did not directly engage in this conflict provides an optimal environment to address sensitive matters with an objective and solution focused manner. Cross-cultural intelligence will be an added advantage when these two sides gather.

[100] See Milton J. Esman, "Can Foreign Aid Moderate Ethnic Conflict?", *Peaceworks*, Mar. 1997, <http://www.usip.org/pubs/peaceworks/pwks13.pdf>.

[101] For example, a 2002 lawsuit accused several corporations and banks of aiding and abetting South Africa's apartheid government. See Erbe**,** *supra* note 3, at 394.

[102] David R. Smock, "Humanitarian Assistance and Conflict in Africa," *Peaceworks*, Feb. 1996, <http://www.usip.org/pubs/peaceworks/pwks6.pdf>.

[103] A similar warning was issued by Ndungu Wainaina, the director of the International Centre for Policy and Conflict, which is a member of the Kenyans for Peace with Truth and Justice Coalition. Ndungu Wainaina, "What Citizens Should Expect from a Truth Commission," *The Daily Nation Kenya*, May 17, 2008. *Id.*

[104] Neba Mbonifor is one of coauthor Ndi Richard Tanto's neighbors and colleagues, a historian, teacher, and community activist.

[105] See Susan Shepler, "The Rites of the Child: Global Discourses of Youth and Reintegrating Child Soldiers in Sierra Leone," 4 *J. of Human Rights* 197-211 (2005); see generally Frank Faulkner, "Kindergarten Killers: Mortality, Murder and the Child Soldier Problem," 22 *Third World Q*, 491-504 (2001).

[106] See Faulkner, *supra* note 105, at 500; see Shepler, *supra* note 105.

[107] Voker Druba, "The Problem of Child Soldiers," 48 *Int'l Rev. Educ.* 271, 271-77 (2002) (concluding that rehabilitation and reintegration are greatly hampered by lack of funds, and inadequate personnel and social institutions).

[108] Faulkner, *supra* note 105, at 492.

[109] *Id.* at 495.

[110] Id.

[111] *Id.* at 496.

[112] *Id.* at 500. The challenge of refugee children is more complex. *Id.*

[113] See Faulkner, *supra* note 105.

[114] See, e.g., John Dugard, "Reconciliation and Justice: The South African Experience," 8 *Transnat'l L. & Contemp. Probs.* 277, 310 (1998) (discussing restitution and public forgiveness in South Africa).

[115] See, e.g., Shepler, *supra* note 105.

[116] *Id.*

[117] Jeffrey D. Sachs, The *End of Poverty: Economic Possibilities for Our Time* ( Penguin Press, 2005, 81-84, 203-04) (describing how development aid has fallen in the last decade as diseases like AIDS and malaria have been endemic and how the IMF and World Bank have failed Africa).

[118] Stewart Frances, Lall Sanjaya, and Wangwe Samuel, *Alternative Development Strategies* (New York, 2003).

[119] S. Adepoju and R. Stewart, *African Studies Review* (2001, 103-74). George Mubanga is a journalist and radio commentator from Zambia who helped lay the foundation for South Africa's Truth and Reconciliation process through quietly meeting with communities and persuading their participation.

Africans living in Africa have benefited a lot from programs designed by organizations and countries in the western world that are aimed at improving the standard of living. This is very critical to planting the necessary seeds for building cultures of peace. For example, volunteers from Scandinavian countries, the United States, and Japan are playing a critical role helping millions of disadvantaged Africans and orphans who have lost their parents from AIDS.

[120] *Id.*

[121] Paul Vallely, "Gleneagles Did Succeed," *New Statesman*, July 3, 2006, at 4-26.

[122] Economist Sachs, like authors George Mubanga here and Ndi Richard Tanto earlier, promotes a clinical, or case-by-case, diagnostic evaluative approach, exemplified by conflict resolution's reflective practice, rather than a "one size fits all" approach to financial recovery. Sachs, *supra* note 117, at 83-84; see also *id.* at 101 (describing his negotiation of Bolivia's debt cancellation agreement, which became a template for debt cancellation).

[123] Journalist Mubanga plans to use conflict cost-risk-benefit analysis to explore the dire need for these options in a documentary film.

[124] Author Mubanga would appreciate hearing from bankruptcy lawyers concerned with the African debt crisis who could educate him about contemporary bankruptcy law and proceedings and help him explore possible correlations and avenues for African countries. He is particularly interested in learning more about Chapter 15, which incorporates the Model Law on cross-border bankruptcy drafted by the United Nations Commission on International Trade Law (UNCITRAL) in 1997. *11 U.S.C. § 1501* (2008). The law allows U.S. courts/judges to issue subpoenas (orders) as circumstances dictate on bankruptcy proceedings that involve foreign countries. The main consideration of U.S. courts and judges when handling cases of this nature depends on whether the conduct of a creditor or debtor violates laws of public policy in the United States and does not conform to basic rules of procedural fairness. See *11 U.S.C. § 1506.*

[125] Sachs, *supra* note 117, at 90-92. He had studied the Great Depression and mechanisms to help "extricate countries from bankruptcy." *Id.* at 90. He currently acts as an impartial, trusted outside advisor to many countries in such crisis. See The Earth Institute at Columbia University, Full Bio: Prof. Jeffrey D. Sachs, <http://www.earth. columbia.edu/articles/view/1770> (last visited Mar. 20, 2009).

[126] Sachs, *supra* note 117, at 190-209 (emphasizing that corruption is only one of many complex variables responsible for Africa's deep poverty).

[127] M. Lancet, "Making Healthy a G8 Priority," *The Lancet* 368:259 (2005).

[128] Adepoju and Stewart, *supra* note 119.

[129] Lancet, *supra* note 127.

[130] Adepoju and Stewart, *supra* note 119.

[131] See *supra* note 3 and accompanying text.

[132] See Africa Action, <http://www.stwr.org/africa/cancel-africas-debt.html> (last visited Mar. 20, 2009).

[133] *Id.*

[134] Global Issues, "New Report Reveals Third World Debt Package Failings," <http://www.globalissues.org/article/227/new-report-reveals-third-world-debt-package-failings> (last visited Mar. 20, 2009).

[135] Gunter G. Bernhard and Hussain M. Nureldin, "External Shocks and the HIPC Initiative: Impacts on Growth and Poverty in Africa," 17 *African Dev. Rev.* 461-92 (2005).

[136] See generally Erbe, *supra* note 3, at 393.

[137] See *id.*

[138] See *id.* at 371, 393.

[139] See generally *id.* at 393.

[140] See generally *id.*

[141] See Erbe, *supra* note 3, at 393.

[142] See Lancet, *supra* note 127; see also Sachs, *supra* note 117, at 192.

[143] Lancet, *supra* note 127; see also Sachs, *supra* note 117, at 192.

[144] See Dominick Salvator, "African Development Prospects: A Policy Modeling Approach" 49 (N.Y.: Taylor and Francis Ltd., 1989).

[145] See generally Lancet, *supra* note 127.

[146] *Id.*; see also Sachs, *supra* note 117, at 92. See *id.* for case study analysis of how he has helped other countries reverse this downward spiral and an argument that Africa must drastically increase its crop yields and transportation networks.

[147] See Gerald Lenoir, "Shaping the Debate, American Friends Service Committee," <http://www.afsc.org/AfricaLifeOverDebt/ht/d/ContentDetails/i/18919>.

[148] *Id.*

[149] See Sachs, *supra* note 117.

Section VI

# Mediation at Its Best Builds Democratic Capacity

> "I thought that democracy comes from government. I realized that we . . . have to create healthy democratic society. . . . Conflict seminars are very helpful for increasing the well-being of our society. He did a great and important job. He directed our mind to think about democracy! I discovered that I'm not as democratic as I thought. . . . All of this showed me that I am not what I hoped . . . and how to become what I like . . . open-minded and democratic" (Erbe 2004).

> "Lincoln's role with slavery models requisite impartiality in regards to stakeholder and institutional alliances and pressure. If political fraternity had been a priority, Lincoln may have allowed states to spread slavery without interference. If he had revered the judicial system as sacred, slavery would have prevailed. While Lincoln obviously did not mediate the end of slavery and held strong personal convictions regarding slavery, his ability to act with independent integrity under pressure from powerful interests provides inspiration for mediators of political and other high stake battles" (Erbe 2006).

Mediation's potential for remedying our most pressing global concerns, while increasingly recognized by practitioners and local communities, is still largely unnoticed by scholars. Good governance—the optimal exertion of societal influence for effective democratic culture—is arguably our most pressing global need.[1] As introduced in earlier sections, one of mediation's ideal contributions is democratic capacity-building.[2] In Latin America, mediation has served as a "catalyst for judicial reform."[3] The role of the ombudsman,[4] which is increasingly one of mediation, has proven effective at combating corruption.[5] Mediation can be more impartial, fair, and reliable than any one party's courts. This section's analysis of international interviews and case studies suggests that mediation advances good governance, at micro and macro levels of society, by heightening inclusive participation, decision-making by all, and stakeholder responsiveness. Impartiality is critical to mediation's governance legacy, along with transparency and accountability. Yet these keys to good governance are vulnerable to abuse given the private setting in which mediation occurs. If mediators and parties to mediation fail to safeguard the integrity of their process, mediation's growing popularity may erode rather than elevate good governance.

This section further serves as a foundation for future research[6] by identifying the many links between mediation and good governance. It introduces mediation's global contribution to academics and practitioners in the fields of dispute[7] and conflict[8] resolution. Simultaneously, it describes the mediation process that can best serve the needs of international development.

The role that stakeholders play in mediations is an important focus. Inclusive participation and accountability benefit the public good since they tend to safeguard impartiality and transparent access to information. When done properly, mediation responds to the needs and interests of all stakeholders.[9]

This section examines many forms of mediation: ombuds mediation, mediated decisions, policy and rule making, facilitated dialogues in ethnic conflicts that mirror mediation, and mediated litigation. In the global context, mediation includes intractable conflict involving complex issues of ethnicity and identity.[10]

This section argues that the relationship between growing uses of mediation and good governance deserves scrutiny. The goal is to facilitate mediation's positive contribution to good governance by guarding against abuses of power. Civil society mediation, while less visible, may be growing faster than the traditional international mediation that occurs between nation-states. At the very least, it is important to understand the impact of such dynamics.[11] For example, as the United Nations (U.N.) has reported, "there is a dearth of works that go deeply beyond the rhetorical and give practical guidance on ways that governance systems and structures can address power inequality."[12]

To this end, this section utilizes academic literature, available case study data,[13] and interviews with experts. The list of experts includes: (1) a mediation faculty member who consults with business throughout Latin America, (2) a scholar from Northern Ireland who focuses on South Africa's truth and reconciliation process, (3) a mediation friendly corporate counsel for a Fortune 500 transnational corporation, (4) a prominent entertainment mediator with an international practice, (5) a mediator working throughout the Pacific Rim, (6) a published expert on mediated environmental process who consults with the U.N., (7) the former head of ADR for one of the leading U.S. bar associations who has consulted internationally, (8) an artist-mediator who was born and continues to work in Israel, (9) the Secretary General for an international NGO, (10) a restorative justice practitioner working internationally with her focus in Latin America, and (11) the International Development Policy Officer for a member country of the European Union. Their perspective is integrated throughout this section and shaped its organization.[14]

The case studies analyzed here illustrate the links between mediation and the most popular criteria for evaluating governance.[15] International references for analyzing these evaluative criteria include South Africa's mediated Peace Accords, the International Monetary Fund's (hereinafter "IMF") ombuds-mediator, and the United Nations Economic Commission for Europe's (hereinafter "UNECE") Convention on Access to Information, Public Participation in Decision-Making and Access to Justice in Environmental Matter (hereinafter "AARHUS"). Although AARHUS was not mediated, it is nevertheless lauded as advancing the democratization of international institutions and illustrates mediation's potential for advancing good governance. The research evaluating multicultural mediation led by civil society[16] introduced earlier in this book (and reviewed again here in Part 4) provides data to further analyze mediation and governance. Feedback from students of mediation representing over 70 countries supplements this global evaluation.[17]

How do outsiders discern whether mediation is likely to advance governance with diverse communities around the world? This section asserts that academics, practitioners, and stakeholders must strive collectively to identify common ground as they evaluate mediation's role in governance. Such common ground is a prerequisite for evaluating mediation's multicultural and global usefulness.

This section is primarily descriptive, noting patterns of mediation and governance in diverse contexts at various levels of society, reflecting the stakeholder influence identified by scholars of multitrack diplomacy and governance. Mediation is increasingly the mechanism of choice in a wide range of global forums for exerting influence in the face of conflict. This is not to suggest that the mediations reviewed in this book are the same—in impact or process. Much research potential exists for contrasting these small- versus large-scale efforts in detail and depth. Nevertheless, the mediation reviewed here, whether small or large, demonstrates its undisputable and growing global popularity. Most important for this book's purpose, the range of diverse contexts provides the data needed to begin noticing and questioning the relationships between mediation and good governance, or true democratization.

The time is ripe for scholars to note mediation's impact in the global context. This section begins by defining good governance. The definition acknowledges the interaction of various players and identifies criteria for evaluating governance. It then goes on to define mediation in relation to evolving global governance, particularly its popular capacity for impartiality which empowers local communities and brings them together with societal leadership. This section, like section four, distinguishes between traditional authoritative and non-traditional, facilitative mediation.

It is tempting to become prescriptive. The significant overlap between facilitative mediation at its best and the criteria proposed for evaluating governance naturally leads to the prescriptive question: Should mediation be promoted for advancing good governance globally? Discerning the answer is quite an ambitious task and requires longitudinal study beyond this book's capacity.[18] It does attempt two modest prescriptive arguments: (1) global mediation and its role with good governance deserve more attention, and (2) the remarkable parallels and overlaps between mediation and the most popular criteria for evaluating governance indicate that mediation is well-suited for promoting good governance. Outside researchers, as well as those intimately connected with a particular mediation process, can scrutinize these conclusions, case by case, asking whether that process is internally and externally advancing or eroding governance. Assessing whether mediation's internal satisfaction of the criteria for good governance contributes to broader societal and global governance will vary depending on each mediation's import. Easier to imagine is that allowing mediations to circumvent the criteria for good governance will hurt broader governance by, for example, allowing stakeholders to "hide behind closed doors" or feign broad and diverse participation, and equal and inclusive decision-making.

The section ends stressing mediation's capacity for building consensus between diverse interests, building relationships, and creating durable resolutions for efficient use of resources, thus satisfying two criteria used for evaluating the quality of governance. A myopic focus on efficiency can create rather than resolve problems. Relationships must be strong enough to build a lasting consensus. Practical suggestions are offered on how to discern whether mediation is the most efficient alternative for effective dispute resolution.

## Defining Good Governance

In its literal meaning, governance is the act of governing. Understanding how acts of governing have changed in recent years and continue to change lays an essential foundation for beginning to evaluate governance and mediation. Many assume that governance merely describes governmental activities. Governance, as defined by contemporary scholars, however, is much different. It is nontraditional and defies easy explanation. The nation-state's nature and role has altered dramatically in recent decades. It is increasingly dependent on and constrained by civil society, regional and international bodies, and transnational mechanisms such as the global market.[19] At contemporary governance's core is the transfer of powers, responsibilities, and rights from governments to civil society's groups and movements, requiring collective action around shared interests.[20] As will become evident throughout this section, historic boundaries and distinctions between nation-states and their communities are increasingly blurred.[21] New players affecting governance include regional and international groups, transnational corporations and NGOs, as well as global communities. Shifting networks of influence and information rather than predictable discrete entities are more and more likely to shape dispute and conflict resolution. As a result, collaborative mechanisms seeking to encourage deliberative and interactive relationships between these new networks, stakeholders,[22] and government are necessarily emerging.[23]

Once the reader starts to understand the web of relationships and influence now described as governance, the next step is to appreciate mediation as the growing thread connecting these relationships. Mediation, or third-party facilitation, for reasons yet to be explored here, is one of the few predictable constants bridging diverse, seemingly unrelated, contexts:

> Many studies have noted that an actor with high centrality to a network will act as "facilitator" . . . to bring otherwise dispersed actors together to engage in mutually beneficial cooperation . . . entailing a change from an exclusive emphasis on turf to a more inclusive attitude toward integrative approaches that can bring together diffuse authority and resources . . . unique configurations of actors around specific projects.[24]

Could mediation prove to be the core of contemporary governance? Its frequent presence as the mechanism for organizing and navigating diverse stakeholders at all societal levels[25] facing a range of issues motivated this section's inquiry.

Scholars go so far as to include mediation in their descriptions of governance, at times interchanging mediation and governance. The UN Economic and Social Commissions for Asia and Pacific (hereinafter "UNESCAP") is one noteworthy example, defining governance as "the process of decision-making and the process by which decisions are implemented. . . . It is the complex mechanisms, processes, relationships, and institutions through which citizens and groups articulate their interests, exercise their rights and obligations, and mediate their differences."[26] In short, mediation might represent the contemporary paradigm for governance.

This modern evolution may challenge those envisioning traditional government which does not include mediation among diverse interests. In light of shifting political and social realities, however, governance must now encompass what former Ambassador McDonald coins "multitrack diplomacy."[27] This comprehensive term acknowledges the influences of many different actors: NGOs,[28] professional and ethnic groups, businesses,[29] citizens, academics, activists, religions, philanthropists,[30] the media, and governments.[31] Negotiations between these key groups[32] influence, and often determine, the state of governance globally.[33]

Astute observers of international events will readily accept the growing influence of the powerful, organized, and visible interests of civil society, including transnational organizations, NGOs, businesses, churches, and the media, but may struggle with comprehending the role of more diffuse, seemingly less powerful groups of civil society, such as citizens or professional and ethnic communities. Scholars describing emerging global governance do not restrict their lists of stakeholders or processes to the most powerful. Instead, they emphasize negotiated networks, "associative governance," and "state-society synergy."[34] Less powerful roles, responsibilities, and rights, particularly those exercised in social movements and informal as well as formal social networks, are also key to a comprehensive understanding of emerging global governance and influence. For example, like academics, a range of professions are present at the mediations reviewed in this book. Of course, their power will differ from process to process, but their global networks spread information and build influence.

Civil society includes social movements, with shared ideology and goals, as well as groups. The noteworthy global surge in human rights awareness and litigation exemplifies the influence of a civil society initiative in the form of a social movement. Under human rights law, any alleged victim-citizen is free to initiate international dispute resolution. With civil society's support and leadership, many are exercising their rights.

Citizen power, in relation to the mediation studied here, looks like that of an informal social movement,[35] or a network, as well as the power exercised in discrete mediations where governance mandates citizen participation. "Ordinary" community members are considered important stakeholders in mediations along with more powerful interests, such as those of business and government. They are present in the international mediations reviewed in this book, negotiating concerns regarding the community impact of a Peruvian mine and South Africa's post-apartheid future, as two striking examples. Citizen participation is increasingly personal as well as representative. Citizens elect representatives to negotiate certain issues, while simultaneously participating in conflict processes in which they personally negotiate the resolution.

One discrete case of citizen-to-citizen mediation is miniscule compared to the mediation described above involving powerful stakeholders and international decision-making. Yet the global movement of citizen mediation is a growing alternative to traditional government decision-making—strong enough to attract the attention of political scientists. Obviously mediation between powerful interests will differ from that which occurs between citizens, but that difference only builds the case for giving the relationships between governance and mediation the scholarly attention they deserve. Less powerful interests are generally less visible and do not receive the media scrutiny of more powerful interests. As a result, their mediations are more likely to raise the concerns related to the good governance criteria of transparency and accountability analyzed later in this book. Can we assess the global cumulative impact of these individual cases? Not likely, but nevertheless we must consider: How does one concerned about mediation and good governance evaluate a popular global "movement" promoting a mechanism of informal and private governance that is uncoordinated and unpredictable? Studying this trend is key to satisfying governance criteria that require broad participation and consensus-building among diverse interests and that a state empower its citizenry.[36]

Like multitrack diplomacy and peace-building, the relationships between mediation and good governance must be examined at all levels of society. Once again, UNESCO describes these contemporary acts of governing as:

> The ceaseless culture-creating activity that characterizes the social body involves interaction at every level, from the intrapersonal . . . to the interpersonal—in

> household, neighborhood, community, on through successive levels of civic organization from city to the United Nations. . . . There is a constant interpenetration of levels . . . [with] patterns developed in every domain, from the individual and the interpersonal to the national, and interenvironmental.[37]

Thus, this book presents a range of case studies, small-scale corporate and citizen mediation, along with international processes. Once again, they are not equated—in process or impact. They represent numerous distinctions for future comparison. The threads that bind them, however, are central to this book's purpose: all demonstrate mediation's growing popularity around the world. All provide data for questioning mediation's role in governance at various levels of societies, particularly the criteria proposed for evaluating governance.

The four community focus regions of this book—Cameroon, the Balkans, Nepal, and Ukraine—illustrate the growing role of mediation within this new paradigm for governance. In Cameroon, readers will remember, a religious NGO, Ecumenical Service for Peace, prepares political leaders and community members for mediation. As a result of its efforts, there are now nonviolent conflict resolutions instead of the prior violence that had claimed two hundred lives.[38]

In the Balkans, the Nansen Network, another NGO, facilitated cross-ethnic dialogue among citizens, diverse professions (psychologists, educators, and engineers) and the media.[39] Their initiative aimed to "overcome consequences of recent wars through interethnic dialogue and cooperation."[40] Participants in these dialogues reported increased optimism.[41]

In both Nepal and Ukraine, citizens mediated disputes with each other through a court mandate and NGO leadership, respectively. Mediated disputes were their alternative to relying on government determination and enforcement.[42]

To grasp mediation's far-reaching role in changing global governance, the reader must first grapple with modern governance's complex and dynamic network of stakeholders, relationships, movements, and influences. Interplay between diverse interests and forces—powerful through status, organization, influence and popularity—increasingly governs global society. How does one evaluate the effectiveness of process and outcome? A body of international experts and social scientists devote themselves to evaluating governance.[43] Their consensus is reported here. Experts agree on the following attributes for evaluating both process, such as participation and rule of law, and outcome, such as efficient use of resources. These recommended attributes listed below will be referenced throughout this section when examining the relationships between mediation and governance.

Eight interdependent characteristics are most often identified with good governance: (1) broad participation in governance that reflects the diversity of the community (ethnic and gender) as well as freedom of association and expression,[44] (2) the rule of law, including human rights,[45] enforced fairly and impartially,[46] (3) transparency,[47] (4) consensus-based mediation between the diverse stakeholders stressed in the first criterion above where all discuss and agree to sustainable decisions,[48] (5) inclusive decision-making, once again between the myriad societal interests referenced earlier, (6) efficient use of resources, (7) responsiveness to stakeholders' interests,[49] and (8) accountability.[50] Exploring global scholars' rationale for selecting these particular criteria for good governance is beyond this section's scope, but readers are referred to the extensive scholarship.[51]

## Mediation's Relationship with Good Governance

As defined earlier, mediation[52] is any force outside of a particular conflict that assists with negotiation,[53] resolution,[54] and transformation of that conflict.[55] The mediation reviewed in this book is much more narrowly defined, emphasizing the particular type of mediation that overlaps with and has the potential for advancing good governance as described above. Traditionally, government leaders have mediated international disputes. While state-compelled mediation is still seen, particularly in response to political crisis, it is increasingly complemented by informal, collaborative, and facilitated processes initiated by international organizations, such as the U.N., and members of civil society, such as NGOs, business, and citizens—all the groups identified earlier as influential with informal diplomacy.[56]

One Pacific Rim mediator observes that "sophisticated parties are now no longer willing to allow a third party (whether government or mediator) to . . . make decisions that impact matters fundamental to their personal and business lives."[57] These stakeholders want to control their disputes. Development experts concur.[58] Sustainability requires participation and local ownership.[59] Excessive reliance on outside experts who attempt to act for parties rather than empower them to act on their own behalf has not worked.[60]

At the same time, the growing popularity of facilitative mediation (large and small scale) where parties and communities (professional and expert) are empowered to come together, make their own decisions through consensus-building, and take responsibility for the consequences, is impossible to ignore.[61] For this book, mediation's scope encompasses "facilitated face-to-face dialogue . . . allowing communication, understanding, rehumanization of the enemy, reframing of the conflict as a shared problem to be solved[,] . . . moving towards inclusive processes of mutual empowerment" and "drawing on integrative methods . . . emphasizing the joint responsibility of the parties for approaching their problems in a way that respects the interests, need and values of all."[62]

As introduced earlier, in facilitative mediation the parties lead their own process. The mediator simply facilitates and coaches parties.[63] The University of Washington's Institute for Environmental Mediation describes mediation as a process in which "those involved in a dispute jointly explore and reconcile their differences. The mediator has no authority to impose a settlement."[64]

Lebanon is one archetype of postwar reconstruction embracing facilitative mediated processes at the community level, with a focus on development.[65] Lebanon is a culturally rich nation with religious (Muslim and Christian) and social diversity (including Arabs, Palestinians, Kurds, and Armenians), which disintegrated into civil war in 1975. Among Lebanon's innovative postwar grassroots mediation processes is a community relations board that will mediate local dispute resolution.[66] Intracommunity and interreligious dialogue is also being used to elicit local views and guide expression in constructive ways. It is being used to bring local and national leaders together on priority issues of shared concern and create ideas for reconciliation.[67]

The overlap between the mediation as defined here and the most popular criteria proposed for evaluating governance is undeniable. Thus each part of this section will focus on one or more of these governance criteria and explore mediation's specific contribution to that particular criterion as reported from the field. They will include concerns and recommendations related to advancing mediation's positive contribution to good governance. The first part focuses on criteria four and six—sustainable consensus-building and efficiency, the second on criterion one, broad, diverse community participation, and the third, equal, inclusive decision-making; then criteria two and seven: impartial responsiveness to stakeholders, and last, criteria three and eight: transparency and accountability.

## Part 1: Build Efficient Consensus between Diverse Interests for Sustainability

Mediation naturally comes to mind when considering the good governance criteria of consensus-building among diverse interests for sustainable resolution and efficient use of resources, whether mediating a cross-ethnic dialogue across a nation or litigation between those from different countries.[68] Simple logic advocates that agreements reached by consensus are more sustainable and easier to implement than those imposed or forced. With community stakeholders consciously creating space for dialogue, communication and positive debate naturally increases civil society's buy-in and the resultant responsibility for implementing change.[69] Both are essential characteristics of sustainable reform.[70] With both community and business stakeholders, some cultures prefer informal opportunities to resolve disputes rather than formal, adversarial forums. Mediation is often lauded for being less expense and time-consuming than litigation.[71] Mediation's legitimate potential for efficiently using resources reduces expense and time through collaborative consensus-building rather than adversarial dispute resolution. This is one of its recognized contributions to good governance, satisfying criterion six as well as part of criterion four described above. In evaluating whether mediation advances good governance, though, the fourth and sixth criteria, in their entirety, must be satisfied through efficient and long-term sustainable consensus-building. Increased speed alone does not constitute good governance unless the resolution lasts. Presumably all participants must accept the legitimacy of the process and the outcome. "It is of the highest moment that those who administer justice should always act under public responsibility, and that every citizen should be able to satisfy himself with his own eyes [that] . . . a public duty is performed."[72] Only then, when mediation builds lasting agreement among diverse interests, is there true efficiency as described by scholars evaluating governance. Thus, if litigation resolves conflict entirely but mediation leads to a series of disputes, litigation may be the most efficient route. Conversely, if on-going mediation is necessary to move forward with seemingly intractable conflict like that in South Africa and the Middle East, where no other conflict mechanism shows potential, mediation, when contrasted with the costs of on-going escalating conflict, is arguably the most efficient alternative in line with good governance.

## The Efficiency Illusion

Efficient use of resources is the sixth criterion recommended for evaluating governance. A myopic focus on costs alone, however, can hinder good governance by prohibiting lasting sustainable consensus among diverse interests.[73] Economic concerns can overwhelm the dispute resolution process and impede deliberation.[74] Rewarding quick results, for instance, discourages a participatory process. Cost pressures often curtail work with the most marginalized.[75] A short-sighted view of efficiency can even create the illusion of success while masking ineffectiveness, breaking trust, and creating backlash.[76] Interestingly, dispute resolution experts fault contracts for their failure to accommodate the complex terms of collaborative efforts.[77] Myopic contracts sabotage efficiency. Contract clauses are needed that represent and require the best of what is described throughout this book.

The experts interviewed here understand that taking the time to recognize and address real differences in stakeholder perspectives is critical. Agenda-setting prevents oversimplification and elucidates important issues.[78] Social, economic, and equity questions "may take time to emerge."[79]

In the face of contentious conflict, a collaborative process like mediation may be the most efficient of options. "Political wrangling" and judicial review can prolong conflict for years, without any benefit.[80] Mediated process is sometimes the only way to move forward when there is an impasse or costly escalation.[81] The reader will remember that after two years of violent conflict resulting in several deaths, the Bafanji and Balikumbat villages in Cameroon received over three years of targeted assistance in mediation techniques. Community members from these villages are now resolving a variety of issues via mediation.[82]

An on-going process, rather than ad hoc meetings, can improve the likelihood of success.[83] Some mediations only take five to ten months, but others may last for years.[84] The Nansen Network, for example, started mediating cross-ethnic dialogue in the Balkans before the first NATO bombs in 1999,[85] and is still aspiring to improve cross-ethnic relationships throughout the region. To address such violent and complex conflicts, the parties may have to abandon time limits.[86] Efficacy, or the power to achieve desired, sustainable results, is the key to ferreting out flawed attempts at efficiency that avoid addressing tough issues and thus create additional conflict and costs for the future.

## Start with Sufficient Relationships

Fortunately, scholars of good governance acknowledge the need for both the efficient use of resources and the sustainability, or efficacy, derived from consensus. Mediation's growing popularity and contribution to good governance may be due to its ability to facilitate agreement between diverse contentious interests to create durable resolutions.

Those interviewed for this book recognize the importance of balancing the competing goals of cost-effectiveness and relationship-building.[87] They further value mediation's role in crafting creative resolutions and preserving party reputations.

The criteria used here for evaluating governance do not explicitly mention relationships. They do stress mediation of diverse interests, consensus-building, and sustainable resolution. All, like facilitative mediation itself, implicitly require some degree of relationship, communication, and interaction. Thus, literature and interview data commending mediation's role in relationship building is referenced below.

While business is often identified with efficiency, here business provides substantial data that emphasize mediation's global contribution to building sustainable relationships between those from different countries and cultures. Professor Antonio Mendoza, who consults throughout Latin America, believes that mediation facilitates foreign direct investment, and more specifically, joint ventures requiring horizontal relationships, between foreign corporations or business and local government, for example.[88] While investment agreements will contain traditional rule-of-law provisions, joint ventures also require cooperative relationships and consensus-building among diverse interests.[89] When investment agreements only consider the company's self-interest, or neglect to attempt consensus-building among the diverse interests affected by the agreement, they risk sacrificing durable relationships with those possessing less clout.[90] This awareness motivated IMF's creation of an ombuds-mediator in response to NGO complaints.[91] The IMF mediator now prioritizes listening to diverse perspectives and otherwise building relationships with those affected by investments. With a Peruvian mine, for instance, community members, employees, academics, NGOs and other interested stakeholders were invited to participate in conflict resolution process.[92]

Dr. Kishan Khoday concurs with Professor Mendoza, further asserting that relationships, and not rules, have "emerged to manage conflicts between the mandates of public agencies, the interests of business and the values of civil society groups in defining the . . . boundaries of the new global economy."[93] While some formal rule of law has emerged, most law is "de facto . . . being developed and overseen by a diverse configuration of social relationships."[94]

As these global relationships grow, so does mediation and its popularity. In conversations with counsel for multinational corporations doing business in Asia, one researcher found that companies preferred mediation over the court system.[95] "Mediation cuts through a great deal of bureaucracy and can allow parties to face each other and resolve their differences in an informal way."[96] There are cultures and countries, like Japan, that prioritize relationships and inherently wish to avoid adversarial proceedings.[97] In a study of 60 major corporations, 81 percent of respondents judged mediation as more satisfactory than litigation, with 59 percent highlighting the preservation of relationships.[98] The most popular corporate dispute resolution option is mediation. Arbitration, mediation-arbitration, in-house grievance and fact finding, peer review, and ombuds intervention are secondary.

Mediation's success in the Philippines shows its interpersonal and analytical strengths for building sustainable consensus. Mediators were rated highly for both communication and problem-solving skills. Evaluating parties described the traits of their effective mediators as: (1) the ability to identify problems and issues, (2) patience, (3) sensitivity, (4) listening with no pressure to settle, and (5) impartiality.[99]

As introduced earlier, community evaluations of mediation in the Balkans, Cameroon, Nepal, and Ukraine also report successful strengthening of relationships: "I found helpful the knowledge to resolve conflicts peacefully and restoratively in my community pregnant with conflict . . . the improvement of my social relationships with friends, neighbors and even long time enemies."[100]

In Cameroon, these relationships helped form consensus between community members and political leadership.[101] Since receiving mediation training, both have cooperated in conflicts over construction, alleged theft, health care, and education.[102]

Likewise, the Ukrainian Center for Common Ground encourages diverse groups to confront issues involving unemployment, religious tensions, and discrimination. The project starts with discussion and the goal of building sustainable relationships between participants so they will continue to work together in their communities.[103]

The Balkans dialogue project explicitly states that it "provides social interference (in ethnic wars) through personal contacts."[104] Dialogue participants appreciated opportunities for cross-cultural teamwork.[105] They specifically valued opportunities to hear and understand others' feelings, views, perceptions, needs, and ideas. As a result, participants self-reported the strengthening of cross ethnic relationships.

How do the stronger cross-cultural relationships, understanding, and collaboration resulting from the mediation described above contribute to good governance? The community case studies from the Balkans, Cameroon, Nepal, and

Ukraine strongly illustrate mediation's value to good governance. In all, mediated consensus-building served many diverse interests, satisfying part of the fourth criterion for evaluating governance. Participants recognized their growing understanding of complex conflict dynamics within their broader communities.[106] Many express faith in consensus, viewing it as easier to implement than less collaborative forms of decision-making.[107] Cameroon's experience provides particular hope. While it may be sui generis, it builds a case for the importance of testing mediation's potential to advance nonviolent governance. If the process results in more efficient, sustainable decision-making than alternatives to mediation, both the fourth and the sixth good governance criteria are met. In short, "[a] good working relationship allows us to handle our differences efficiently."[108]

## Design Mediation for Maximum Efficiency

It makes sense to consider mediation only if it adds value or creates resilient efficiency, strategically balancing efficiency with relationship-building as needed. Mediation's facilitated consensus-building benefits more complex conflicts involving diverse stakeholders and long-term relationships.[109]

Can we design models for assessing conflict intricacy and educating those concerned of the value of mediation in facilitating durable resolution of the most challenging disputes? The optimal guide would help parties maximize efficiency and ensure durability through investment in the mediation of diverse interests as necessary. It can begin to do this by linking and delinking issues. This same or another model could further guide parties in agenda setting or prioritizing of issues. A transnational mining corporation and a global network of environmental NGOs developed the beginnings of such a guide.[110] Their matrix rates the biodiversity importance of 57 different operational areas, thereby directing attention to the areas of greatest importance.[111]

Mediation inherently delineates and prioritizes party issues. The process envisioned here would be similar but occur prior to mediation—it would help parties decide whether mediation is necessary and represents their most efficient alternative. It makes sense to reserve mediation energy for the most intractable problems, rather than squandering scarce resources on trivial disputes.[112] Arbitration, for example, often efficiently creates lasting resolution with straightforward business issues involving two parties from different countries. Such dispute resolution can eliminate easily resolved issues. Mediation, however, may be essential to progress with disputes involving more than two parties, issues that are not readily resolved, or the valuing of reputations and lasting relationships.

## Part 1, Notes and Questions

1. Start to identify your global concerns. Possibilities identified (directly and indirectly) in this section include: (1) environmental sustainability, (2) human rights, (3) democracy capacity building, (4) sustainable development, (5) eradication of poverty, and (6) ethnic conflict.

   Do you know how mediation, negotiation and other conflict skills are being used with your particular concern(s)? Research and find at least one case study example. Share and discuss.

2. How could mediation, negotiation, and other conflict skills be used with the concern(s) you identified above? Outline your utopian vision. Share and discuss.

3. Identify a decision, involving two or more decision-makers, that felt good to you and otherwise met your criteria for optimal decision-making. List your criteria in concrete specific detail. Compare your criteria to this section's criteria for measuring good governance. How are they the same? Different? Share and discuss.

4. Over a period of time, like the next week, notice and journal all issues of concern to you. Once you have a list, for each issue consider many ways it might be effectively addressed, including avoidance and passage of time, some form of interpersonal communication, skilled negotiation and mediation.

   Which of the options you have identified above are the most efficient and likely to lead to satisfactory resolution that lasts? When is mediation necessary?

   In other words, when and how does mediation add value? Share and discuss.

5. Try acting as a mediator in a negotiation or conflict process. Considering the skills and attitudes introduced in this book's first chapters, what might you try to improve relationships? What might promote cooperation or advance consensus? Try at least one of your ideas; share and discuss the results.

6. What aspects of a democracy are most important to you—important enough that you would invest in preserving if in danger of losing? Freedoms protected by law (speech, association . . . )? Equal protection (against violence in your home or community . . . )? Equal opportunity (education . . . )? Protection against corrupt leaders? Social security?

    Which of the above seem idealistic to you and not yet part of your life experience?

    Do any matter enough for you to work for their advancement and fruition? If so, how might you do this?

## Part 2: Including All

While mediation is inherently a multi-stakeholder process,[113] satisfying part of the fifth criterion for evaluating governance, inclusive decision-making with true power sharing, not all multistakeholder processes constitute mediation. In fact, many of the ineffective multistakeholder processes that occur are not mediated.[114] These processes exclude important constituencies.[115] This type of exclusion is unlikely to occur in a well-run mediation. Inclusion can be described in two ways characterizing mediation's contribution to optimal governance through the facilitation of broad, diverse participation. First, inclusive conflict process is thorough and includes all significant interests. Second, it consciously seeks the participation of the most contentious and potentially difficult stakeholders, including the most marginalized. Arguably their presence, when skillfully mediated will increase the likelihood of a lasting resolution.

### Facilitate Inclusive Process

Actors concerned with pressing international issues, such as ethnic conflict, are enthusiastically pioneering the mediated multistakeholder process.[116] They aspire to overcome feelings of exclusion, to engage diverse stakeholders and their opinions, and to facilitate inclusive decision-making. Engaging diverse participants is particularly important in ethnic conflicts. Burmese activists, for example, are asking international bodies, such as the U.N., for inclusive participation. They would like to be welcomed to negotiate.[117]

Ethnic conflicts are often the product of regimes that promote feelings of exclusion with certain groups. If the purpose of transitional justice is to move toward greater egalitarianism, it is essential to overcome feelings of exclusion and ensure that decision-making about basic rules will enhance feelings of participation and inclusion.[118]

The results are promising, even revolutionary. Inclusion at its best offers ground-breaking, face-to-face contact for those warring parties who have never met.

The international experts interviewed here reiterate the importance of participation that includes local community leadership. It is particularly important to include those representing the groups historically most excluded or marginalized in decision-making to ensure equal inclusive decision-making.[119] One World Trust has devoted much research to evaluating effective participation ("engagement") in collaborative process.[120] Once again, its results highlight the importance of including the most marginalized groups. Susan Opotow proposes inclusion at all societal levels and across all subpopulations, as aspired to in South Africa.[121] Those interviewed further commend care in maintaining the participation of those who lack time and resources.[122] "Before . . . any consensus process . . . can claim democratic legitimacy, one must know among whom the consensus was struck and that it in fact represented the consent of those whose assent is necessary."[123]

## Global Mediation's Inclusiveness

In tackling the toughest of conflicts, particularly those involving marginalized groups, the mediated multistakeholder process advances democratic self-determination by including those most often excluded in consensus-building. One of the most famous examples of mediated inclusive process leading democratic transition is the South Africa's Peace Accords. The mediating NGOs broadly included political organizations and parties, civic organizations, minority groups, security forces, businesses, trade unions, churches and the government. This mirrors the groups recognized earlier for their roles in multitrack diplomacy and contemporary governance.[124] A media campaign on television, radio, and the Internet, meetings in communities lacking media access, and wide circulation of a draft constitution for review, comment, and objections actively solicited opinions of marginalized and hard-to-reach groups.[125]

The IFC ombuds-mediator, in publicized work, likewise demonstrated comprehensive and inclusive participation of many, if not all, stakeholders affected. In response to NGO complaints about a mine financed in Peru, the mediator organized a series of conflict resolution and mediation trainings for 63 participants, including politicians and government staff involved with mining, community delegates selected for this particular process, mine employees, academics, members of the local chamber of commerce, and staff from various NGOs.[126]

Likewise, Kofi Annan praises AARHUS as "the most impressive elaboration of Principle 10 of the Rio Declaration, which stresses the need for citizens' participation in environmental issues and for access to information on the environment held by public authorities."[127] This process is lauded, compared to the negotiation of other environmental treaties, for its focus on the process of decision-making as well as its outcomes.[128] It is heralded as a model for multilateral policy-making, emulating the democratization of global institutions through the broad participation of diverse interests. Fifty-five countries of North America, Western, Central and Eastern Europe, and Central Asia participated.[129] Contentious NGOs engaged from the very beginning of the process, acting as advisors to UNECE while designing the process.[130]

## Equipped to Address Critique

Scholars and practitioners around the world regularly evaluate whether a multistakeholder process truly reflects the broad, diverse participation of stakeholders mandated for good governance. Even though AARHUS is noted for its allowance of NGOs as equal partners, it is also critiqued for its apparent failure to identify all of the necessary stakeholders, particularly those representing the general public, the interests of economic and social development, and others affected by the process.[131] Environmental NGOs may have dominated the AARHUS negotiation process, particularly "a handful of western NGOs with a very clear agenda."[132] The lawyers and academics present were aligned with these NGOs. It is uncertain whether business interests were involved at all.[133] NGOs may attempt to circumvent coordination of government and intergovernmental bodies, along with business, perceiving that well-coordinated government or business involvement dominates the process and distorts outcomes.[134]

While collaborative partnering occurred from the very beginning of AARHUS, apparently no consideration was given to mediation's ability to promote inclusive participation. An impartial third party would have advanced AARHUS's governance taking merely the steps followed in a "typical" mediation. Skilled convening of mediation, described in the next two paragraphs, increases the likelihood of the presence and direct voice of a broad array of interests rather than simply those who are more organized or powerful.[135] Lawsuits and party-initiated mediations often define disputes and identify stakeholders. Seasoned facilitative[136] mediators will nevertheless ask whether all of the parties who are crucial to creating a lasting resolution are present.

While mediators cannot force parties to include marginalized or contentious stakeholders, those who abide by popular ethical precepts will share their concerns regarding exclusion privately with resistant stakeholders.[137] Some mediators brainstorm options and propose ideas that address stakeholder concerns about including certain stakeholders. If these stakeholders insist on the exclusion of interests judged vital to good faith process, mediators can withdraw.[138] While mediator withdrawal does not solve the parties' conflict(s), at least withdrawal protects the integrity of the mediation process.

Mediating cross-ethnic conflict with the communities themselves almost ensures inclusion of marginalized groups. The community case studies referenced throughout this book self-identified and evaluated cross-ethnic mediation. Nepal's multicultural discussion demonstrated inclusion.[139] The Cameroon mediations likewise had diverse participants, from traditional political leadership to community members.[140] The Norwegian mediators who started the Balkans dialogue invited community members and professionals from conflicted and marginalized regions across the Balkans. These participants were then asked to recommend new participants, resulting in increasing inclusion and diversity of participants.[141]

Both civil society and government stakeholders must actively engage in mediation. If a government agency decides to be relatively passive, it hurts its own interests as well as those of the civil society (and vice versa).[142] About half of the case studies referenced in this book brought government and civil society together, including South Africa's Peace Accords, the negotiation of the AARHUS treaty, and the IFC ombuds-mediation process.[143]

In Cameroon, it is clear that government actively participated in mediation.[144] Cameroon mediations include traditional councils, rulers, and representatives.[145] Consequently, civil society is learning the value of working with government.[146]

The external study of mediations provides valuable data to help evaluate government and other stakeholder involvement. The IMF evaluation team, for example, found imperative that all stakeholders be prepared to support and monitor the ombuds-mediator's independent role.[147] While government often proclaims independent oversight, in reality, NGOs more often serve as the true watchdogs. Environmental Rights Action, for example, publicly alleged that the IMF ombuds failed to consult with a truly inclusive group of opinion leaders in examining Shell and IFC implementation of the Niger Delta Contractor Revolving Credit Facility.[148]

## Mediation Bridges Difference

Challenges grow with the increased diversity of participation mandated for good governance. Often participants addressing contentious issues like ethnic and environmental disputes bring assumptions and approaches quite alien to the collaboration needed to find common ground and develop the shared platform and culture of communication and negotiation.[149] As described in the AARHUS process, bringing all contending forces "to the table" is easier planned than implemented when facing power inequity and tension.[150] Difference in culture, perspective, and power requires in-depth consideration.

Moreover, an inevitable "clash of cultures," such as styles of problem-solving, surfaces even without ethnic and power differences. Those interviewed for this book mention the following experience. Engineers, scientists, and other experts are used to being acclaimed for professional achievement rather than their partnership with clients and community served or those affected by their findings.[151] Business leaders' focus on "making a profitable deal" may challenge the government's expectation of mandated, top-down authority. Various stakeholders may tolerate whatever means advance special interests.[152] Political culture can attract personalities who view mediation's open communication as foolish and who are used to manipulation and domination instead.[153] Lobbyists are rewarded for advocating for the interest that they represent as competitively as possible. Likewise, activist culture may be feared as it vilifies those with more privilege, while simultaneously facing accusations of co-option for participation alone. As a result, these groups are too often working at cross purposes.

The IMF ombuds-mediator epitomizes this challenge in its annual report. "The reality is that there is often a huge gap between the . . . cultures of the private sector companies that undertake IFC/MIGA projects and the communities . . . impacted by them. One of our basic jobs is to help IFC and/or MIGA to bridge that gap."[154]

Professor Naomi Roht-Arriza vividly captures the innate concrete conflict emerging from professional difference alone:

> Integrating post-conflict reconstruction and collective reparations seems . . . promising. Attempts to do so will, however, encounter difficulties based on differences in vocabulary, professional biases, restrictive mandates and ease of goals. Neither UNDP or the World Bank frames issues in terms of . . . justice . . . but rather in terms of repair . . . and . . . growth. . . .In part, this may be due to the predominance of lawyers in framing reparations . . . and the predominance of economists and engineers in . . . development. . . . Post-conflict work . . . involves merging . . . perspectives of conflict prevention, humanitarian assistance, human rights monitoring and traditional development cultures, each with its own "turf," time frame and policy prescriptions. Development . . . involves . . . shorter term and more measurable goals than moral and social reconstruction. It is easier to rebuild roads and bridges.[155]

She goes on to share this valuable insight. Sustainability for the private sector has some relationship to cost recovery, for NGOs it has a bearing on empowerment and community voice, and for the public sector it generally means technically sound and thus not needing to be addressed again in the future. These are not mutually exclusive concepts but they are significantly different starting points.

Fortunately, mediation once again provides recourse, offering several proven tools that have already been introduced and advocated. The first is in-depth interest analysis—fundamental to integrative bargaining with possible joint gains for parties.[156] Using integrative bargaining, those from different "cultures" do not necessarily need to change their thinking, or perceptions of risk and value, to move toward options satisfying more than one party. Experts in the fields of dispute and conflict resolution may assume integrative awareness with negotiators holding different goals, such as the protection of endangered species, creation of jobs, reduced infant mortality, and the production of essential resources.[157] Global practitioners, however, describe how many, if not most, stakeholders are entrenched in the distributive paradigm. Polarizing disputes by framing them as simple "either/or" win-loss assumes traditional distributive bargaining with an elementary linear logic where parties simply distribute or divide. Integrative bargaining, on the other hand, is designed for complexity and interdependence. When parties are confused and approach an integrative negotiation with distributive tactics and strategies, they unnecessarily limit themselves by focusing on differences; thus missing possibilities for progress. Integrative bargaining starts by presuming that expected and desired outcomes differ according to each stakeholder's views. By analyzing these "positions" for underlying interests rather than requiring change in mandates or frameworks, integrative bargaining reframes the conflict as a shared search for options that maximize satisfaction for all.

Integrative bargaining cannot be expected to be a magic panacea, particularly with complex conflict like that which is described here. Agreement to options for mutual gain requires rigorous evaluation of parties' aspirations, with in-depth appreciation of costs, risks, and benefits. Skilled or facilitated integrative bargaining, however, is designed to guide opposing parties through this creative search for satisfactory options in a tough and systematic way. In short, it is designed to meet challenges.

Those interviewed here further commend the importance of qualified and competent mediators.[158] Skilled mediators are facilitators and coaches in integrative negotiation, bridging cultural difference as explained above.[159] Most stakeholders need to learn how to truly broaden their decision-making approaches.

The partnership between Rio Tinto, a multinational mining company, and Bird Life International, a global network of environmental NGOs, exemplifies the integrative approach. Their objectives reflect mutual, or integrative, benefit, focusing equally on their diverse stakeholder interests of biodiversity, mining operations, and reputation.[160]

Optimally, interest analysis identifies common needs shared by parties to a conflict. Skillful mediation, through its building of party relationships, may even have potential to transform cultural identity as well as conflict. Susan Opotow describes a new conception of identity, the relational self, arising through recognizing affinity or "perceived resemblance to those with whom one has a common interest."[161] Opotow is a colleague of Yale psychologist Morton Deutsch, who pioneered related research demonstrating how recognizing and creating cross ties between ethnic groups can reduce conflict. Opotow theorizes that the process of identifying shared interests alone changes identity.

Mediation is well-suited for responding to the challenges posed by good governance's first criterion: broad participation of diverse stakeholders. As mentioned often throughout this book, through careful listening, insightful interest identification, particularly common interests bridging difference, and other tools of integrative bargaining, mediation effectively facilitates creative problem-solving by diverse stakeholders. It also furthers good governance's requisite consensus-building for sustainable resolution. In the face of contemporary "clash of cultures," mediation provides rare links.

# Part 3: Balance Power and Facilitate Equal Inclusive Decision-Making

International experts increasingly advocate the use of "transformative party-driven . . . bottom-up," or mediated, conflict resolution.[162] They recommend that citizens initiate the consensus-building of good governance in emerging democracies.[163] Others stress the importance of "allowing conflicts to be raised, fought over and resolved."[164] In many parts of the world, truly participatory institutions are needed to satisfy good governance's fifth criterion: equal and inclusive decision-making.

## Mediation, At Its Best, Builds Democratic Capacity

Some communities assert that the practice of mediated dialogue goes beyond broad participatory governance and actually instills a culture of peace into their violent societies.[165] Without an option like mediation, filling critical gaps in legal capacity, minority ethnic groups may see a violent struggle for independence as their only alternative.[166]

Cameroon's mediating NGO describes itself as creating a "society of participation based on peace, justice, reconciliation, and compassion."[167] Its ultimate goal is to empower self-sustaining collaboration. The participants in mediated cross-ethnic dialogue throughout the Balkans specifically described the concrete benefits of conflict resolution training in mediation[168] within an emerging democracy. They appreciated discovering new principles and ideas for building good governance through equal inclusive participation of diverse interests. Mediation, as described by Balkans participants, can train effective citizens of a democratic state. It provides concrete opportunities for individuals to wrestle with understanding others' perspectives, expressing their own interests, and otherwise exercising freedom of expression in conflict resolution. These are all essential to good governance's fifth criterion: inclusive decision-making with power balancing. The truly impartial mediator gives all parties an equal and public opportunity to be heard as part of providing democratic mediation (Note: readers are given questions and models later in this section to assist them in helping parties determine who is "truly impartial." This book does not attempt to introduce the many cultural challenges involved with encouraging open and public disclosure).[169] Although confronting differences can be difficult, those involved receive the opportunity to reach understanding, abandon "costly" attitudes,[170] and successfully balance rights and responsibilities in order to create lasting resolutions, further satisfying another criterion of good governance: sustainable consensus-building.

## Inclusive Power-Sharing Is Key

Up to this point, mediation's inherent capacity for advancing good governance has been stressed. Mediation, by the nature of its process, facilitates broad participation among diverse interests, freedom of expression, consensus-building for sustainable resolution, and efficiency. With the remaining criteria for good governance, however—equal and inclusive decision-making, impartiality, transparency, and accountability—mediation's presence has strong potential to either advance or erode governance. The IFC ombuds capture the challenge of mediating the power-balancing needed for equal and inclusive decision-making.

It is not easy for any major institution—be it a multinational corporation, a government agency, or a major financial institution—to become comfortable and proficient in doing business in a climate of escalating expectations regarding transparency, public trust, and accountability. . . . Senior management . . . will . . . contribute . . . best when there is sufficient sophistication within the corporate and on-site team to support healthy long-term enlightened self-interest.[171]

Likewise, a mediator working throughout the Pacific Rim sees the greatest challenge of global dispute resolution as mediation's evolution "from an ad hoc process to a more institutionalized one, whether that be within large global corporations, state court systems, or government to government."[172] How do we ensure the good governance criterion of equal inclusive decision-making, or power sharing, with mediation in the face of entrenched power accustomed to top-down decisions?

As processes from around the world are reviewed here, mediation's potential for either promoting or eroding good governance, particularly equal and inclusive decision-making, becomes clear. Good governance must be consistently linked by both mediators and stakeholders to conscious internal scrutiny of potential power abuse.

Such assessment is particularly important when a stakeholder has a history of power abuse, conscious or complicit. Transnational corporations have been involved, directly and indirectly, in the most violent and challenging of disputes, particularly in developing countries with oil, gas, and mineral resources. In one instance, guerrilla groups extorted money from contractors in Colombia.[173] Oil and gas rents can support corrupt governance. Even though Shell invested more than $33 million per year in community development for the Niger Delta, critics allege that corrupt officials and contractors siphoned off much of the money and that Shell aimed to "buy favors."[174] In a related example, a 2002 lawsuit accused several corporations and banks of aiding and abetting South Africa's apartheid government through their investments.[175]

Moyer and Haynes assert that a "properly functioning democratic society fosters the 'delimitation of government prerogatives and [creates] context for constraining arbitrary and intrusive state power.'"[176] When those with power abuse and ignore the rights of those they serve, they cannot be trusted to govern.[177] A government oppressing a group of citizens certainly cannot claim to be impartial.[178] Likewise, corporations aligning with corrupt governments cannot pretend to be mediating in good faith, as honest collaborators.

Can influence ever be equal in a decision-making process where some stakeholders are politically more powerful? To answer this critical question, three issues will be explored: (1) Are those concerned with a particular mediation, mediators and stakeholders, aiming for true power-sharing or tolerating corruption? (2) Do the most powerful stakeholders commit to decisions made with the less powerful? (3) Do all stakeholders, irrespective of power, perceive and report equal treatment and participation?

Democratic mediation, as used here, describes the mediation process in which participants themselves describe internal democracy. As a start, equal treatment of all parties, irrespective of power, is necessary.[179] Specifically, all concerned—mediators and stakeholders—must consider and respect everyone's input. Researcher Baruch found that the most satisfied parties to mediation report the highest process control, participation in decision-making, and freedom of expression.[180] Students of mediation from over 60 countries identify multicultural equivalence (i.e., inclusion of all voices) as the most important variable of exemplary cross-cultural mediation.[181]

Yet the institution of mediation itself can be corrupt. It is not enough for one participant in a mediation to assert equality. All participants must confirm inclusive decision-making and power-sharing. To preserve credibility and garner support, mediation must find ways to generate sincere collaboration that adequately considers power imbalance. Aspiring to genuine collaboration requires the naming and confrontation of power abuse, partiality, bad faith, and the other corrupt behaviors described earlier. As mentioned above, including victims of corruption in mediation with the actors whose behavior is allegedly corrupt increases the likelihood that these concerns will surface.

Developing civic society strong enough to weaken, or at least check, the monopoly of power can prevent a reversion to violence.[182] Strong citizens are less likely to be manipulated by government and other powerful interests. Civil society can easily play the dual role critically needed with the most troubling conflicts: continuing to check power abuse but also advocating for equal and inclusive decision-making through mediation. In a comparison of violent and nonviolent strategies used by Chechen, East Timorese, and Palestinian separatists, peace researcher Yo'av Karny from Israel concluded that nonviolent conflict strategy showed the most promise of success.[183] Once again, Cameroon's success with mediation in transitioning from violent to nonviolent conflict resolution serves as an encouraging example.

Despite challenges and difficulties, attempting inclusive decision-making through mediated conflict is a prerequisite to good governance throughout the developing world, particularly where a history and practice of community protest exists.[184] The parties' agreement—and the dispute's resolution—will naturally be tested by time and impact on society. Critiques by concerned civil society and communities may be necessary for genuine power-sharing or the sustainability and effectiveness of dispute resolution over time. Nevertheless, mediation advances governance in emerging democracies when it both emulates and spreads democracy.

All global parties to mediation must somehow find their way to this end.[185] Furthermore, fundamental reform of all institutions involved with governance is vital to moving forward with good governance.[186] In Latin America, for example, masses of citizens criticize the administration of justice as "slow, [and] tending to favor those in power."[187] This is one of the reasons international experts laud a participatory conflict-resolution process that includes the grassroots community. As in Latin America, citizens and other stakeholders bearing the costs of corruption can raise and problem-solve their concerns in participatory processes like mediation.

Collective desperation and increased violence motivated South Africa's Peace Accords,[188] with government stakeholders purportedly taking the lead in power-sharing. According to Susan Collin Marks, a South African mediator and principal with the global NGO involved with Ukraine's mediations, the negotiation of South Africa's Peace Accords included everyone as equals. "In many cases the government became just another player, not a referee or participant with extra powers. One international observer . . . was astonished at the government's readiness to be equal partners at the table."[189]

Mediation can also play a role in alleviating broader corruption. One World Trust, a global NGO, evaluates effective participation with collaborative processes like mediation. It stresses linking macro and micro decision-making, or connecting the (macro) policy decisions of the most powerful stakeholders, like business and government, with the decisions made in micro process like mediation.[190] If government and business share power through their commitment to follow through in their agreements with less powerful stakeholders, they demonstrate the equal and inclusive decision-making of good governance.

The AARHUS process mentioned earlier is a model for linking micro and macro decision making. Yet it apparently gauged its success solely on progress, or the fact that it included more NGO participants than any similar process, only addressing the first criterion of good governance through broadening diverse participation. Good governance also requires equality of influence in relation to final decisions. No data was found evaluating this criterion in the AARHUS negotiation process.

The external evaluation of the IMF ombuds detailed later also does not mention equality of influence or decision-making. The reader is left to wonder whether the diverse list of citizens, employees, NGO representatives, and other participants with the Peruvian process described earlier, reflects token, true but unequal, or truly equal influence.[191] The evaluation data describing tensions between the mediator and NGOs, as well as the mediator and the most powerful stakeholders, though, infers the mediator's aspirations for equal participation and treatment.[192] NGOs criticize the ombuds mediator as biased toward IMF and MIGA, while these same institutions criticize the same mediator as preferencing NGOs. Apparently, the ombuds-mediator considered opposing perspectives well enough to raise concern among both parties.

## A Popular Alternative to Untrustworthy Legal Systems

Mediation is growing in popularity around the world for its ability to fill critical gaps where the rule of law is unreliable, corrupt, or missing. Mediation has the capacity to create a trustworthy rule of law that transcends domestic systems and combines civil and common law and other legal traditions.[193] When groups from different countries and conventions are mediating a dispute, mediation allows them to include institutional heritage that is important to each of them. Some mediated international multistakeholder processes have established binding legal agreements.[194] South Africa's Peace Accord is one noteworthy example. If mediated, the AARHUS convention would have produced similar law. Ideally, the rule created is truly impartial—created to oversee all groups and individuals, no matter how powerful, and applied equally, to ensure justice.[195]

Those interviewed here expressed the need for impartial enforcement mechanisms with mediation like those available with arbitration and judicial proceedings.[196] Otherwise, users are "forced" into a dual track process—with court or arbitration necessary to enforce mediated agreements.

Growing promise and use of mediation worldwide, however, also brings concerns. What causes lawyers most trepidation is a mediator privately caucusing with each side.[197] "As a result of private caucus sessions, the mediator may feel biased to one side or another on the basis of what he or she hears in confidence."[198] This is noteworthy because ex parte communications are also present in the corrupt systems that mediation seeks to circumvent. A related concern arises when an autocratic mediator pushes parties into making "premature and unnecessary concessions that interfere with the attainment of high joint benefit."[199]

The external evaluators of the IMF ombuds-mediator stress that impartiality, inevitably tested with tough political pressure, must be strictly maintained.[200] They found "the risk of perceptions from within the institutions that [the mediator] too consistently adopts the NGO perspective, and from civil society that it represents the institutions of which it is a part."[201]

Traditionally, common law holds judicial precedent in high esteem in order to promote impartiality, or equivalent treatment through case-by-case application without bias.[202] Procedural safeguards have been built to limit state power abuse.[203] Yet law cannot advance good governance without impartial enforcement. Likewise, government-initiated mediation must be scrutinized for its observance of impartiality.[204] "Conflict is often resolved superficially, and the transformative potential of mediation, in imparting skills and engaging in structural change, is neglected. . . . Mediation centers . . . are often perceived as government agents."[205]

Independent alternatives are needed in countries where courts are controlled and pressured politically by the executive branch.[206] As described throughout this book, communities, professionals, and other members of civil society around the world are enthusiastically embracing mediation as a trusted alternative to deficient courts. In a study of 16 countries, all but two (Argentina and Chile) report a much higher trust in community and indigenous dispute resolution than formal courts.[207]

What is purportedly happening with mediation in the Philippines demonstrates the need and reasons for zealous reform. The Philippine courts urgently need vital changes addressing backlog, corruption, and systemic biases and inefficiencies.[208] In 1999, during a two-week National Settlement Period, the Department of Justice referred 1,800 cases to mediation. Most reported satisfaction with both the process and the mediator whether or not their case settled.[209]

The above success sparked a societal trend. The Supreme Court started mediation in the Court of Appeals and the Department of Trade in its consumer protection bureau. The Departments of Environment and Natural Resources and Agrarian Reform "are encouraging greater private sector participation in . . . communitywide conflicts over land and resources."[210] The Board of Investments and Intellectual Property Rights office hope to gain a competitive edge over other Asian investment destinations through the use of mediation.[211]

Mediation's global surge in popularity is due in part to the alternative it offers parties who cannot trust their legal systems to decide disputes impartially. Mediation, however, must also be scrutinized to ensure impartiality. It lacks the procedural safeguards of legal systems. Thus, parties and mediators themselves must safeguard mediation's impartiality.

## Impartiality Is Pivotal to Good Governance

"[The] stability of all democratic institutions rests upon a justice system founded on principles of equal access, impartiality, and independence."[212] Like impartial rule of law, mediator impartiality throughout the mediation process is key to whether mediation advances rather than erodes good governance.[213] For this book, impartiality will be characterized as the mediator's lack of bias or favoritism toward parties.[214] It is foundational to building trust between stakeholders, particularly those from different countries.[215] Parties who evaluated cross-cultural mediation in the Balkans, Cameroon, Nepal, and Ukraine stressed how they disliked partiality. The least effective of mediators were described as biased, indifferent, judgmental, close-minded, and disrespectful.[216]

One proposed way to increase public confidence and decrease the potential for political manipulation during mediation is to appoint multiple mediator panels, including mediators chosen by each of the communities concerned—similar to the current model for international commercial arbitration.[217] Multilateral and NGO groups abiding by principles of impartiality and neutrality, like those of the International Committee of the Red Cross, may be the most independent and trustworthy mediator if their participation in a particular mediation process is feasible.[218]

Lincoln's role with slavery models requisite impartiality in regards to stakeholder and institutional alliances and pressure. If political fraternity had been a priority, Lincoln may have allowed states to spread slavery without interference. If he had revered the judicial system as sacred, slavery would have prevailed. While Lincoln obviously did not mediate the end of slavery and held strong personal convictions regarding slavery, his ability to act with independent integrity under pressure from powerful interests provides inspiration for mediators of political and other high stake battles.

Without impartiality, mediation can be a pawn for powerful interests. Although multiple parties are involved, mediation by a partial mediator can thwart the achievement of common objectives that are effective and last. Given multicultural mediation's stakes and challenges, this section recommends the impartial mediation teams described above.

## Create Optimal Conditions

Those interviewed here recommend the following strategies for increasing inclusive decision-making around the globe. First and foremost, stakeholders need to be persuaded to talk with each other. Interviewees identify corporations as one of the global stakeholders needing to better understand mediation's value. As one corporate interviewee expressed, many are still unaware of mediation and its benefits—education is needed.[219] Interviewees relate this lack of appreciation of mediation, for reasons unexplained, to their suggestion that corporations need closer coordination between government and community affairs. Furthermore, in interviewees' experience, having a designated senior-level corporate and government visionary who is responsible for piloting and otherwise spearheading innovative efforts can be instrumental to whether dispute resolution such as mediation occurs.[220]

Mandated participation, however, like IFC requirements, is problematic. Mediation is a voluntary process, fundamentally resting on the principle of party self-determination. Mandating participation violates this principle. Exploring viable options that respect self-determination, while increasing participation, is required. Sophisticated convening of mediation, described earlier, is the most popular response.[221] In the convening stage of mediations, mediators privately talk with parties, help them identify their interests, look for ways to respond to party concerns, and otherwise encourage inclusive participation.

Corporations and other businesses can be guided in recognizing their interests in managing the risks of conflict, such as protecting their local and global reputations from the negative press and protest that can result from destructive conflict. Seasoned business stakeholders do recognize that social license to operate is essential.[222] Respect for what each stakeholder can contribute and the reality that absent collaboration end results cannot be achieved should motivate inclusive processes.[223] One corporation found that inviting community participation moderates "escalating . . . expectations of unconditional benefit."[224]

Advances are also possible with mediation itself. A realistic first step is attempting to measure progress in the concrete process challenges faced with mediation's internal governance. Questions are provided at the end of this section for this purpose. They can also be used to help stakeholders create equal and inclusive decision-making that is responsive to their interests through designing the mediation process itself.

Conflict resolution scholar Susan Opotow and book interviewees advocate for mediation's inclusion across time, beginning prior to and continuing after mediation.[225] They believe community engagement is best built into complex dispute resolution from "the very beginning" when disputes are first named. Global interviewees recommend starting with diverse representation of stakeholders, perhaps through a coordinating group of stakeholders who convene other stakeholders and design the mediation.

Mediation's capacity for facilitating equal inclusive decision-making between stakeholders of varying power is pivotal to its contribution to governance, particularly in emerging democracies where citizens may be new to participatory institutions and dialogue across difference. Mediation optimally trains citizens for these tasks. Powerful stakeholders, however, must be willing to share power —linking their decisions with those made by less powerful stakeholders—for equal inclusive decision-making to occur. Once powerful stakeholders are willing to negotiate with the less powerful, however, mediation provides several avenues for advancing governance, such as designing conflict and dispute resolution to increase stakeholder responsiveness during and after mediation.

## Parts 2 and 3 Notes and Questions

1. Pick a conflict that concerns or interests you. List all those who have a connection to this conflict; then all who need to be included to discuss and negotiate a lasting and satisfactory resolution. Is there anyone else you would include for optimal response?

   Go through the above lists and note which parties you would readily invite and easily work with in a mediation process, assuming you are the mediator. Are there any parties that you would hesitate in inviting to the mediation? Note your reasons.

   Are there any parties that you would worry about inviting to the mediation process? Once again, note your reasons.

Share and discuss the above reflection. Brainstorm ways you might reduce your hesitation or address your worries.

2. Several faculty at California State universities have recently researched students' disposition towards social justice. One survey with a range of dispositions is included in appendix 5. Students of negotiation, conflict resolution and peacebuilding define social justice in a variety of ways. Examples include responsiveness to the needs of those suffering injustice such as lack of access to adequate education, or the freedom to live in ways that do not harm others, including the natural environment. How do you define social justice?

3. Use your definition(s) of social justice to create and list specific criteria for evaluating and guiding a just mediation process. Share and discuss.

4. Not surprisingly, students of negotiation, conflict resolution, and peacebuilding at California State University Dominguez Hills, from diverse cultural groups, with many identifying as African and Latino Americans, often report a positive disposition towards social justice. Most importantly, they report that they feel empowered to act on behalf of justice by their education in the skills of cross cultural communication, negotiation, and mediation.

    Identify injustice, local and global, that concerns you. What role does negotiation and mediation play in empowering you to act regarding this injustice? Share and discuss.

5. A few students are wary that others will attempt to impose their definition of social justice on them rather than learn about their definitions and facilitate their resolution. What do you think about self determination as the basic premise of mediation? What are some concrete ways you can facilitate?

6. Balancing power when some of the parties to mediation are initially much more powerful than others requires reflection, skill, moment to moment observation, and commitment. Think of a conflict that concerns or interests you where there is a power imbalance. How exactly would you, as mediator, proceed to balance power so that all participate and are treated equally? Share and discuss.

## Part 4: Custom Design Multicultural Responsiveness

All stakeholders are free to craft mediation that is more aligned with their interests than formally established forms of dispute resolution. Ideally, they will transform the "pursuit of privilege (power) into the responsibility for governance, or responsiveness to all stakeholders."[226] Arguably, a "civil service that is strongly oriented and committed to service" demonstrates the regard for stakeholders required for good governance.[227] Civil society, and religious, academic, and other mediation stakeholders can also insist on genuine respect for their interests before they agree to proceed in mediation with a historically corrupt and disinterested government. While no stakeholder can force another to participate in mediation, each stakeholder can refuse to participate unless good faith parameters for honest collaboration are honored. Or, since stakeholders are free to participate without pressure to reach an agreement or resolve a conflict, they may derive value from mere face-to-face communication with corrupt civil servants and other stakeholders acting in bad faith. Stakeholders hold the power, with the help of skilled mediators, to persuade opposing parties that benefits to be gained in proceeding with honest collaboration outweigh the costs of entrenched, escalating conflict.

If authentic power-sharing does occur, heightened responsiveness to the populace, one of good governance's conditions, naturally follows. Likewise, mediation plays a foundational role in advancing the good governance condition of stakeholder responsiveness if all concerned and interested stakeholders design the mediation process itself.[228] Conversely, mediation loses credibility and legitimacy when a powerful stakeholder designs or imposes the mechanism for mediation.[229]

Ironically, the AARHUS treaty negotiation, introduced earlier, emulates both. It is lauded as advancing democratization of multilateral decision-making for including environmental NGOs, academics, and lawyers in the process design.[230] Such private stakeholders are often best situated to respond to the needs they know and understand.[231] Civil society groups throughout societies and around the globe can also be more flexible than government bureaucracies, allowing them to respond more quickly and creatively to newly arising issues and concerns. Civil society is likewise acknowledged for its closeness to the public, particularly when representing citizen interests.[232] The latter's practical insight and information may not otherwise be available to government. Yet, since government, NGOs, and academic and legal representatives did not invite business and other affected interests to the AARHUS table, this process is simultaneously vilified as a form of domination with an environmental agenda. Civil society is admonished to maintain its legitimacy by convening broadly inclusive dispute resolution to ensure diverse responsiveness.[233]

## Rare Multicultural Responsiveness

Once a broadly inclusive group is created, mediation gives all stakeholders the opportunity to heighten responsiveness to their interests and needs. Parties from different countries, cultures, and legal systems are free to craft mediation to include a variety of approaches to conflict and thus respect all concerned.[234] The cross-ethnic dialogue mediated throughout the Balkans presents an intriguing organic design model, improving its stakeholder inclusiveness and responsiveness with each subsequent dialogue. Stakeholders from conflicting ethnic groups and diverse professions were nominated, recruited, and invited to join the mediating NGO. Thus, a wide spectrum of conflicting communities intimately designed and delivered the NGO's next mediated dialogues, inherently ensuring responsiveness to those communities' needs and interests.[235]

To preserve mediation integrity and to heighten effectiveness, process conflict must be reconciled before attempting substantive discussion. Openly addressing procedural challenges helps facilitate stakeholder understanding of expectation and risk.[236] Ideally all concerned will carefully define the desired role of mediation, agree to multicultural ground rules[237] for decision-making, and design mediation to meet particular needs and interests.[238]

Not surprising to those intimately acquainted with mediation, the author's students from an estimated 70 countries enthusiastically commend mediation's democratic process. Many see its underlying premise of self-determination crossing cultural barriers. Mediation gives parties several tools that help them to engage in dialogue in the face of difference. Ground rules allow parties to craft procedural mechanisms that are well-suited to their needs and expectations.[239] Reframing culturally charged language can sensitively convey essential meaning. (Note: Impartial cultural insiders may be needed to help mediators reframe skillfully and astutely.)

Mediation's myriad benefits responsive to cross-cultural conflict resolution include its emphasis on story-telling. Sharing cultural, personal, or collective stories humanizes stakeholders. Elucidation of difference enhances creative option generation.[240] Discovering cultural uniqueness helps imaginations open to new possibilities.[241]

To satisfy good governance's remaining criteria: transparency and accountability, all stakeholders must scrutinize information sharing and follow through to ensure that transparency and accountability are present.

## Part 5: Safeguarding Transparency and Accountability

While the remaining criteria for evaluating governance, transparency, and accountability, are distinct concepts and practices, they will be analyzed together in this section because they overlap and depend on each other. Stakeholder accountability often requires transparency, where stakeholders openly consult with each other and share vital information.

Traditionally, representative democracies hold civil servants and government agencies accountable to citizens by way of elected representatives. Accountability simply means that individuals and institutions are answerable for their actions and the consequences that follow from them. Transparent, or open sharing of information regarding the exercise of mandated functions, is necessary. Government and business often need independent parties to oversee and stimulate their best behavior.

With mediated governance as it is described throughout this book, all stakeholders must hold each other accountable. Transparency and accountability are shifting from vertical processes, where representatives share and follow through with constituents, to horizontal processes, where stakeholders in a particular mediation or negotiation share and follow through with each other.

Governmental and intergovernmental bodies can be less than transparent in sharing how dispute resolution relates to official decision-making. Naturally promises made but not kept—that mediated decisions will be honored in official decisions—trigger and escalate conflict. Ideally, however, the stronger the nation-state and intergovernmental body, the more it allows, even seeks, strong voice and questioning within mediations and other conflict processes.

Disputants alienated from corrupt legal systems and governments are demonstrating their faith in mediation. Some explicitly embrace mediation as creating "new spaces of transparency in the justice system."[242] The IFC creation of its ombuds mediator is one noteworthy example, recognizing mediation's benefits, including its facilitation of important information sharing. One can easily imagine the same corporations criticized earlier likewise benefiting from the increased information flow found in sound mediated participatory process.

Truly democratic mediation requires honest information sharing. Parties should be able to verify their mediation's transparency to secure mediation's contribution to good governance. Parties to mediation contract, for example, to honestly share information relevant to the decisions mediated.

Mediators can also play a role with ensuring accountability. Mediators can encourage, even require, stakeholder commitments to honest collaboration and follow through with contractual provisions in their agreements to mediate.

Open and honest disclosure and information sharing headed the list of optimal cross-cultural processes evaluated in the Balkans, Cameroon, Nepal, and Ukraine.[243] This was particularly true throughout the Balkans. Conversely, parties to mediation in Nepal criticized violations of their agreements to mediate, deceit, and the failure to share important information as the principal roadblocks to successful mediation.[244]

## Mediation Can Result in Heightened Transparency

In common law systems, accountability is equated with public record and scrutiny, particularly judicial review. Optimal accountability for good governance with a society as a whole requires independent and critical media, a representative decision-making body that is separate from police and military forces, and education of individuals so they are aware of their rights.[245]

Most mediations, however, are protected from such scrutiny. Only the education of parties in mediation such that they are aware of their rights, risks, and options is allowed. As a result, mediations necessarily depend on their own parties to safeguard transparency and accountability. While mediators may require that parties agree to open information sharing before proceeding, the mediator has no standing to enforce such agreement. Instead, confidentiality provisions prohibit mediator disclosure. Thus, the potential for power abuse and bad faith is great unless the parties guard against them themselves.

Mediation can incorporate a formal commitment to greater transparency. The AARHUS Treaty mentioned earlier concluded with an explicit commitment by the government to "provide enhanced access to information. . . . This will be used to produce a culture of greater openness so that decisions taken are more transparent."[246] While no data was found regarding transparency and South Africa's mediated Peace Accords, transparency was one of the criteria for negotiating South Africa's transitional constitution.[247] Meetings were open to the public and all materials were accessible through the Internet.[248]

As with the IMF, many companies and some intergovernmental organizations commit to transparency after suffering "untold reputational harm" from historic lack.[249] They wisely adopt their own proactive policies and practices of full transparency and have been so advised by NGOs.[250] Some establish independent community mechanisms with impartial oversight. A class action of African-American employees alleging discrimination at Coca-Cola illustrates mediation's commitment to transparency. After the Northern District of Georgia ordered all stakeholders to engage in mediation, their resultant agreement created a taskforce to oversee its implementation for a period of three years, as well as conduct internal investigation of on-going complaints.[251] As proposed earlier, taskforce selection paralleled the selection of international commercial arbitration panels—three appointees nominated by Coca-Cola, three by the class counsel and one chairperson agreed to by both.[252] All appointees needed to satisfy criteria negotiated in mediation.

Mediation also naturally facilitates transparency with its decision-making process, in addition to the contractual agreements mentioned above. Parties to court mandated mediation in Nepal lauded first and foremost party disclosure and mediator questioning.[253] Participants to mediated cross-ethnic dialogue throughout the Balkans similarly commended open, honest discussion.[254] One party in Ukraine appreciated allowing all to talk freely.[255]

On the other hand, those interviewed for this book also valued the ability to ensure confidentiality with mediation[256] as a means to avoid constraining the free expression of opinions and ideas.[257] Related is their interest and mediation's role in preserving reputations.[258] Mediators, which are agreed to and trusted by all parties, can be indispensable. They assist with face-saving by, for example, fielding tough questions that participants truly do not know how to answer immediately themselves.[259]

Fear of scrutiny has led some parties to reject the presence of outsiders entirely, even impartial mediators. This allegedly occurred with South Africa's prenegotiation talks between Afrikaners and ANCS in the late 1980s.[260] Transparency must somehow be balanced with confidentiality. Optimally, disclosure of information does not materially harm business and political interests. Once again, Mozambique's peace process provides an intriguing twist. Participants agreed to confidentiality of communication but transparency of results.[261]

A more common response is a provision in agreements to mediate, which is reviewed and signed prior to proceeding with mediation. Parties contract a degree of open, honest information sharing determined by the degree of relevance to the resolution while also agreeing not to use or reveal the information outside of mediation. Thus, parties to mediation create their own legal avenue for holding a less than transparent party accountable for contract breach, both within and outside the mediation, while also protecting confidentiality.

In summary, mediation facilitates transparency in several ways. Mediators encourage disclosure through open-ended questions and by allowing full discussion among mediation participants. Parties initiate and monitor information sharing. Mediators and parties may also commit to good faith transparency, informally or in their agreement to mediate. A resolution can result in a commitment to transparency, including monitoring by impartial panels.

## Evaluate Potential Concerns

While mediation is normally protected from the public scrutiny ordinarily deemed necessary to ensure accountability, occasionally ombuds-mediators provide windows into the mediation process. This occurred with the IMF-MIGA ombuds mediator through external and independent evaluation of parties' experience and perceived mediator impact. A team of three outsiders having no apparent relationship with those being evaluated reported progress and concerns with transparency and accountability.

In 1995 the IFC and MIGA created an ombuds division in response to harsh criticism of the World Bank by a Chilean NGO. This ombuds office investigated complaints involving IFC and MIGA projects. In one case, it arranged an independent study of water quality, with monitoring of transparency and impartiality. The study, similar to the mediated Coca-Cola agreement described above, featured a diverse and collectively chosen group of local community representatives.[262]

The IFC ombuds' most publicized work[263] occurred in Peru in response to local and NGO complaints of pollution by a local investment in the mine sector. The intervention exemplifies options that are remarkably similar to those available to mediators. As one example, the IFC ombuds organized a series of trainings for 63 participants in apparent preparation for mediation.[264]

The external reviewers mentioned earlier concluded that the ombuds-mediator was beneficially impacting IFC and MIGA "by influencing the agenda and terms of internal debate on challenging issues central to successful development."[265] They also found that "senior management and some middle management, and most environmental and social development specialists, seem to particularly value . . . early warning."[266]

Reviewers learned that the NGOs valued opportunities for review and comment provided by the ombuds but perceived that the IFC and MIGA are not yet comfortable operating in a climate that demands accountability, openness and trust . . . the natural tendency is to have conversations in private. . . . Change and learning with respect to uncomfortable or painful issues are seldom sought out and embraced by any large institution. . . . Not all potential or active clients [however] understand the business value of properly managing environmental and social risks and aggressively growing environmental and social opportunities.[267]

The evaluators recommended that the IMF ombuds "carefully evaluate the willingness and ability to engage in productive problem solving of the senior management of any company."[268] Party unresponsiveness should be a reason for refusing to proceed with mediation. This would educate all parties, particularly those with most power or resistance, that mediation requires accountability and transparency.

The above evaluation raises critical questions about what is happening "behind closed doors." None of the interview data gathered for this book, asking global mediators and related practitioners to evaluate mediation and good governance, even mention transparency or accountability. Are the most powerful parties in these mediations likewise resistant to open conversations and information sharing, or transparency? Are the impartials routinely subject to stakeholder criticism about taking the other party's side? How empowered do the parties need to be to effectively guard transparency and ensure accountability?

The evaluations of cross-cultural mediations from the Balkans, Cameroon, Nepal, and Ukraine are reassuring. While not asked the above questions, participants praise genuine power-sharing and free communication. Parties self-policed and reported being exceedingly satisfied, explicitly with their mediators' impartiality and their own sense of empowerment. Only one recommendation, that serious participation be encouraged, indicated any concern with accountability, or that stakeholders hold each other responsible for their actions and consequences.

The above data also provide an example of how mediation, its dangers and contribution to good governance, can be scrutinized without violating confidentiality provisions. If anonymous, participant evaluations of their mediator's competence and mediation's integrity can become a regular practice.

## Part 6: Questions Evaluating Mediation

This section ends with sample questions scrutinizing mediation's role with governance. They parallel the most popular criteria affiliated with good governance and can be used to guide both evaluation and research, internal and external, of efficient mediation of diverse interests, inclusive participation, impartiality, equal and inclusive decision making, stakeholder responsiveness, transparency, and accountability.[269] Parties to mediation can evaluate all criteria anonymously without intruding on substantive negotiations and otherwise violating confidentiality provisions. Mediators can self-police, using evaluation questions to solicit diverse cultural perspectives regarding mediator performance and ethics. Competition among mediators and their spirit of professionalism might move mediators to market client satisfaction and continuous improvement. Independent bodies, like the IMF team or academia, can lead more elaborate research aspiring to raise mediation standards and enhance stakeholders' ability to protect themselves. A body of opinion research would be built within the field of global mediation, allowing for future statistical analysis.[270]

### Questions for evaluating efficient mediation of diverse interests

1. Were diverse interests mediated for the common good?

2. Did mediation effectively balance necessary relationship-building and relationship-maintenance with the efficient use of resources? Was mediation needed? Justifiable?

Consider the following circumstances where mediation can be beneficial

Was there community/organizational/political resistance?

Did relationships matter?

Were there more than two significant interests (making dispute resolution such as arbitration awkward)?

Was there potential for resolution of some/all issues in collaborative bargaining, custom designed solutions and other mediator guidance?

Was there a need to preserve, even build, reputation?

Questions for evaluating inclusivity (Space is provided for your notes regarding specifics)

1. Were all significant interests included, including:
   a. Marginalized stakeholders:

   b. The most contentious and challenging stakeholders (e.g., business for environmental NGOs; protestors for business):

   c. Individuals reflecting ethnic, cultural, professional, intellectual diversity:

   d. Those in conflict whose face-to-face communication was previously lacking:

   e. Those lacking time and resources:

2. Did the mediator recognize, elucidate, and effectively bridge all significant interest present? If so, how? Please describe.

   Checklist of Mediator Behavior Key to Bridging Interest
   ___ Careful listening
   ___ Accurate understanding across culture
   ___ In-depth interest analysis-identification
   ___ Identification of parties' commonalities
   ___ Generation of options for mutual gain

**Questions for evaluating equal inclusive decision-making (and space for notes):**

1. Was the decision-making process equal?

2. Were all parties treated equally? Please describe.

3. Where parties treated equally during introductions?

4. Did parties participate equally?

5. How would parties describe all interactions with mediator(s)?

6. Were power imbalances present and recognized?

If so, what helped most powerful stakeholders feel comfortable participating in transparent and inclusive process?

7. Was the potential for power abuse present? If yes, how was this scrutinized and prohibited?

### Questions for evaluating stakeholder responsiveness/mediator impartiality

1. Did a diverse, inclusive group of stakeholders design the mediation process through discussions with the mediator or a coordinating group?

2. Were process challenges openly addressed?

3. If more than one culture was present, how was a multicultural process crafted to respect all stakeholders' self-determination? Please describe details for each category listed below.

   Ground rules:

   Option generation:

4. Did the mediator effectively use multicultural tools? Please describe for each category below.

Ground rules:

Storytelling:

Reframing to diffuse culturally-charged language, while preserving essential meaning:

Creative option generation:

2. How would you rate and describe responsiveness to each stakeholder's interests and concerns in this mediation? (Separate rating for each stakeholder is recommended).
3. How would you rate and describe mediator impartiality?

Impeccably Impartial Biased Partial to One Side

Three-member mediation team selected by stakeholders:

Ex Parte Communication

Frequent Non-Existent

Parties Safeguarded Impartiality:

At all times No

4. If agreement was reached, is a diverse inclusive group committed to evaluating the resolution's long-term impact? If yes, please describe.

## Questions for evaluating transparency and accountability

1. How would you rate and describe the mediation's transparency?

   Open, Honest Sharing of All Important Information No

   Agreement to mediate contracted transparency?

2. How would you rate and describe the good faith honest collaboration of parties to mediation?

   Outstanding Bad Faith
   Agreement to mediate contracted good faith?

## Parts 4, 5 and 6 Notes and Questions

1. Design your own multicultural process for discussing and negotiating conflict with a group of friends or acquaintances from a variety of cultural backgrounds and identities.

   Note: If you are unable to easily connect with those you already know who identify with cultures other than your own, make a conscious effort to connect with someone new who identifies with a culture other than your own for the purposes of this exercise. The most sensitive and skillful students of multicultural conflict resolution have often grown up in multiple cultures as a result of immigration to another country, marriage across cultures, and other circumstances. It is highly recommended that you consider Fulbright programs, Peace Corps, international study abroad, and other extended cultural immersion to broaden your cultural experience, especially if you have not already experienced multiple cultures as part of your life experience.

   Step 1: Imagine you are being asked to openly and publicly discuss, negotiate, or participate in a mediation of one of your conflicts with others concerned with this conflict. What conditions do you need before you will feel comfortable proceeding? Create a list with specific needs.

One example of a conflict process condition that is common in the United States is confidentiality or the promise that no one will share your participation or link your name and other identifying description with conversation about the conflict process with anyone outside of the process.* Californians often expect no interruption no matter how long a participant decides to speak. In the author's experience, Japanese expect a quiet time of reflection before speaking or responding to someone else.

*This represents two possible definitions of confidentiality.

Step 2: Ask all others involved in this exercise to complete step 1 privately, without consulting others involved in this exercise (to avoid pressure regarding group conformity, which might distort the results). They are welcome to consult with nonparticipants from their cultural groups for help with identifying the conditions they need.

Step 3: Each participant shares their list with other participants.

Step 4: As you listen during step 3, attempt to identify all common shared conditions and any others that are similar or related to each other. Create a comprehensive list for your group.

Step 5: With each condition shared that is different from yours, ask yourself: can I live with and respect this condition? Create a second comprehensive list for your group of all conditions that can be easily respected even though not shared.

Step 6: Consider each condition that another shares that you cannot easily respect such as a desire for yelling or interruption. Brainstorm ways you might create space for that condition while simultaneously respecting your own needs, principles. . . . For example, you might agree to mediation with private meetings, or caucuses, where conditions can be satisfied without your direct presence.

2. Review the process you created above. Do your resulting conditions create multicultural equivalence?

   What, if anything, do you need to add to balance power? Ensure equal participation? Equal treatment of all concerned? Freedom from bias? True impartiality?

3. Review the conditions you created in the exercise above. Do they address and ensure accountability of all participants? If not, how could they?

4. Do the same analysis regarding transparency (open honest sharing of information).

5. Evaluate your process conditions with the questions provided at the end of this section. Share and discuss.

## Notes

[1] Tom Farer, Presentation at the Annual Meeting of the American Association of Law Schools (Jan. 4, 2003). In the simplest terms, good governance is effective democratic culture. See Transparency International, <http://www.transparency.org> (last visited Feb. 28, 2006). Other attempts at defining good governance are presented in chapter 5. See, e.g., Julius Court et al., *Assessing Governance: Methodological Challenges* (United Nations University, 2002, 4).

[2] See Alison Taylor and Jay Folberg, *Mediation: A Comprehensive Guide to Resolving Conflict Without Litigation* (Jossey-Bass, 1984) ("Using mediation to facilitate conflict resolution and encourage self-determination strengthens democratic values and enhances the dignity of those in conflict."); ("Democracy building is an intrinsic part of conflict management, and vice versa.") International Institute for Democracy and Electoral Assistance, <http://www.idea.int/utindex.cfm> (last visited Sept. 3, 2004); ("Sustainable human development, economic growth, security, conflict prevention, and conflict resolution as well as good governance are all intricately intertwined.") United Nations Development Programme: Management Development and Governance Division and Bureau for Development Policy, Promoting Conflict Prevention and Conflict Resolution Through Effective Governance: A Conceptual Survey and Literature Review, available at <http://magnet.undp.org/Docs/crisis/mapexercise.htm> (last visited Oct. 29, 2003) [hereinafter United Nations Development Programme]; see also Aeyal M. Gross, "The Constitution, Reconciliation, and Transitional Justice: Lessons From South Africa and Israel," 40 *Stan. J. Int'l. L.* 47, 56-57 (2004); John Davies and Edward Kaufman, *Second Track/Citizens' Diplomacy* 3 (Rowman & Littlefield, 2002).

[3] Thomas J. Moyer and Emily Stewart Haynes, "Mediation as a Catalyst for Judicial Reform in Latin America" 18 *Ohio St. J. on Disp. Resol.* 619, 648 (2003).

[4] "[One] who investigates complaints and mediates fair settlements, especially between aggrieved parties such as consumers or students and an institution or organization." Dictionary.com, <http://dictionary.com> (last visited Feb. 26, 2006).

[5] Transparency International, *supra* note 1.

[6] Establishing mediation's success in reducing systemic corruption, and otherwise building good governance, requires sophisticated longitudinal inquiry attempting to document less tangible macro change. Evaluating and measuring good governance alone is a complex undertaking. Court et al., *supra* note 1, at 2. Measuring issues of governance poses challenges that are not encountered in the economic or social development fields. While it is easier to provide firm indicators of such things as economic growth or primary school enrollment, it is much more difficult to find and agree upon indicators of a political macro development like governance. . . . Perhaps because it is a broad and complicated concept, there exists no regular, systemic, and cohesive data collection effort centered on the concept of governance. *Id.*

Measuring development shows parallel challenges. Analyses exist of failure, but "it is not easy to . . . determine which factors accounted for success." United Nations Development Programme, Capacity Development for Sustainable Human Development: Conceptual and Operational Signposts (1997), available at <http://magnet.undp.org/cdrb/CAPDEV.htm> (last visited Mar. 5, 2006). "The process is nonlinear. It is a learning and experimenting process in which people test ideas, gain experience, and feed back their experience into the process." *Id.*

Existing evaluation of mediation focuses on relatively straightforward disputes in contexts with long-standing use. See, e.g., Francis O. Spaulding, "The Rand Report, the

Federal Judicial Center Study and Alternative Dispute Resolution in United States District Courts" (1999), available at <http://www.fos-adr.com/fos-art3.html>. Simple studies offer valuable information and insight but only begin to tackle the challenges involved with correlating mediation and governance. The article by Moyer and Haynes, *supra* note 3, provides a persuasive argument for judicial reform throughout Latin America but fails to establish that mediation is catalyzing change apart from providing an alternative to corrupt processes. *Id.* This research gap may reflect barriers inherent in studying mediation. Confidentiality agreements block collection of comprehensive data. Researchers are forced to rely on anecdotal selective reports by parties concerned. Nevertheless, despite all barriers, related research is beginning to analyze more complex dynamics like those of multilateral negotiations. See, e.g., Mary Jo Larson, "Low-Power Contributions in Multilateral Negotiations: A Framework Analysis," 19 *Negot. J.* 133, 139 (2003) ("An understanding of multilateral negotiations requires a comprehensive and systemic perspective, one that recognizes multilevel structures, a variety of processes and the different roles of different actors.").

Those scrutinizing multistakeholder process identify the need for more research. See, e.g., Minu Hemmati, "Multi-Stakeholder Processes for Governance and Sustainability: Beyond Deadlock and Conflict" 2 (2002), available at <http://www.earth summit2002.org/msp/book.htm>. Even building a databank of opinion research, beginning with this book's example, would facilitate valuable statistical analysis. Spaulding, *supra.*

[7] A dispute arises when a claim is made against another. William Ury et al., *Getting Disputes Resolved* 4 (Jossey-Bass, 1988). Some define dispute as requiring a communication break-down or barrier needing third-party assistance. Roxanne S. Lulofs and Dudley Cahn, *Conflict from Theory to Action* 341 (Allyn and Bacon, 2000). Both definitions are incorporated here.

[8] Conflict is defined as the broader context of disputes, or any "perceived divergence of interest." Dean G. Pruitt and Sung Hee Kim, *Social Conflict: Escalation, Stalemate and Settlement*, 3d ed. (McGraw-Hill, 2004, 7-8).

[9] See Christopher W. Moore, *The Mediation Process: Practical Strategies for Resolving Conflict*, 2d ed. (Jossey-Bass, 1996, 231).

[10] See, e.g., Nancy Erbe, "The Global Popularity and Promise of Facilitative ADR," 18 *Temp. Int'l and Comp. L.J.* 343 (2004).

[11] United Nations Development Programme, *supra* note 2, at 4. ("There is a very real need for a major text that synthesizes the disparate lessons of individual cases into some broad sets of conclusions.").

[12] *Id.* See Erbe, *supra* note 10, at 349 (citing Frank E. A. Sander, "Some Concluding Thoughts," 17 *Ohio St. J. on Disp. Resol.* 705 (2002)).

[13] Ideally, case study data is rich in detail. See, e.g., Ronald J. Fisher, *Paving the Way: Contributions of Interactive Conflict Resolution to Peacemaking* (Lexington Books, 2005, 203).

[14] One interviewee notes that practitioners too often fail to share lessons learned. Nancy Erbe, "Survey Regarding ADR and Governance" (2004) (on file with author).

[15] See Court, *supra* note 1.

[16] Ethnomethodology aimed to elicit how participants to mediation framed and judged their own experience. Relying on human consent, participants were given the option of requesting an electronic or phone interview. The challenges of securing information about sensitive cross-cultural conflict were evident. None of the participants elected more personal conversations. Instead, they requested complete anonymity. Erbe, *supra* note 10, at 350-51. Mediators facilitating cross-cultural conflict face similar chal-

lenges. Mediators must somehow build context where participants feel safe sharing their experience openly. Often confidentiality or privacy is requisite.

[17] This section also references additional case studies to illustrate mediation's potential to advance or erode governance.

[18] Yet, "even the social research whose design prevents useful generalizations of its conclusions can provide a gold mine of inspiration and ideas." Spaulding, *supra* note 6, at 22. What might be of some use, and what is offered here, is . . . neither a melody line of ADR nor a base obligator of support structure but rather a free-ranging pizzicato accompaniment—one with no pretense to completion or even to internal coherence . . . its greatest pretension is that some of it might suggest ways to make the opus . . . more satisfying to composers, performers or audience. *Id.*

[19] Mark Bevir, "The Hollow State," in *Encyclopedia of Governance*, ed. Mark Bevir (Sage, 2006).

[20] See SAGE Reference Tracking, Encyclopedia of Governance Project Description, <http://www.sageapps.com/SRT/> (follow link to *Encyclopedia of Governance*) (last visited March 22, 2006).

[21] See, e.g., Chris Ansell, "The Networked Polity: Regional Development in Western Europe," 13 *Governance* 303-33 (2000).

[22] Stakeholder is broadly defined to include "any group or individuals who can affect, or is affected." Caroline Neligan, *Increasing Accountability through External Stakeholder Engagement* (One World Trust, 2003, 4).

[23] See, e.g., Martha Feldman and Anne Khademian, "Inclusive Management: Building Relationships with the Public, Center for the Study of Democracy" (2004), <http://repositories.cdlib.org/cds/04-12> (last visited Mar. 7, 2006).

[24] *Id.*

[25] See Ansell, *supra* note 21, at 310.

[26] United Nations Development Programme, *Reconceptualizing Governance* (1997) (emphasis added); see also Marita Thornhill, et al., "The Environment as Catalyst: Understanding Environmental Governance for Sustainable Development" 2, available at <http://www.phelamanga.co.za/Environment%20as%20Catalyst.doc> (quoting Ian Kooiman, "Societal Political Governance: Overview, Reflection and Design," 1 *Pub. Mgmt.* 67, 70 (1999)). ("All those interactive arrangements in which public as well as private actors participate aimed at solving social problems, or creating social opportunities, and attending to the institutions within which these governing activities take place.").

[27] Davies and Kaufman, *supra* note 2, at 49:

[Multitrack] diplomacy may be broadly defined as the bringing together of professionals, opinion leaders, or other currently or potentially influential individuals from communities in conflict, without official representative status, to work together to understand better the dynamics underlying the conflict and how its transformation from violence (or potential violence) to a collaborative process of peace building and sustainable development might be promoted. It complements "first track" or official diplomacy . . . when official dialogue is blocked or constrained . . . [and] is increasingly recognized as an essential component in a multilayered diplomatic process aimed at transforming the contentious power dynamics of complex, protracted conflict into processes of constructive engagement and joint problem solving.

[28] In a recent global survey, NGOs were ranked as the second "most publicly trusted group or organization," second only to national militaries. Kumi Naidoo, "Civil Society, Governnance and Globalization," Address at The World Bank Group Presidential Fel-

lows Lecture Series (Feb. 10, 2003), available at <http://info.world bank.org/etools/ bspan/PresentationView.asp?PID=133andEID=63>.

[29] General Electric, as one example, is credited with promoting peaceful conflict resolution of the 2002 nuclear showdown between India and Pakistan. Timothy L. Fort and Cindy A. Schipani, "Adapting Corporate Governance for Sustainable Peace," 36 *Vand. J. Transnat'l L.* 377, 423 (2003).

[30] Philanthropy has great influence. Private funders supported international tribunals adjudicating Holocaust claims as one noteworthy example. Norbert Wuhler Lecture at Master's Forum, Straus Institute for Dispute Resolution (2003). On the other hand, poor coordination is judged as key to failure of donor-driven development efforts. United Nations Development Programme, *supra* note 2, at 7. In one reported case, United States Aid for International Development funded a restorative justice dispute resolution process in Colombia. Yet when a restorative justice expert from the United States visited Colombia and asked about the program, no one had heard of it. Lynette Parker, "Restorative Justice: A Vehicle for Reform?" presented at 2004 Annual Meeting of Latin American Studies Association (Oct. 7-9, 2004).

[31] See generally Mark E. Warren, "Civil Society and Good Governance," in *U.S. Civil Society Project* (Georgetown Public Policy Institute, 1999); see also United Nations Development Programme, *supra* note 2 ("Capacity development has concentrated on governments with little or no attention to the need to develop the capacities of the other . . . partners, whose contributions are critical for the success of national development programs, such as civil society and the private sector.").

[32] The UNESCAP acknowledges government as one formal actor along with many others, formal and informal, such as associations of farmers, political parties, labor unions, finance institutions, organized crime syndicates, and multinational corporations. Andrea Strimling, "The Federal Mediation and Conciliation Service: A Partner in International Conflict Prevention," 2 *Pepp. Disp. Resol. L.J.* 417, 424 (2002).

[33] A recent World Governance survey proceeded accordingly, surveying government, academic, business, NGO, legal, media, and religious "well-informed persons." Court et al., *supra* note 1, at 15.

[34] See, e.g., Ansell, *supra* note 21, at 303-33.

[35] See, e.g., Symposium, Intentional Conversations about the Globalization of ADR, Dispute Resolution Institute, Hamline University School of Law (Oct. 29-30, 2005) (A group of scholars and practitioners from nine countries describe global mediation as "a movement of ideas".).

[36] Ansell, *supra* note 21, at 304.

[37] Elise Boulding, *Cultures of Peace: The Hidden Side of History* (Syracuse University Press, 2000, 1).

[38] Erbe, *supra* note 10, at 380-83.

[39] *Id.* at 348.

[40] *Id.* at 377.

[41] at 378-79.

[42] See generally Erbe, *supra* note 10.

[43] See, e.g., Court et al., *supra* note 1.

[44] See, e.g., Kristian S. Gleditsch and Michael D. Ward, "Double Take: A Reexamination of Democracy and Autocracy in Modern Politics," 41 *J. Conflict Resol.* 361 (1997); see also Monty G. Marshall and Keith Jaggers, "Polity IV Project," <http://www.cidcm.umd.edu/inscr/polity/index.htm#data> (last visited Mar. 5, 2006) (measuring "autocracy" and "democracy" in most independent states).

[45] Minorities and the most vulnerable must be considered and, optimally, included in decision-making. Freedom House, Freedom in the World 2004: The Annual Survey of Political Rights and Civil Liberties (2004); see also "Freedom House," <http://www.freedomhouse.org> (last visited Mar. 5, 2006) (surveying human rights).

[46] See, e.g., Luis Pasara, "Judicial Reform and Civil Society," in *Justice Delayed: Judicial Reform in Latin America*, ed. Edmundo Jarquin and Fernando Carillo (Johns Hopkins University Press, 1998, 83), cited in Moyer and Haynes, *supra* note 3.

[47] *Id.* ("Good decisions require access to good information.")

[48] Focus on increasing the privilege of a few elites rather than the well-being of the rest is destabilizing.

[49] Neligan, *supra* note 22, at 4.

[50] Paula Dobriansky, "Principles of Good Governance," 8 *Econ. Persp.* (2003), <http://usinfo.state.gov/journals/ites/0303/ijee/dobriansky.htm> ("Development cannot flourish where people cannot make their voices heard, human rights are not respected, information does not flow, and civil society and the judiciary are weak.").

[51] See, e.g., Court et al., *supra* note 1.

[52] Nancy Erbe, "Conflict Mediation," in *Encyclopedia of Governance*, *supra* note 19.

[53] Defined here as "communication for the purpose of persuasion." Stephen Goldberg and Frank E. A. Sander et al., Dispute Resolution: Negotiation, Mediation, and Other Processes (Aspen Publishers, 2003, 17).

[54] Defined for this book's purposes as problem-solving through generating agreements acceptable to all stakeholders. Robert A. Baruch Bush and Joseph P. Folger, *The Promise of Mediation* 12 (1994).

[55] Transformation definitions vary depending on emphasis. Some focus on consciousness and character of individuals while others on the restructuring of social institutions. All are relevant here. For the purposes of this article, transformation is broadly defined as leading change, both individual and social. *Id.* at 24.

[56] *Id.*

[57] Erbe, *supra* note 14 (emphasis added).

[58] See, e.g., Strimling, *supra* note 32, at 418.

[59] United Nations Development Programme, *supra* note 2, at 5; see also Mary Jo Larson and Xiapong Tian, "Strengthening Women's Role to Sustainable Peace: The Benefits of Flexibility," 23 *Conflict Resol. Q.* 53, 54 (2005).

[60] Women's Status: Vision and Reality, New Delhi, India (2001). As the largest democracy in the world, India has vast potential for demonstrating mediation's role with good governance.

[61] See, e.g., Centre de Mediation et d'Arbitrage de Paris, Programme Grotius MARC (2000) (survey throughout Europe); Janet Murdock, "Forging New Frontiers: Spreading ADR in Brazil," ACResolution, Summer 2003, at 26; Lynette Parker, Circles and Restorative Practices, Presentation at the Third International Conference on Conferencing (2002).

[62] Davies and Kaufman, *supra* note 2, at 5.

[63] See, e.g., John Lande, "How Will Lawyering and Mediation Practices Transform Each Other?" 24 *Fla. St. U. L. Rev.* 839, 839 n.1 (1997) (citing Moore, *supra* note 9, at 8, 41-53).

[64] Hemmati, *supra* note 6, at 15.

[65] In the global context, mediation includes intractable conflict involving complex issues of ethnicity and identity. See, e.g., Erbe, *supra* note 10, at 343.

[66] See, e.g., Institute of World Affairs, Community-Building in Post-War Lebanon: A Project to Enhance Ethnic Tolerance and Civic Identity (best citation available).

[67] Institute of World Affairs, *supra* note 66.

[68] *Id.*; see also Fort and Schipani, *supra* note 29.

[69] See Nancy Erbe, "Optimal Strategy with Global Disputes: Blending the Best of Distributive and Integrative Bargaining," XII *Bus. Res. Y.B.* 748 (2005).

[70] Parker, *supra* note 30.

[71] *Id.*

[72] Spaulding, *supra* note 6.

[73] United Nations Development Programme, *supra* note 2, at 29.

[74] Robert F. Cochran, Jr., "Lawyers and Virtues: A Review of Mary Ann Glendon's *A Nation Under Lawyers: How the Crisis in the Legal Profession is Transforming American Society*" and Anthony's T. Kronman's "The Lost Lawyer: Failing Ideals of the Legal Profession," 71 *Notre Dame L. Rev.* 707, 710-11 (1996) (book review).

[75] Naidoo, *supra* note 28.

[76] See, e.g., United Nations Development Programme, *supra* note 2, at 4.

[77] See, e.g., Michael P. Pappas, "A Flexible Framework for the Prevention and Resolution of Construction Disputes," Paper presented at Conflict Studies, *supra* note 1.

[78] *Id.*

[79] *Id.*

[80] Philip J. Harter, "A Plumber Responds to the Philosophers: A Comment on Professor Menkel-Meadow's Essay on Deliberative Democracy," 5 *Nev. L.J.* 379, 380 (2005).

[81] *Id.* at 382-83.

[82] Erbe, *supra* note 10, at 380-83.

[83] Hemmati, *supra* note 6, at 114; see also Roger Fisher and Danny Ertel, *Getting Ready to Negotiate* (Penguin Books, 1995, 128) (commending multiple meetings).

[84] Hemmati, *supra* note 6, at 98.

[85] Erbe, *supra* note 10, at 377-79.

[86] This is exactly what occurred in the mediation-negotiation of Mozambique's peace process. Fisher, *supra* note 13, at 96.

[87] Erbe, *supra* note 14.

[88] Interviews with Antonio Mendoza, Professor, Pepperdine University School of Law, Malibu, Calif. (Fall, 2003).

[89] *Id.*

[90] *Id.*

[91] Compliance Advisor Ombudsman (CAO), Report of the CAO Expert Mission to Cajamarca: April Meetings (May 2002), available at <http://www.cao-ombudsman.org/pdfs/CAO%20APRIL%20REPORT%20english.doc>. The complaint involved a hydroelectric dam. While civil society criticism can be uncomfortable, the World Bank acknowledges that it has moderated its activities in response.

[92] *Id.*

[93] Dr. Kishan Khoday, *Partnership as Governance Reform: Negotiated Rule-Making in the New Economy, Partnership Matters* 23 (The Copenhagen Centre, 2003).

[94] *Id.* at 24 (emphasis added).

[95] Sally A. Harpole, Global Center for Dispute Resolution Research Barcelona Symposium on International ADR Research Issues (Feb. 22-23, 2002).

[96] David B. Lipsky and Ronald L. Seeber, "The Appropriate Resolution of Corporate Disputes: A Report on the Growing Use of ADR by U.S. Corporations" 3 (1998).

[97] Harpole, *supra* note 95, at 13. Such nonadversarial cultures often have long-standing traditions of elders mediating disputes within their cultures. This traditional mediation, however, is not the cross-cultural, transnational mediation reviewed here.

[98] Lipsky and Seeber, *supra* note 96.

[99] Belle Abaya, "The Philippine Mediation Experience: From Community Justice to Judicial Reform," ACResolution 12 (2003).

[100] Erbe, *supra* note 10, at 373.

[101] *Id.*

[102] *Id.* at 382-83.

[103] Erbe, *supra* note 10, at 388. Nepalese respondents described themselves as personally providing valued cultural education. *Id.* at 360.

[104] *Id.* at 378.

[105] *Id.* at 362.

[106] *Id.* (elected anonymity with human subjects protection).

[107] Erbe, *supra* note 10, at 346. Readers interested in going further with exploring the reasons global scholars include mediation among diverse interests for sustainable resolution in their criteria for evaluating governance are encouraged to read their extensive body of scholarship. See Court et al., *supra* note 1.

[108] Fisher and Ertel, *supra* note 83, at 86. It is too early to discern mediation's long-term impact in the Balkans or Nepal. Inspiring, though, are reports of participants bridging ethnic difference in the midst of violent conflict and long-standing tensions. Where government proved ineffectual or unconcerned, citizens, professionals and NGOs moved forward.

[109] Mediation mechanisms that proactively prevent crisis and anticipate challenges are unarguably valuable to transnational corporations. Developing Tri-Sector Partnership "Markers," Report from Natural Resources Cluster/Business Partners for Development Workshop (June 23-25, 1999), available at <http://www.bpd-naturalresources.org/ media/pdf/wshop/markers.pdf>; see also Nancy Erbe, "Communications Theory and Restorative Justice: Approaches to Proactive Conflict Resolution," IXX *Bus. Res. Y.B.* 696 (2005).

[110] Jonathan Stacey, "A Global Partnership with a Mining Multinational: Exploring and Realizing the Capacity for Strategic Biodiversity Conversation," *Partnership Matters* 34-35 (2003).

[111] *Id.*

[112] *Id.*

[113] Literally interpreted as more than one party. See Neligan, *supra* note 22. "Multi-stakeholder processes [are] processes which aim to bring together all major stakeholders in a new form of communication, decision-finding (and possibly decision-making) structure on a particular issue" (emphasis removed). They cover a wide spectrum of structures and levels of engagement, comprising dialogues and growing into processes encompassing consensus-building, decision-making, and implementation, or partnerships." Hemmati, *supra* note 6, at 2. Pioneering businesses, civil society and government form actual working partnerships. See Developing Tri-Sector Partnership "Markers," *supra* note 109, at 5.

[114] See generally Hemmati, *supra* note 6.

[115] See, e.g., AARHUS treaty negotiation discussed later.

[116] While arbitration is an increasingly popular method for global dispute resolution, "the consensual basis of arbitration, and aspects of its basic format, make it an awkward

method when the dispute in question involves more than two parties." Jack Coe, *International Commercial Arbitration* (Transnational Publishers, 1997, 66).

[117] Erbe, *supra* note 10, at 355.

[118] Gross, *supra* note 2, at 58.

[119] Erbe, *supra* note 14.

[120] Neligan, *supra* note 22. As a result, detailed questions have been designed to help participants structure effective process.

[121] See generally Susan Opotow, "Psychology of Impunity and Injustice: Implications for Social Reconciliation," in *Post-Conflict Justice*, ed. M. Cherif Bassiouni (Transnational Publishers, 2002).

[122] Erbe, *supra* note 14.

[123] Harter, *supra* note 80, at 387.

[124] Susan Collin Marks, *Watching the Wind: Conflict Resolution During South Africa's Transition to Democracy* (United States Institute of Peace Press, 2000, 18). See also a list of multitrack diplomacy actors earlier in book.

[125] *Id.*

[126] See CAO, Report on the Training Activities of the Mesa De Dialogo Y Consenso CAO/Cajamarca (2001-2002), available at <http://www.cao-ombudsman.org/ html-english/documents/MesadeDialogoyConsensoCAOCajamarcaAssembly07August2003 englishtranslation.pdf>.

[127] Hemmati, *supra* note 6, at 121.

[128] See *id.*

[129] *Id.* at 122.

[130] Hemmati, *supra* note 6, at 121.

[131] *Id.* at 122-24. (One NGO forecasts a future lawsuit.)

[132] *Id.* at 122.

[133] *Id.* at 123.

[134] Erbe, *supra* note 14. Civil society stakeholders are generally more independent than government and business stakeholders. Their presence in mediations should enhance accountability by ensuring broad, diverse participation. Some NGOs, however, are the problem. Critics report that NGOs discourage popular participation, waste resources and unknowingly support corruption. They, too, must be held accountable. Uganda and South Africa have both initiated "Installing Codes of Conduct" for civil society organizations to ensure accountability. Alexander Their and Jarat Chopra, "Considerations for Political and Institutional Reconstruction in Afghanistan," *The Journal of Humanitarian Assistance,* January 2002, 8).

[135] Harter, *supra* note 80, at 2; see also Straus Institute for Dispute Resolution, Pepperdine University School of Law, "Advanced Mediation Practice" 114-160 (description of convening); see, e.g., Moore, *supra* note 9, 114-60.

[136] Facilitative mediators are diametrically different from the evaluative third parties described earlier as failing to build effective relationships with concerned communities. In fact, facilitative mediators start the convening process described above by listening to all of the parties and otherwise building rapport and trust.

[137] Model Standards of Conduct for Mediators (Apr. 2005); see also Robert A. Baruch Bush, Symposium, "The Dilemmas of Mediation Practice: A Study of Ethical Dilemmas and Policy Implications," 1994 *J. Disp. Resol.* 1 (1994).

[138] See *supra* note 137.

[139] Erbe, *supra* note 10, at 360.

[140] See *id.* at app.II, 382 (appendix authored by Ndi Richard Tanto).

[141] *Id.*

[142] Harter, *supra* note 80, at 8.

[143] The Ukrainian mediation NGO mentions including political and government stakeholders but does not detail specifics. Erbe, *supra* note 10, at 387-88.

[144] While the Cameroon mediations sound highly successful, in general, representatives claiming to speak for groups must be checked to ensure legitimacy. Representatives who lack close working relationships with their constituencies are a problem. They may not even attempt the ratification needed for broader buy-in. Such representatives sometimes attempt to conceal conflict with vague language. Needless to say their approach is not sustainable.

[145] See Erbe, *supra* note 10, at app. II, 380 (appendix authored by Ndi Richard Tanto).

[146] As one example, the International Landmine Campaign in Africa obtained leverage through engaging rather than confronting the state. All stakeholders, including civil society, as another example, benefit from creating a stable and reliable legal structure accountable to many rather than a special interest group.

[147] Government and NGO evaluation of their experience is elaborated later in this section.

[148] Ben Dysart et al., "Beyond Compliance?" An External Review Team Report on the Compliance Advisors/Ombudsman Office of IFC and Mica, at iv (2003).

[149] *Id.*

[150] Erbe, *supra* note 14.

[151] United Nations Development Programme, *supra* note 2, at 4. ("There is a dearth of works that go deeply beyond the rhetorical and give practical guidance on ways that governance systems and structures can address power inequality.")

[152] Erbe, *supra* note 14.

[153] *Id.*

[154] CAO, Response by the Office of Compliance Advisor/Ombudsman of the External Review (July 2003).

[155] Naomi Roht-Arriaza, "Reparation Decisions and Dilemmas," *27 Hastings Int'l. and Comp. L. Rev.* 157, 191 (2004).

[156] See Howard Raiffa et al., *Negotiation Analysis: The Science and Art of Collaborative Decision-Making* (Belknap, 2003, 191).

[157] Erbe, *supra* note 14.

[158] Erbe, *supra* note 14.

[159] Nancy Erbe, *Holding These Truths: Empowerment and Recognition (An Interactive Case Study Curriculum for Multicultural Conflict Resolution)* (Berkeley Public Policy Press, 2003, 149).

[160] Jonathan Stacey, "A Global Partnership with a Mining Multinational: Exploring and Realizing the Capacity for Strategic Biodiversity Conversation," *Partnership Matters* 26 (The Copenhagen Centre, 2003). Most readers familiar with environmental activism will appreciate this rare partnering between the hotly warring factions of mining and environmental NGOs.

[161] *Identity and the Natural Environment: The Psychological Significance of Nature*, ed. Susan Clayton and Susan Opotow (MIT Press, 2003, 3).

[162] Robert A. Baruch Bush, "Realizing the Potential of International Conflict Work: Connections Between Practice and Theory," 19 *Negot. J.* 97 (2003); A. Marco Turk, "Democratized Restorative Justice As a Lesson for Criminology: Cyprus 1997-2003," 29 *The Criminologist*, May/June 2004, at 1-3 (noting though that diplomatic elites appear to

lack faith in civil society and constrain themselves to traditional legal and political process).

[163] *Id.*

[164] United Nations Development Programme, *supra* note 2, at 23.

[165] Parker, *supra* note 30. What is the relationship between equal inclusive decision-making and a culture of peace? Unfortunately, no elaboration was given, once again providing fertile ground for future research.

[166] Oliver P. Richmond, "Mediating Ethnic Conflict: A Task for Sisyphus? International Studies Association" (1999), <http://www.ciaonet.org/isa/rio01/index. html>; see, for example, Keith Swartzendruber, Eliciting Peace: Mediating the Sandinista-Miskito Conflict (2002), <http://www.geocities.com/keithswartzendruber/ eliciting peace1.htm>.

[167] Erbe, *supra* note 10, at 362. This book's interviewees recognize community training in dispute resolution skills as a "premium." They commend training in negotiation, cross-cultural communication, process awareness, strategic thinking, group facilitation, trust, and team-building—all means through which to empower the most effective of mediation. Erbe, *supra* note 14.

[168] While facilitative mediation is optimally democratic, guiding inclusive decision-making through encouraging party design of the mediation process and treating parties equally, as elaborated throughout this book, the reader should not presume that the mediation reviewed here is democratic or optimal. Mediation's internal structure must also be evaluated case by case.

[169] Buck-passing, elitism, and dogmatism are named as attitudinal barriers within Nigeria's government as one example. Christina Atako, University of Cambridge and International Business Leaders Forum, Partnership Matters 18 (2003) (hereinafter "University of Cambridge"). Legal ethicists likewise stress that citizen attitudes matter as well as the rule of law. Cochran, *supra* note 74, at 720-23.

[170] Erbe, *supra* note 14.

[171] CAO, *supra* note 91; see also Aidan Davy, Companies in Conflict Situations: A Role for Tri-Sector Partnerships? Business Partners for Development (2001). ("Tri-sector partnerships that explicitly seek to prevent conflicts need to aspire to equal representation of all parties.")

[172] Erbe, *supra* note 14.

[173] See generally Davy, *supra* note 171. Corporations risk accusations of human rights violations through the acts of contractors and acquiescence, or other involvement.

[174] *Id.*

[175] Penelope E. Andrews, "Reparations for Apartheid Victims: The Path to Reconciliation?", 53 *DePaul L. Rev.* 1155, 1163 (2004).

[176] Moyer and Haynes, *supra* note 3, at 652 (quoting Alexis de Tocqueville, cited in Andrew Levin, "Civil Society and Democratization in Haiti," 9 *Emory Int'l L.Rev.* 380, 400 (1995)).

[177] Davy, *supra* note 171, at 6.

[178] Aneta Wierzynska, Note, "Consolidating Democracy through Transitional Justice: Rwanda's Gacaca Courts," 79 *N.Y.U. L. Rev.* 1934 (2004). Wierzynska cites Rudolph J. Rummel's study, concluding that "every instance of mass murder by a state against its own people has happened under authoritarian rule." *Id.* at 1948 (citing Rudolph J. Rummel, "Focus On: Power, Genocide, and Mass Murder," 31 *J. Peace Res.* 1 (1994)). Rwanda is a classic example. Additional research provides striking correlation between corruption and violence. Countries ranked highest for corruption resolved dis-

putes with violence 60 percent of the time, while countries ranked lowest used violence 14 percent of the time. Fort and Schipani, *supra* note 29, at 419.

[179] *Id.*

[180] Robert A. Baruch Bush, "What Do We Need A Mediator For?: Mediation's "Value Added" for Negotiators," 12 *Ohio St. J. on Disp. Resol.* 1 (1997).

[181] See Marks, *supra* note 124, at 16. What did it mean to include all as equals? No concrete descriptive detail was found. Given such process's import, chronicling this detail with future conflict mediation would prove invaluable.

[182] Parker, *supra* note 30.

[183] Yo'av Karny, *Fateful Choices: Violence and Nonviolence in the Independence Struggles of Small Nations* (United States Institute of Peace, 2004).

[184] *Id.* No published data was found, however, to discern whether civil society is attempting mediation with the most powerful stakeholders.

[185] United Nations Development Programme, *supra* note 2, at 17.

[186] Thornhill et al., *supra* note 26, at 31.

[187] Moyer and Haynes, *supra* note 3, at 640.

[188] See Marks, *supra* note 124. Yet, post Peace Accords, increasing violence has been reported. Assessing how mediated inclusive participatory dispute resolution can be both exemplary in process and immediate results yet fall short in sustainable resolution is hotly debated among South African communities and academics worldwide and beyond the scope of this book.

[189] *Id.*

[190] Neligan, *supra* note 22.

[191] CAO, *supra* note 126.

[192] Likewise, Burmese activists stress the importance of "a level playing field" in advancing democratic governance. Erbe, *supra* note 10, at 359 n.76. Once again, mediation provides tools, such as negotiation of multicultural ground rules, as pragmatic ways to balance power and build cross-cultural respect.

[193] Muslim and indigenous law are other examples of prevalent global traditions. See Eric Luna, "A Place For Comparative Procedure," 42 *Brandeis L.J.* 277 (2004). The emerging economies of Eastern and central Europe show that quickly establishing rule of law can be instrumental to growth and development. Fort and Schipani, *supra* note 36. The resulting contract and property protection facilitates development of the free market. Trustworthy rule of law is likewise an essential prerequisite for good governance. Tolerating selective illegality erodes public confidence and discourages participation. Moyer and Haynes, *supra* note 3, at 638. See also U.S. Agency for Int'l Dev., New Partnerships Initiative Resource Guide (1997) ("Without a minimal level of human rights . . . local empowerment is an illusion.").

[194] The AARHUS Convention mentioned earlier is one example noted for linking environmental and human rights.

[195] At its worst the rule justifies status quo injustice. In circumstances like South Africa's apartheid, transitional justice requires transformative law. Gross, *supra* note 2, at 50. ("The analytical tool of transitional justice becomes both an interpretative tool that helps to elucidate the concept of justice during transitions, and a normative tool for evaluating change and the degree of commitment to correcting injustice.")

[196] Unfortunately, the converse still occurs—law and enforcement that discriminate and preference the most powerful or elite.

[197] Erbe, *supra* note 14.

[198] In caucus, mediators divide parties and communicate separately for various strategic reasons. Moore, *supra* note 9, at 319. Mediators differ greatly in their use of caucusing. Some engage in frequent private conversations with parties, or shuttle diplomacy, to evaluate distributive positioning. Others will only use caucus in rare circumstances due to the concerns mentioned in the text above, perhaps after perceiving stubborn impasse or that a party is uncomfortable sharing vital information publicly.

[199] *Id.*; see also Barry C. Bartel, "Med-Arb as a Distinct Method of Dispute Resolution: History, Analysis and Potential," 27 *Willamette L. Rev.* 66 (1991).

[200] CAO, *supra* note 91.

[201] *Id.*

[202] Luna, *supra* note 193.

[203] *Id.*

[204] Ngoh-Tiong Tan, "Community Mediation in Singapore: Principles for Community Conflict Resolution," 19 *Conflict Resol. Q.* 289 (2002).

[205] *Id.* at 299. Not surprisingly, government agents rate the quality of governance significantly higher than nongovernment agents. Court et al., *supra* note 1, at 15.

[206] Emily Stewart Haynes, "Mediation as an Alternative to Emerging Postsocialist Legal Institutions in Central and Eastern Europe," 15 *Ohio St. J. on Disp. Resol.* 257 (1999). While judicial corruption is the natural focus for an examination of ADR and good governance, Transparency International's Global Corruption Barometer found that political party corruption is the leading citizen concern, found in 33 of the 47 countries surveyed (including the United States) and followed by concerns regarding corruption with police and medical services. In many industrialized countries, voting is declining, along with party affiliation, due to alienation from the decision-making process. Judicial corruption is ranked third or fourth. Transparency International, *supra* note 1. In the United States, corrupt medical services are the second leading priority. Corruption in the legal profession, however, represents a growing trend. Cochran, Jr., *supra* note 74.

[207] Court et al., *supra* note 1.

[208] Abaya, *supra* note 99.

[209] *Id.*

[210] *Id.* at 13.

[211] *Id.*

[212] United Nations Development Programme, *supra* note 2.

[213] See, e.g., Alma Abdul-Hadi Jadallah, "The Arab-Israeli Conflict: Challenges for American Third-Party Intervenors," *ACResolution* 36 (2003).

[214] Erbe, *supra* note 10, at 361 n.95. NGOs that fully depend on mediation income are not seen independent.

[215] *Id.*

[216] *Id.* at 347, 360, 364.

[217] *Id.* at 291; Haynes, *supra* note 206, at 282.

[218] The mediation-negotiation of Mozambique's Peace Process is an intriguing case study. While those alleged to be instrumental to its progress were inside members of the community and did not pretend to be impartial, the words used for describing their facilitation were "respectful and faithful." Fisher, *supra* note 13, at 96.

[219] Erbe, *supra* note 14.

[220] *Id.*

[221] Erbe, *supra* note 10, at 347; 367-70.

[222] Ken Kaplan, University of Cambridge, *supra* note 169, at 33.

[223] *Id.* at 34.

[224] Business Partners for Development, Emerging Lessons for Tri-Sector Partnerships: A Review of Four Case Studies (2000).

[225] See, e.g., Erbe, *supra* note 14.

[226] Their and Chopra, *supra* note 134, at 8.

[227] United Nations Development Programme, *supra* note 2, at 44.

[228] *Id.*; Harter, *supra* note 80.

[229] Hemmati, *supra* note 6, at 118.

[230] *Id.*

[231] Contra Harter, *supra* note 80 (citing argument that government alone should determine public interest).

[232] Naidoo, *supra* note 28; see also Harter, *supra* note 80, at 10 ("For the process to meet its goal of reconciling competing values and insights into a "public interest"—a vision shared by the populace and not just imposed by the bureaucracy—it must . . . be democratic and hence broadly representative.")

[233] Civil society is also advised to use approaches which mobilize constituencies, develop shared platforms, and create internal democracy (rather than claim to speak for people who are not consulted or considered). Naidoo, *supra* note 28.

[234] Coe, *supra* note 116, at 108.

[235] Erbe, *supra* note 10, at app I.

[236] Ken Kaplan, University of Cambridge, *supra* note 169, at 32.

[237] Ground rules are process parameters, principles or boundaries agreed to by the parties to mediation. Erbe, *supra* note 159, at 166.

[238] *Id.*

[239] *Id.* at 168.

[240] *Id.*

[241] Erbe, *supra* note 159, at 148. See Michelle Lebaron, *Bridging Cultural Difference* (Jossey-Bass, 2003, 232).

[242] Parker, *supra* note 30.

[243] Erbe, *supra* note 10, at 347, 370.

[244] *Id.* at 368.

[245] Roberta Jamieson, "Shaping The Future: Taking the Initiative in a Turbulent Environment," Keynote Address at the Second Ombudsman Leadership Forum Conference, Our Common Work: Trends and Tools for the Millenium (June 7-10, 2000).

[246] Hemmati, *supra* note 6, at 124.

[247] Gross, *supra* note 2, at 54.

[248] *Id.*

[249] CAO, *supra* note 126.

[250] Global Witness and Human Rights Watch advised companies operating in Angola to publicize all payments. See generally Davy, *supra* note 171.

[251] Abdallah v. Coca-Cola Co., 133 F. Supp. 2d 1364 (N.D. Ga. 2001).

[252] *Id.* at 1369.

[253] Erbe, *supra* note 10, at 370.

[254] *Id.*

[255] *Id.*

[256] Erbe, *supra* note 14.

[257] Fisher, *supra* note 13, at 178 (discussing the Peru-Ecuador peace talks).

[258] Erbe, *supra* note 14.

[259] See, e.g., Kinga Goncz and Sandor Gesko, "Ethnic Minorities in Hungary: Democracy and Conflict Resolution," 552 *Annals Am. Acad. Pol. and Soci. Sci.* 28, 28-

30(1997) (describing how Partners for Democratic Change successfully facilitated meetings between government and the Roma regarding complaints of police discrimination); see also SPIDR Environment/Public Disputes Sector Critical Issues Committee, Guidelines for Using Collaborative Agreement Seeking Processes (2004), <http://www.mediate.com/articles/bestpracticespiderC.cfm>.

[260] Fisher, *supra* note 13, at 110, 116.

[261] *Id.* at 96.

[262] The complaint involved a hydroelectric dam. While civil society criticism can be uncomfortable, the World Bank acknowledges that it has moderated its activities in response. Naidoo, *supra* note 30.

[263] CAO, *supra* note 91. Historically, the ombuds' role was more of an impartial investigator, with quasi-judicial powers. For example, an ombuds-like process was established in South Africa as part of negotiating the Peace Accords. The Goldstone Commission of Inquiry Regarding the Prevention of Public Violence and Intimidation, composed of a judge, senior advocate and three other legally qualified persons "investigated the nature and causes of violence, identifying those responsible and recommending action to the state president." *Id.* at xii. Likewise, the Civil and Political Rights Covenant (and its accompanying Protocol) and the Convention on Racial Discrimination created Ombuds committees, with representatives from 18 ratifying countries, to oversee worldwide human rights. *Id.* Ex officio experts "investigate [on petition] and criticize what the governors do that the governed do not like." *Id.* Criticized governments are mandated to respond with remedies. This work continues today through the use of classical ombuds.

[264] It appeared to be the most publicized work during this book's research.

[265] CAO, *supra* note 91.

[266] Their and Chopra, *supra* note 134, at 18.

[267] Dysart et al., *supra* note 148, at 20.

[268] *Id.* at 5.

[269] *Id.*

[270] Spaulding, *supra* note 6, at 23-24.

# Conclusion

Our warring world deserves to practice seriously what dispute resolvers preach, a willingness to suspend judgment long enough to impartially inquire whether our profession has yet to tap its potential. Sustained exertion and experimentation are essential.

[Peacebuilding is a] multigenerational task involving the gradual transformation of a conflictual society and, secondly, of ensuring that peace-building becomes an organic phenomenon, at work at all levels of our society rather than the traditional, narrow view of peace being negotiated by political leaders alone. . . . Peacemaking involves more than the condemnation of violence. "Peace" is built, gradually, over decades and generations.1

While scholars scrutinize legal systems around the world, domestic and international, a quiet revolution grows. Practitioners from many fields, including law, development, public administration, and business, along with citizens and NGOs, are crafting alternative forums. They seek access, inclusion, and fair consideration of their needs, optimally, through efficient and sustainable resolution—in short, good governance.

In many countries, parties to conflict face legal ineptitude and are barred from access to legal forums. Private deals occur behind closed doors. Mediation, or skilled facilitation, provides a ready option where accountability, impartiality, rule of law, and transparency can be contracted.

Reflecting on his work in the Balkans, Dr. Tauber proposes facilitative inter-ethnic teams—community building, counseling, conflict resolution, and reconciliation.2 He views conflict resolution as key to an integrated strategy for transgenerational rehabilitation and capacity building.3

It is hoped that experts among us will give the reports of community members surveyed here credence—enough to stimulate their own inquiry and research with the facilitative approach and global dispute resolution. In the worst of cross-cultural conflict, these communities engage, inspire, and empower, offering us a rich opportunity for reflective practice, through increased competence and consciousness, as we internationalize our practice. Fundamental to both multicultural "sea legs" and our influence as third-party interveners with conflict is the awareness of "self." Peacemakers around the world show us that the most powerful persuasion requires conviction. What do we stand for? "Interveners . . . who believe that mediation can serve important political agendas and social harmony infuse the profession [of mediation] with a higher purpose that serves the interests of all practitioners. . . . When they succeed the field may be energized with a sense of purpose and vision."4

Of course, the global surge in mediation raises questions. Mediation has the capacity to circumvent the rule of law and create more corruption as well as to promote good governance. What safeguards are necessary to enhance mediation's contribution to the best of governance around the world? One premise behind this book is that mediation and its relationship to good governance deserve attention and guidance.

Nevertheless, mediation is demonstrating unbridled promise. Mediation's internal democracy, or good governance, creates outcomes truly responsive to diverse needs at all levels of society through consensus building. Mediation has potential to transform broader society, encouraging democracy through training citizens, impartially guiding power sharing, effectively bridging cultural difference, building durable relationships and sustainable solutions, and otherwise enhancing the parties' ability to work together efficiently and effectively through, for example, ensuring requisite transparency and accountability.

Nelson Mandela recently shared his new vision: a world order based on partnership and mutual respect, in which the benefits of collective human endeavor accrue to all, and the imbalances of the past and their legacy are redressed, mirroring contemporary scholars' description of global governance, where collective will negotiates sustainable consensus responsive to diverse interests.5 Mediation plays an important part in fostering respectful and effective global partnering—but it is a part that demands scrutiny.

## Notes

[1] "Each side [in Northern Ireland] is normally suspicious of 'outsiders' and especially suspicious of those who spend time with the opposition. . . . There are very few, if any truly neutral people. . . . While we need not to feign neutrality, we do . . . need to remain impartial. . . . Impartiality is an important hallmark of a mediator." Brendan McAllister, "Mediation: A Tool for Change: Northern Ireland Experience," 18 *Conflict Resol. Notes* No. 3, 28-29 (2001). Impartiality is later described as "open-minded."

[2] Charles David Tauber, M.D., "Psychological Trauma, Physical Health, and Conflict Resolution in Croatia, Serbia, and Bosnia: Lessons for the Future," 18 Conflict *Resol. Notes* No. 4, available at <http://www.conflictres.org/vol184/tauber.html> (last accessed Oct. 26, 2004).

[3] *Id.*

[4] Thomas Princen, "Joseph Elder: Quiet Peacemaking in a Civil War," in *When Talk Works: Profiles of Mediatiors*, Deborah M. Kolb (Jossey-Bass, 1994).

[5] Nelson Mandela, Nobel Peace Prize Address (Dec. 10, 1993), available at <http://www.anc.org.za/ancdocs/speeches/nobelnrm.html>.

# Glossary

**Arbitration:** The informal quasi legal process of resolving disputes between people or groups or nations by referring them to an impartial third party, either agreed on by them or provided by law, who makes a judgment.

**Civil Society:** The totality of voluntary social relationships, civic and social organizations, and institutions that form the basis of a functioning *society*, as distinct from the power-backed structures of a *state* and the commercial institutions of the *market*. Together, state, market, and civil society constitute the entire society.

**Concessions:** An act of yielding, admitting, or compromising in some way. Also something, e.g., a privilege, right, or kindness, that is granted to a person, group, or nation, usually in view of special circumstances.

**Diplomacy:** Managing communication and relationships between nations. It involves skill and tact in dealing with other people of different cultures, language, or ethnicity.

**Impartial:** Not biased (not inclined) to any person, group, institution, or nation. Having no direct involvement or interest and not favoring one entity or side more than another.

**Multilateral:** Involving more than two parties or countries.

**Reconciliation:** The ending of conflict or renewing of a friendly relationship between disputing people or groups.

**Restorative Justice:** An approach to *justice* that focuses on the needs of victims and offenders, instead of satisfying abstract legal principles or punishing the offender. Victims take an active role in the process, while offenders are encouraged to take responsibility for their actions, by apologizing, returning stolen property or community service. It is based on a *theory of justice* that considers crime and wrongdoing to be an offense against an individual or community rather than the state. Restorative justice that fosters dialogue between victim and offender shows the highest rates of victim satisfaction and offender accountability.

**Sovereign:** The ruler or permanent head of a state (like a king or queen in earlier times). Ruler who is independent, self-governing and not ruled by any other state or authority. Having supreme authority.

**Stakeholder:** Something, somebody, or group with direct interest, involvement, or investment in something.

# Appendix 1: Interethnic Dialogue in Western Balkans

By Goran Lojancic, Nansen Network
Edited by Daniel Perez, Fulbright Scholar, Albania

There is not much more to say that has not been said already regarding interethnic relations in the Western Balkans, the former Socialist Federative Republic of Yugoslavia. During the last decade of the twentieth century, the world press, as well as many social scientists, was forced to learn and understand the complex map of ethnicities in this region. Therefore, this short article will only give an overview of the present situation in the region, and introduce the Nansen Network, which is an initiative made with ambition to overcome consequences of recent wars through interethnic dialogue and cooperation.

## A. Nothing To Be Taken for Granted

It appears that the season of wars in the Western Balkans is about to come to an end. The last attempts at war in Macedonia and Southern Serbia were prevented by both a determined and robust intervention by the international community and the frightening experience that the Balkan nations gained from previous wars in Bosnia and Kosovo.

The challenges facing the region are not easy. The reconstruction of mutual relationships is heavily burdened by the partial and unsustainable resolution of wars and the high level of hatred and resentment. This burden almost halted creativity of all major initiatives, making investors, both political and economic, follow "elephant paths," inert and proven activities, which have shown some results in the past. The European Union integration process, at least for now, is encouraging economic cooperation and political moderation between politicians of former Yugoslav countries. The sustainability of this cooperation and moderation, however, is questionable.

Aside from the political and psychological consequences of recent wars, there is also a set of physical consequences that cannot be overcome easily: a high rate of criminal activities—which are not surprisingly, interethnic—connected with politics, criminal accumulation of capital (war profiteers), hundreds of thousands of refugees and internally displaced persons, demolished infrastructure, etc. After World War II, it took a decade of reconstruction in Europe for each year the war was waged. And this was Western Europe, with all its potential and standards. In the Western Balkans, the picture is even less pleasant.

Nonetheless, there is still some reason for optimism. The main warlords are imprisoned, dead, or politically insignificant. The patriots' last attempt to take power in Serbia, through the assassination of the Serbian prime minister, provoked a determined and unconditional state response and turned out to be a glorious loss. In less than a month, the whole pyramid of violence and criminal connections in government bodies collapsed. It is significant that Serbian police could count on political support and police cooperation in all the countries of the region. Further, the public appearance of this ugly criminal scene seriously decreased doubts that the Serbian public had toward the International War Crime Tribunal in Hague, which is a solid side effect.

The importance of right wing political parties with nationalistic politics is slowly decreasing. Those parties that were overthrown in Croatia, Macedonia, Serbia, and even in Bosnia are constantly losing electorate percentage. In Kosovo, the first elections after the war brought a less radical political option to power than was expected. Additionally, old economical and cultural connections have been reestablished; visiting theatre shows, concerts, movies, sporting events are no longer bizarre attractions any more.

## B. Nansen Network: Think Realistic, Ask for the Impossible

Optimism was on thin ground when the idea to begin dialogue work between ethnic communities in Western Balkans landed. It started as an exclusive project for a small number of people in the Nansen Academy in Lillehammer, Norway, and now has around 40 employees and thousands of beneficiaries. The unexpected question from two participants in the course in Lillehammer, one Serbian and one Albanian from Kosovo— "why can't we do these things in our home town"—resulted in the first Nansen Center in Pristina, the capital of Kosovo. This Nansen center organized a series of dialogue workshops, which came as a surprise to everyone, including participants in those workshops, society in general, and international donors.

Although the center in Pristina had a short life, interrupted by first NATO bombs in March 1999, the results were not forgotten. The Norwegian Foreign Ministry expanded the venture and several months after the end of the war in Kosovo, four centers were restarted in Belgrade, Skopje, Podgorica, and Pristina, followed shortly by five more in Sarajevo, Banja Luka, Mostar, Osiijek, and Mitrovica.

Nansen dialogue provides social interference through personal contacts. Each of our participants is both a representative of her ethnic group and, at the same time, our advocate in her community. It can, obviously, create problems when the target group numbers millions and capacities are limited. Our general strategy had to acknowledge a population of more than twenty million people. That is why we created a series of workshops and combined interethnic dialogue with education in Nansen dialogue work. We encouraged the most successful participants to continue their education until they were ready to take over a different level of activities, such as organization, marketing, facilitation, and cofacilitation, under the Nansen umbrellas in their own communities. Through that work these participants brought our ideas and the basic aspects of our work to the many people we could not reach from one center. Many of our participants are now assistants in Nansen offices, independent trainers, and founders of local NGOs, but they all share one thing—specific education in Nansen dialogue. In Serbia, our participants often call themselves Nansen people, with ambition to show identity in NGO work.

Thanks to the fact that we are present everywhere in the region, the most difficult cross-border or cross-ethnic activities became just a usual activity to conduct. This relaxation spreads to our participants, as well. Almost all of them are aware that they are part of a big picture. The phenomenon of ethnic boundaries is starting to lose its significance. Influential political and social subjects recognized this, which is a great reward for the small steps we try to make and a powerful motivation for future work.

# Appendix 2: Cameroon

By Ndi Richard Tanto, Ecumenical Service for Peace

The North Western and Western provinces of Cameroon have gone down in record as violent provinces. In the 1990s, these provinces experienced violent conflicts between the Balikumbat and Bafanji ethnic groups in the North Western province and between the Bagam and Bamenyam in the Western province. In 1995 and 1998, during two major clashes between the Balikumbat and Bafanji killed more than 200 people, destroyed more than 2.7 billion Cameroon francs in property, and forced many families to move out of the area. Cohabitation for these two communities was impossible and nonexistent. Suspicion, bitterness, and misery reflected these people's trauma.

## The Case of Bafanji/Balikumbat

Bafanji and Balikumbat are villages in the Balikumbat Sub-Division. This Sub-Division has five villages: Balikumbat, Bafanji, Bamukumbit, Baligansin, and Baligashu. For a first level training in Non-Violent Conflict Resolution (NVCR), we first targeted opinion leaders and identified the resident stakeholders in the area. In 2000 and 2001, we organized a series of workshops in all the villages of the Sub-Division for these leaders. We organized this series because we did not want to give the impression that we came to mediate the conflict.

After these workshops, we set up structures called Peace Forums in each of the villages. These forums sought to set the basis for the dissemination of knowledge, practice the learned skills, and exchange peace ideas in their communities. These structures organized monthly meetings and became an attraction to their communities. Before long, some of the traditional leaders recognized that these forums provided an effective structure for conflict resolution and sent them local conflicts.

Convinced that this first step had the desired impact, we brought all the Peace Forums in the Sub-Division to a second level training. Our second level trainings focused on techniques of mediation. Five delegates represented each Peace Forum. This five-day workshop brought together, for the first time in four years, participants from Balikumbat and Bafanji in the Balikumbat village. At the end of this workshop, all participants made a commitment to work towards restoring peace in the area. They made landmark resolutions to contact their traditional village councils and talk about the need for the councils to be trained in NVCR techniques.

Next, we targeted the traditional councils of Balikumbat and Bafanji. The traditional council is responsible for resolving conflicts at the village level.

When we contacted them for training, there was no hesitation. We began by giving them a first level training separately in their respective villages as a prelude to bringing them together in a second level training. This proved very successful for at the end of the workshops they all resolved to face the conflict dividing them.

This training prepared the conflicting parties with the same basic understanding of the issues involved in conflict so they could meet and discuss with the same framework of understanding. It was therefore easy for the traditional councils to meet because they had received similar training.

In October 2002, the Balikumbat and Bafanji traditional councils, representatives of Peace Forums, and traditional councils of the three other villages in the Sub-division, about 90 people in all, met in Bafanji for an evaluation and planning meeting. This was the first time all of them had come to Bafanji since the war of 1995. They were exposed to the cost of conflict on development in their area. After discussions, the parties committed themselves to working with the Ecumenical Service for Peace (SeP) and the administration to find a way out of the conflict. They will submit a report describing what they consider the issues at stake and how they think this conflict should be resolved. The events of these meetings so elated the Fon of Bafanji that he personally entertained all the members of the Balikumbat Traditional Council.

When this phase is complete, the traditional rulers will work out a final solution that all parties will accept. This will not be a workshop but high-level discussions, involving the administration of the division. A series of follow-up meetings to this effect have already been planned. It is hoped that before the year runs out, we will celebrate reconciliation in the area. All of these activities have made visible impact. After only three years working intensively in the area, we have made such progress that it would now be difficult for violence to occur even if we were to leave.

The SeP contributes to Non-Violent Social Transformation their creation of a society of participation based on justice, peace, reconciliation, and compassion. The SeP works mainly in Cameroon's conflict areas. The SeP organizes trainings in conflict resolution at three levels. The first level focuses on concepts such as peace, justice, reconciliation, and general notions of mediation and negotiation. Second level workshops concentrate on mediation, and third level workshops analyze conflicts. When invited, members of the SeP often participate as mediators in third level workshops. Other training activities focus on socio-political leadership, citizenship education, and paralegals. SeP also trains vulnerable groups, those that have problems with government they cannot to resolve because of the government's greater power, in Non-Violence.

SeP hopes that after their interventions, conflicting parties will be empowered such that they are able to collaborate in the search for conflict solutions. The following are some examples of such collaboration.

In September 2002, there was tension between Balikumbat and Bafanji concerning the building of a Government Secondary School in Bafanji. The Fon of Balikumbat felt the school was being built on disputed territory and ordered the building destroyed. This caused tension, and some members of the Traditional Council in Balikumbat rushed to the site and protected the school. The Fon then used his political influence and encouraged the Senior Divisional Officer for Ngoketunjia to issue an injunction, which stopped construction of the school. The people of Bafanji formed a delegation led by the leader of the Peace Forum and met the Fon in his palace to discuss lifting the injunction and continuing with construction. The method of seeking redress has drastically changed since the 1990s.

In January 2003, another incident occurred which would have led to a clash, but the communities, especially those who have been trained, approached the problem peacefully. A native of Bafanji took his motorbike to Bamukumbit for repairs. The Fon of Balikumbat came, took the bike from the repairer, and accused the owner of stealing it from a Balikumbat person during the war. The owner provided documents to prove that the bike was his own but the Fon refused to hand back the motorbike. The traditional council and peace forum worked hard to calm the situation and violence was avoided.

The Senior Divisional Officer and the Medical Officer for Balikumbat have joined SeP in their crusade for peace. A committee of the Divisional Officer, SeP, and the traditional councils of the two villages has been formed. The statistics of the Balikumbat Hospital show a steady increase in the number of Bafanji people visiting the hospital. The same situation has been observed at the Divisional Officer's office to the great satisfaction of the Divisional Officer.

Before 1995, the head teachers of primary schools in the Balikumbat Sub-Division had an association whose meetings rotated from one village to another. These meetings stopped with the war of 1995. The teachers have relaunched the association and all the head teachers in the Sub-Division are again actively taking part.

It is also becoming fashionable to see people give names to their businesses such as Peace Lover's Saloon or No Peace No Business. There is a steady increase in the number of people from Balikumbat who attend the Bafanji market. In a Bafanji region decimated by war and abandoned by its citizens, people have started rebuilding their homes.

Before this year, Bafanji did not have a member in the Balikumbat Rural Council because it met in the Balikumbat village, and thus the interests of Bafanji were not represented in the council. Today, that council has three members of the Bafanji Peace Forum who effectively take part in deliberations. The number of people from Bafanji attending national and political events has tremendously increased.

# Appendix 3: Nepal

By Rishi Pandey

Nepal, a small Himalayan kingdom, is a land of beauty and diversities. The country is landlocked and bound by the world's two largest populations—China to the north and India to the east, west, and south. Nepal is located between the latitude of 26 [degrees] 22' and 30 [degrees] 27' north and the longitude of 80 [degrees] 4' and 88 [degrees] 12' east, having an area of 147,181 sq km. 199 Topography of the country changes dramatically within the short lateral distance. This topographic variation has created diversities in climate, vegetation, human adaptation pattern, and resource utilization system.

The country harbors four castes and 36 subcastes. In the 2001 population census, 103 ethnic groups were registered and these people use more than 93 different mother tongues. Two religions, Hinduism (80.6%) and Buddhism (10.7%) are the major religions of Nepal. In 2001, the population of Nepal was 23.1 million with a 2.2 annual growth rate and an average household size of 5.4.

The country is predominantly rural, only about 14% of people live in urban areas. The distribution of population is highly uneven. Mountain regions comprise about 15% of the total land surface, but provide shelter for only 7.3% of the total population. The Tarai, southern plain of Nepal, is highly fertile and faces of heavy population growth from migration from the mountain regions as well as India. The Hilly and Tarai region is home to 44.3% and 48.4% of the total population, with 68% and 17% of the total land surface respectively.

## Socio-Economic Condition

Agriculture is the means of livelihood for 80% of Nepalese. The GNP for year 1999-2000 was estimated to be about $5.654 billion (U.S.). Per capita GDP and GNP were $241.82 and $251 (U.S.). Compared with other South Asian countries, e.g., Bangladesh and Pakistan, Nepal has the weakest economic condition in terms of GDP. The country has, however, the third largest area and the fourth largest population. The life expectancy is 59.7 years, the literacy rate is 53.7%, and unemployment rate is 1.8%.[206]

By the end of 2000, the country completed four decades of planned development. More than 45% of the total population, however, is below poverty line. Nepal's fragile hill and mountainous topography cannot provide enough available space for food production. A limited growing season and high altitudes act as natural constraints to increasing food production. Machined agriculture is possible only in Tarai region where large cities and industrial areas occupy the cultivable land.

Nepal has faced problems of international, interregional, and intraregional transportation. The Nepalese industrial producers cannot compete in the global market. Countries such as China and India have a sufficient market for mass production and can cheaply produce materials. In Nepal, however, production cost is higher due to small-scale production and inland transportation.

## B. The Political Situation and Recent Change

Nepal has faced political instability since the country's unification. In the 1990s, multiparty democracy was re-established in Nepal. The re-establishment of democracy raised the Nepalese people's expectations. People expected radical developmental change. This was not an easy task for the first elected government. Members of elected government and high level bureaucrats became mired in corruption and abuse of authority. Problems of transparency, commitment, effective administration, and management were raised. These situations showed a weak administration and biased bureaucracy.

With a lack of vision in political leaders, politics for development became directionless. Due to the problem of corruption and the abuse of authority, the Maoist political party introduced the people's war—a new and most serious problem, violence began. In the beginning of the people's war, the contemporary government failed to understand the cause of the war, while the Maoist party won the admiration of unemployed and poor people in remote areas.

Now seven years have passed, claiming more than seven thousand lives. Important pieces of the infrastructure, like telecommunication towers, highways, bridges, airports, hydropower projects, power transmission centers, water supply, schools, post offices, and even health centers and other service centers, were bombed and destroyed. The war ravaged the country's economy and drastically reduced the number of tourists coming to Nepal. Village agriculture has been adversely affected since young men and women either joined in the war or left the villages out fear. The government diverted more than 60% of its development budget to security expenses to stop the war. Insurgency has become a new and very serious problem.

Due to the power struggles, often the proper person is not placed in the appropriate position. Economists who do not take social variables and geographical constraints into account have dominated the National Planning Commission and have failed to adopt development strategies. Without changing the feudal structure of the society by the growth of critical mass of intellectuals, social change, development is unimaginable.

# Appendix 4: Ukraine

By Leyla Mustafaveva

The name of the country itself suggests that it is "at the edge." Bordering Russia and reaching the Black Sea to the south, Ukraine is experiencing its eleventh year of independence since the Soviet Union fell apart and dissolved into the pieces from which it was created. With a continuing currency crisis, wide-spread corruption, an increasing unemployment rate, plummeting life expectancy figures, brewing ethnic conflict in Crimea and the Carpathian Mountains, and a less than stable legal system, Ukraine is indeed on the edge. Understandably, conflicts abound.

The IMF and the World Bank continue to prescribe remedies to set the country on a certain track. The country's leadership does its best to follow the prescriptions. People do what they can to get by. In accordance with the general precepts pertaining to conflict resolution, however, it is important to note that the most effective solutions to ongoing conflicts cannot be dictated from above or outside. This is not merely for moral reasons, but for practical ones—without the participation of all groups involved in a conflict, any prevention or settlement will be of limited efficacy and duration.

In the midst of this discouraging news about the troubled times in the Ukraine, it might be helpful to keep in mind some things that come together as others fall apart. The Ukrainian Mediation Group (UMG) is a network of eight regional centers that provide conflict resolution services. The indigenous effort to systematize practical approaches to dispute resolution began in the 1980s when UMG Director Nikolai Borisov began mediating between striking coal miners and labor management in the Donetsk region of the former Soviet Union. Since that time, the UMG has expanded its repertoire to include projects geared toward promoting dispute management in enterprise restructuring and privatization, court-based mediation, civil society dialogue between ethnic groups in Crimea and the Carpathian Mountains, conflict prevention through mass media operations, and dispute resolution in school systems.

Many projects operate without funding and succeed due to a seemingly endless supply of energy and enthusiasm. The UMG consists of 25 paid staff members and over 100 volunteers, including psychologists, lawyers, judges, teachers, and students. In a country plagued by crippled industries and massive unemployment, the UMG regional centers are encouraging places to be.

In 1994, the UMG entered into a partnership with Search for Common Ground, an international nongovernmental organization dedicated to transforming how the world deals with conflict—away from adversarial approaches toward cooperative solutions. Search for Common Ground in Ukraine (SCG/Ukraine) seeks to strengthen civil society by building capacity and showing institutions how to deal with conflicts constructively and cooperatively by the following means:

Project activities include: (1) supporting and expanding a network of trainers and mediators throughout Ukraine, (2) providing mediation and consulting services, (3) supporting existing conflict resolution institutions and building new ones, (4) providing conflict resolution skills training and educating trainers, and (5) building awareness of conflict resolution as a viable option within Ukrainian society at multiple levels.

Grants from the ARD/Checchi Rule of Law Consortium, Carnegie Corporation of New York, Eurasia Foundation, International Renaissance Foundation (Soros), MacArthur Foundation, C. S. Mott Foundation, Ira Wallach, and the United States Agency for International Development have supported this working partnership.

The SCG-UMG collaboration led to a series of professional exchanges, mediation training seminars, and project developments that encouraged Ukrainians' efforts to influence the ways in which their society deals with conflict. The results have been many. In Donetsk and Odessa, the district courts are creating a place for mediation to alleviate overloaded dockets and promote ADR as an important aspect of legal reform. UMG mediators have consulted Ukrainian and foreign enterprises as they seek to turn conflict management systems into labor agreements and contracts.

Multi-ethnic mediation teams are working together to prevent violence in Crimea, where competing ethno-national ambitions threaten regional stability. During the Soviet era, Crimean Tatars, indigenous people of the Crimean Peninsular, and many other smaller ethnic groups were deported en masse to Central Asia. The return of these formerly deported minority peoples adds considerably to the typical post-Soviet strains on an already fragile social and economic infrastructure. Many people in Crimea claim to live peaceably with their neighbors, however, protests are made which are reminiscent of those in the Former Republic of Yugoslavia in the early 1990s. As of yet, thankfully, there has been no catalyzing force for violence on the peninsula. This parallel, however, should not go unnoticed and demands intervention.

The European Center for Common Ground and the Ukrainian Center for Common Ground have cooperated with government, labor, the private sector, donor organizations, and other NGOs to improve community and ethnic relations in Crimea. Two mediation groups have been established in Crimea and have brought diverse local groups together to resolve issues and problems of common concern (unemployment, citizenship, ecology, discrimination, religious-based issues, etc.). The main work in Crimea involves problem solving skills, which, while second nature in the West, are lacking in post-Soviet Ukraine. The regional organizations' methodology seeks to facilitate group discussions followed by cooperative work in the communities.

In addition to the work of the Local Working Groups, the Ukrainian Center for Common Ground expanded its conflict prevention tools by developing small projects involving the Crimean youth, such as Peace Camps, which focus on

Crimean multi-ethnic heritage and developing cultural diversity management skills. In schools, children learn about conflict resolution as they role-play historical scenes. One will often find children in the school mediation programs lingering in the courtyards after class. They will not go home until they successfully reach an agreement between historical figures such as the Mongol Tatar Sultan and the Kievan Prince or Khrushchev and Nixon. With these children as Ukraine's future, the country may be on the edge of something remarkable indeed.

## Appendix 5: Attitudes Toward Social Justice

Below are a few examples of possible attitudes toward social justice. Extremes are presented to stimulate reflection of how you would describe your attitude toward social justice. Your descriptions can be similar to or very different than any example.

### Examples:

| | |
|---|---|
| **Hostile:** "I feel hostile toward the concept of social justice. It evokes purely negative connotations, e.g., victimhood, entitlement, angry protestors, etc." | **Empowered/Confident/Optimistic:** "I see myself as an activist for social justice and am confident that I am and will continue to influence important change/response." |
| **Apathetic**: "I feel apathetic or neutral toward the concept of social justice—neither negative nor positive. I do not see social justice's relationship to me and have no interest in exploring." | **Involved:** "I see myself as an activist and creator of social justice. It is an important part of my identity." |
| **Concerned But Confused or Uncertain** | **Concerned But Feel Powerless or Overwhelmed** |

**How would you describe your attitude toward social justice?**

## About the Author

Nancy Erbe, J.D., L.L.M., is a professor of negotiation, conflict resolution, and peacebuilding. She has taught conflict resolution for over 15 years at California State University, Dominguez Hills—one of the diverse campuses in the Western States, the Straus Institute for Dispute Resolution, Pepperdine School of Law, University of Denver, University of Oslo International Summer School, and the University of California, Berkeley, where she developed the multicultural conflict resolution concentration in peace studies. At UC Berkeley she also started the Rotary Center for International Studies in Peace and Conflict Resolution and supervised dialogue groups regarding peacemaking in the Middle East and between India and Pakistan as well as U.S. foreign policy after September 11. Her students, clients, and colleagues have been from about 70 countries. She is currently serving on the Fulbright review committee for Senior Specialists in Peace Studies and Conflict Resolution after visiting Cyprus as a senior specialist in 2009. She is the author of *Holding These Truths: Empowerment and Recognition in Action (Interactive Case Study Curriculum for Multicultural Dispute Resolution)* as well as numerous chapters and articles. The United Nations has translated and disseminated her scholarship on human trafficking of girls. After litigating a range of cases with Fredrickson and Byron, she began mediating cross-cultural disputes in 1989, prioritizing social justice and effective management of crisis and violence within the nonprofit and public sectors, e.g., education and government. Her clients have included the U.S. Department of the Interior and Office of Personnel, Colorado Commission on Indian Affairs, Nansen Network (during Balkans War) and Wu Yee.

# Index